STO

ACPL ITEM
DISCARDED

SO-EMF-009

ST THOMAS AQUINAS
SUMMA THEOLOGIÆ

ST THOMAS AQUINAS

SUMMA
THEOLOGIÆ

Latin text and English translation,
Introductions, Notes, Appendices
and Glossaries

NON NISI TE

V.12

BLACKFRIARS

IN CONJUNCTION WITH

McGRAW-HILL BOOK COMPANY, NEW YORK, AND
EYRE & SPOTTISWOODE, LONDON

PIÆ MEMORIÆ

JOANNIS

PP. XXIII

DICATUM

ALLOCUTIO

PAULI

PP. VI

MCMLXIII

HIS HOLINESS POPE PAUL VI

WAS PLEASED to grant an audience, on 13 December 1963, to a group, representing the Dominican Editors and the combined Publishers of the new translation of the *Summa Theologiæ* of St Thomas, led by His Eminence Michael Cardinal Browne, of the Order of Preachers, and the Most Reverend Father Aniceto Fernandez, Master General of the same Order.

AT THIS AUDIENCE

THE HOLY FATHER made a cordial allocution in which he first welcomed the representatives of a project in which he found particular interest. He went on to laud the perennial value of St Thomas's doctrine as embodying universal truths in so cogent a fashion. This doctrine, he said, is a treasure belonging not only to the Dominican Order but to the whole Church, and indeed to the whole world; it is not merely medieval but valid for all times, not least of all for our own.

His Holiness therefore commended the enterprise of Dominicans from English-speaking Provinces of the Order and of their friends; they were undertaking a difficult task, less because the thought of St Thomas is complicated or his language subtle, than because the clarity of his thought and exactness of language is so difficult to translate. Yet the successful outcome of their efforts would undoubtedly contribute to the religious and cultural well-being of the English-speaking world.

What gave him great satisfaction was the notable evidence of interest in the spread of divine truth on the part of the eminent laymen concerned, members of different communions yet united in a common venture.

For these reasons the Holy Father wished it all success, and warmly encouraged and blessed all those engaged. He was happy to receive the first volume presented to him as a gesture of homage, and promised that he would follow with interest the progress of the work and look forward to the regular appearance of all the subsequent volumes.

VOLUMES

GENERAL PREFACE

BY OFFICIAL APPOINTMENT THE SUMMA PROVIDES THE FRAMEWORK
for Catholic studies in systematic theology and for a classical Christian
philosophy. Yet the work, which is more than a text-book for professional
training, is also the witness of developing tradition and the source of
living science about divine things. For faith seeks understanding in the
contemplation of God's Logos, his wisdom and saving providence, running through the whole universe.

The purpose, then, of this edition is not narrowly clerical, but to share
with all Christians a treasury which is part of their common heritage.
Moreover, it consults the interests of many who would not claim to be
believers, and yet appreciate the integrity which takes religion into hard
thinking.

Accordingly the editors have kept in mind the needs of the general
reader who can respond to the reasons in Christianity, as well as of
technical theologians and philosophers.

Putting the Latin text alongside the English is part of the purpose. The
reader with a smattering of Latin can be reassured when the translator,
in order to be clear and readable, renders the thought of St Thomas into
the freedom of another idiom without circumlocution or paraphrase.

There are two more reasons for the inclusion of the Latin text. First,
to help the editors themselves, for the author's thought is too lissom to be
uniformly and flatly transliterated; it rings with analogies, and its precision
cannot be reduced to a table of terms. A rigid consistency has not been
imposed on the editors of the different volumes among themselves; the
original is given, and the student can judge for himself.

Next, to help those whose native tongue is not English or whose duty it
is to study theology in Latin, of whom many are called to teach and preach
through the medium of the most widespread language of the world, now
becoming the second language of the Church.

The Latin is a sound working text, selected, paragraphed, and punc-
tuated by the responsible editor. Important variations, in manuscripts
and such major printed editions as the Piana and Leonine, are indicated.
The English corresponds paragraph by paragraph and almost always sentence by sentence. Each of the sixty volumes, so far as is possible, will be
complete in itself, to serve as a text for a special course or for private study.

THOMAS GILBY O.P.

xi

ST THOMAS AQUINAS
SUMMA THEOLOGIÆ
VOLUME 12

HUMAN INTELLIGENCE
(1a. 84–89)

Latin text. English translation, Introduction, Notes,
Appendices, & Glossary

PAUL T. DURBIN
Lincoln University, Pennsylvania

NON NISI TE

NIHIL OBSTAT

THOMAS A. CLIFFORD O.P.
URBANUS VOLL O.P.

IMPRIMI POTEST

CANICIUS C. SULLIVAN O.P.
Prior Provincialis, Prov. S. Joseph, S.F.A.

die 27 Decembris, 1967

NIHIL OBSTAT

THOMAS A. CLIFFORD O.P.
Censor Deputatus

IMPRIMATUR

✠ RICARDUS CARDINALIS CUSHING
Archiepiscopus Bostoniensis

die 21 Martii 1968

LIBRARY OF CONGRESS CATALOG CARD NUMBER: 63-11128
01987

PRINTED IN GREAT BRITAIN BY EYRE AND SPOTTISWOODE LIMITED

CONTENTS

EDITORIAL NOTES

TEXT AND TRANSLATION

THERE IS as yet no critical edition of the *Prima Pars* of the *Summa,* and the Latin text here presented is, for the most part, that of the Leonine Edition. It has been modified only slightly, here and there, with an eye to general intelligibility for the student. The only other edition that has been consulted is the Piana of the revised Ottawa printing (1953)—textual variations shown in the footnotes refer to this version. They are, it may be noted parenthetically, of practically no importance: the Ottawa version and the Leonine are simply variations on the Piana Edition of 1570, and the lack of significant differences shows it.

As with the text, so with the translation the student has been kept principally in mind. In the view of the present editor all English versions of the treatise on human knowledge presently available are stilted in the extreme. Often the student might as well be reading the Latin text. Hence every effort has been made to produce a smooth translation; that the effort has not everywhere succeeded is witness to the difficulty the translator faces in attempting to render the concise Latin into readable English.

The references for parallel readings in St Thomas, traditionally given at the beginning of each article in most printed editions, have been pared down to include only those that would make a genuine contribution to the reader's knowledge, either as background or as elaboration of the doctrine contained in each article. Scriptural readings also have been considered: St Thomas's Latin version has been respected, but for the English the Jerusalem Bible translation has been preferred whenever it was fitting. Where the divergence between the Latin and the Jerusalem Bible is too great, the old Douay version, which often closely parallels the Latin, has been substituted.

FOOTNOTES

Those signified by a superior number are the references given by St Thomas, with the exception of no. 1, to each article which refers to parallel texts in his writings. Those signified alphabetically are editorial references and explanatory remarks.

In this volume the Notes are fuller than in many of the others, so the reader is recommended to make good use of the Index of Matters.

REFERENCES

Biblical references are to the Vulgate; English translations from the Jerusalem Bible or the Douay. Patristic references are to Migne (PG, Greek Fathers; PL, Latin Fathers). Abbreviations to St Thomas's works are as follows:

Summa Theologiæ, without title. Part, question, article, reply; e.g. 1a. 3, 2 ad 3. 1a2æ. 17, 6. 2a2æ. 180, 10. 3a, 35, 8.

Summa Contra Gentiles, CG. Book, chapter; e.g. *CG* I, 28.

Scriptum in IV Libros Sententiarum, Sent. Book, distinction, question, article, solution or *quæstiuncula*, reply; e.g. III *Sent.* 25, 2, 3, ii ad 3.

Compendium Theologiæ, Compend. Theol.

Commentaries of Scripture (*lecturæ, expositiones*): Job, *In Job*; Psalms, *In Psal.*; Isaiah, *In Isa.*; Jeremiah, *In Jerem.*; Lamentations, *In Thren.*; St Matthew, *In Matt.*; St John, *In Joan.*; Epistles of St Paul, e.g. *In Rom.* Chapter, verse, *lectio* as required.

Philosophical commentaries: On the *Liber de Causis, In De causis.* Aristotle: *Peri Hermeneias, In Periherm.*; Posterior Analytics, *In Poster.*; Physics, *In Physic.*; *De Cælo et Mundo, In De Cæl.*; *De Generatione et Corruptione, In De gen.*; *Meteorologica, In Meteor.*; *De Anima, In De anima*; *De Sensu et Sensato, In De sensu*; *De Memoria et Reminiscentia, In De memor.*; Metaphysics, *In Meta.*; Nicomachean Ethics, *In Ethic.*; Politics, *In Pol.* Book, chapter, *lectio* as required, also for Expositions on Boëthius, *Liber de Hebdomadibus* and *Liber de Trinitate, In De hebd.* and *In De Trin.*, and on Dionysius, *De Divinis Nominibus, In De div. nom.* References to Aristotle give the Bekker annotation.

Quæstiones quodlibetales (de quolibet),Quodl.

Main titles are given in full for other works, including the 10 series of *Quæstiones Disputatæ.*

INTRODUCTION

WHAT St Thomas offers to the reader in his treatise on human knowledge is a succinct and precise summary of the Aristotelian *via media* between Platonism and pre-Socratic sensism. With the latter he deals only very briefly and in a way that is obviously intended as a definitive refutation. Thus most of his attention is focused on a defence of intellectualism that will avoid the extremes of Plato himself, as presented by Aristotle, of Augustine and his medieval followers, or the Neo-Platonic Aristoteleanism of Avicenna and Averroes.

In this defence scepticism nowhere appears as a primary problem. The experience of knowing, and indeed of intellectual knowledge, is simply assumed. The purpose of the treatise is analytical, an analysis of the data of cognitive experience in Aristotelean terms of potentiality and actuality, substance and accident.

There is, moreover, a further, culturally-determined purpose, that of defending genuinely natural knowledge from absorption into some supposed higher mode of knowing. The key doctrine throughout is thus the *abstractive* mode of human intellectual knowledge. But again the defence of abstraction amounts to a simple assumption, namely of the Aristotelean teaching on the body–soul relation. If body and soul are not separate beings but an interrelated composite unity, then the intellectual soul can have no activity that does not involve a bodily contribution. The object of human intellectual knowledge must have the universality and necessity appropriate to intellectual knowledge in general, but it must be a universality grounded in particulars, in the singular existents of our changing physical world. Abstraction seems to St Thomas the only logical mode of attaining such an object—universalized aspects of particular beings are perceived by the intellect, but only in and through sense images (Q. 84, art. 7 is crucial here). He thus concludes simply: abstraction must therefore exist.

It is similarly taken for granted—as an assumption based on the Aristotelean distinction between sciences of the real and the rational—that abstractive knowledge rests, not on abstract entities, but on the real world.

The accusation has been made more than once that in all this there is nothing truly original in St Thomas. It may be granted that he made the so-called 'agent intellect' a part of man, but the concession will be made grudgingly, and it will be added that in doing so he was very likely departing from the true meaning of Aristotle. In a sense this is true—nearly every element in his treatise on human knowledge can be found already present in some other author. Furthermore, a check of his earlier works will show that there is remarkably little advance on individual points of doctrine; this might possibly suggest that much of his cognitive psychology actually comes from his teacher, St Albert the Great.

Yet there is a sense in which he shows the profoundest originality here. In fact the accusations of lack of originality end up disproving themselves. For if it is true that there is little in his cognitive psychology not found in other authors, it is none the less equally true that not one of these authors —even including Aristotle himself—displays an equal degree of mastery in organization and articulation. (Appendix 3 will spell out one instance in some detail.) It may be said, in fact, that this is what hides the originality: subsequent authors take it so much for granted that sometimes they do not notice the lack of tightness in works before his time.

It is safe to say that, in his treatise on human knowledge, St Thomas offers for the first time in the history of cognitional thinking a genuinely comprehensive, internally coherent, realistic theory of knowledge. (Appendix 6 considers his place in the history of theories of knowledge, and Appendix 7 takes up his alleged 'naive realism'.) This is not to disparage the greatness of Plato's *Theætetus*, for instance, or Aristotle's *De Anima*. Nor is it to deny St Thomas's organization may be too neat, as some have said. But it is to recognize the genuine originality displayed in fitting the scattered insights or incomplete treatises into a coherent synthesis.

The place of the present treatise in the total theological synthesis of the *Summa* will be noticed in Appendix 5; the outline of this volume in relation to other volumes in the series is given in note *c* to St Thomas's introduction to his treatise. Additional Appendices, other than those already mentioned, are devoted to his technical terminology on species and images (Appendix 1), to the knowledge of essences (Appendix 2), to the second act of the mind (Appendix 3), and to the kinds of reasoning processes he recognized (Appendix 4).

1a2æ. 84–89

de actibus intellectivæ partis

CONSEQUENTER CONSIDERANDUM est de actibus* animæ, quantum ad potentias intellectivas et appetitivas: aliæ enim animæ† potentiæ non pertinent directe ad considerationem theologi. Actus autem* appetitivæ partis ad considerationem moralis scientiæ pertinent, et ideo in secunda parte hujus operis de eis tractabitur, in qua considerandum erit‡ de morali materia. Nunc autem de actibus* intellectivæ partis agetur.

In§ consideratione vero actuum, hoc modo procedemus:
>   primo namque considerandum est quomodo intelligit anima corpori conjuncta;
>   secundo, quomodo intelligit a corpore separata.

Prima autem consideratio erit tripartita:
>   primo namque considerabitur quomodo anima intelligit corporalia, quæ sunt infra ipsam;
>   secundo, quomodo intelligit seipsam, et ea quæ in ipsa sunt;
>   tertio, quomodo intelligit substantias immateriales, quæ sunt supra ipsam.

Circa cognitionem vero corporalium, tria consideranda occurrunt:

>   primo quidem, per quid ea cognoscit;
>   secundo, quomodo et quo ordine;
>   tertio, quid in eis cognoscit.

---

*Piana (Ottawa: see Editorial Notes, above) in these three places, adds, *et habitibus, et habitus*, and habitual dispositions
†Piana omits *animæ*, of the soul
‡Piana, *erit*
§Piana adds, before this sentence, *Primo quidem de actibus, secundo de habitibus*, First of the activities, then of the habitual dispositions
[a]While the general Latin term is *appetitus*, and the translation seeks to respect this, the reference is to the activities which modern psychology lumps under some such term as 'goal-directed' or (consciously or unconsciously) 'motivated' activity—i.e., human striving in its broadest meaning, from basic biological needs to the highest level of intelligent striving.
[b]Translates the Latin *potentia*. Considering the present-day bad repute of 'faculty psychology', which is disparagingly contrasted with more dynamic behavioural

2

psychology of intelligence

NEXT TO BE CONSIDERED are the activities of the soul using these intellectual and appetitive[a] faculties;[b] the other faculties do not directly concern the theologian.[c] Moreover, the appetitive activities of the soul ought to be considered in moral science and so will be treated in the *Secunda Pars* where moral matters are taken up. Here, then, only the intellectual activities of the soul will be discussed.

In considering them we will follow this order:

first, how the soul understands while joined to the body (84–88);

then, how it understands when separated from the body (89).

The first set of these discussions will have three parts:

how does the soul know material things,[d] which are below its level? (84–86)

how does it know itself and the things contained in it? (87)

how does it understand non-material substances,[e] which are above its level? (88)

Three questions come up with regard to knowing material things:

by what means the soul knows them (84);

how and in what order (85); and what it is that is known in them (86).

---

approaches, it may seem prejudicial to St Thomas to translate *potentia* in this way. In an Aristotelean context *potentia* stands for something thoroughly dynamic. Nevertheless, St Thomas definitely presents a faculty psychology, and it seems better to use the term and attempt in other ways to show its dynamism.

[c]The treatise on human intelligence in this volume is part of what St Thomas refers to as his treatise on man. It presupposes his prior treatment of the soul (1a. 75), its union with the body (76), and its various faculties, cognitive and appetitive (77–83). See Vol. 11. Also Vol. 13, Introduction.

[d]I will so translate *corpora, corporea, corporalia* throughout, so as to make clear the contrast with immaterial reality, crucial to the argument in several places. A 'body-spirit' contrast would do in some places but would be misleading in others.

[e]St Thomas's usage varies; he sometimes speaks of concepts or ideas as non-material *substances* (usually in a context of Platonic Ideas) and not merely as non-material realities.

Quæstio 84. quomodo anima conjuncta intelligat corporalia, quæ sunt infra ipsam

Circa primum quæruntur octo:

1. utrum anima cognoscat corpora per intellectum;
2. utrum intelligat ea per essentiam suam, vel per aliquas species;
3. si per aliquas species, utrum species omnium intelligibilium sint ei naturaliter innatæ;
4. utrum effluant in ipsam ab aliquibus formis immaterialibus separatis;
5. utrum anima nostra omnia quæ intelligit, videat in rationibus æternis;
6. utrum cognitionem intelligibilem acquirat a sensu;
7. utrum intellectus possit actu intelligere per species intelligibiles quas penes se habet, non convertendo se ad phantasmata;
8. utrum judicium intellectus impediatur per impedimentum sensitivarum virtutum.

articulus 1. utrum anima cognoscat corpora per intellectum

AD PRIMUM sic proceditur:[1] 1. Videtur quod anima non cognoscat corpora per intellectum. Dicit enim Augustinus,[2] quod *corpora intellectu comprehendi non possunt, nec aliquod corporeum nisi sensibus videri potest.* Dicit etiam[3] quod visio intellectualis est eorum quæ sunt per essentiam suam in

[1]cf *De veritate* X, 4
[2]*Soliloquies* X, 6. PL 32, 888
[3]*De Genesi ad litteram* XII, 24. PL 34, 474

[a]*species*, images received from things outside the soul; see note *e* below. Note the progression, from *species* here, to *species intelligibilium* in art. 2, to *species intelligibiles* in art. 7.
[b]The reference is to 'innate ideas'; see art. 3, note *a*.
[c]i.e., immaterial substances. 'Non-sensible' here translates the technical Latin *forma separata*; see note *g* below.
[d]1a. 15, 3 makes further precisions with respect to *rationes* and *exemplaria* among divine ideas; they are not called for here.
[e]*species intelligibiles*: this is the technical term for the intellectual-level image used throughout the treatise. A distinction is commonly drawn between an image in the potential state, *species impressa*, and in the actual state, *species expressa*; for St Thomas's own terminology, see Appendix 1.
Because he speaks of *species* in such contexts as the discussion of innate ideas, there was a strong temptation to translate *species intelligibilis* as 'idea'—even though

Question 84. how the soul, while joined to the body, knows material things

Here there are eight points of inquiry:

1. whether the soul knows material things through the intellect;
2. whether it understands them through its own essence or through species;[a]
3. if by means of species, whether the species of all intelligible objects are inborn in the soul's nature;[b]
4. whether these species come to the soul through the influence of non-sensible immaterial forms;[c]
5. whether the things our soul understands are all seen in the divine ideas;[d]
6. whether the soul acquires intellectual knowledge from the senses;
7. whether, using only the species[e] it has, without turning[f] to sense images,[g] the intellect can actually understand;
8. whether intellectual discernment[h] is impeded when the sense faculties are impeded.

article 1. does the soul know material things through the intellect?

THE FIRST POINT:[1] It would seem that the soul does not know material things through the intellect. For Augustine says[2] that *material things cannot be understood by the intellect nor a body seen except by the senses.* Again he says[3] that we have intellectual vision only of those things that

---

Thomists have come to use the term only of the *species expressa*. However, since this could lead to misunderstanding, and since it is possible to transliterate his terminology in an intelligible way alongside 'idea', it was decided to retain 'intelligible species' in some form. The term can also be misleading, however, since what is directly intelligible is not the 'species' itself, but an object by means of it. Thus 'species' will be used with the acceptable English meaning of 'mental image' (see *Webster's Seventh New Collegiate Dictionary* [1963], *s.v.* 'Species', meaning 3). *Species sensibilis* will be rendered as 'image'.

[f]*Convertendo se*: 1a. 89, 1 & 2 will bring out the sense by contrasting the way disembodied or 'separated' soul 'turns to' its objects with the way the soul in the body 'turns to' sense images.

[g]*phantasmata*, images produced by the three so-called 'internal senses'—imagination (re-presentation of sense images in perception, usually synthesized), cogitative faculty (including the quasi-reasoning process, *ratio particularis*, of which sense knowledge is capable), and sense memory. See Appendix 1.

[h]Frequently the meaning of *judicium* in the *Summa*.

anima. Hujusmodi autem non sunt corpora. Ergo anima per intellectum corpora cognoscere non potest.

2. Præterea, sicut se habet sensus ad intelligibilia, ita se habet intellectus ad sensibilia. Sed anima per sensum nullo modo potest cognoscere spiritualia, quæ sunt intelligibilia. Ergo nullo modo per intellectum potest cognoscere corpora, quæ sunt sensibilia.

3. Præterea, intellectus est necessariorum et semper eodem modo se habentium. Sed corpora omnia sunt mobilia et non eodem modo se habentia. Anima ergo per intellectum corpora cognoscere non potest.

SED CONTRA est quod scientia est in intellectu. Si ergo intellectus non cognoscit corpora, sequitur quod nulla scientia sit de corporibus. Et sic peribit scientia naturalis, quæ est de corpore mobili.

RESPONSIO: Dicendum, ad evidentiam hujus quæstionis, quod primi philosophi qui de naturis rerum inquisiverunt putaverunt nihil esse in mundo præter corpus. Et quia videbant omnia corpora mobilia esse, et putabant ea in continuo fluxu esse, æstimaverunt quod nulla certitudo de rerum veritate haberi posset a nobis. Quod enim est in continuo fluxu per certitudinem apprehendi non potest, quia prius labitur quam mente dijudicetur: sicut Heraclitus dixit quod *non est possibile aquam fluvii currentis bis tangere,* ut recitat Philosophus.[4]

His autem superveniens Plato, ut posset salvare certam cognitionem veritatis a nobis per intellectum haberi, posuit præter ista corporalia aliud genus entium a materia et motu separatum, quod nominabat *species* sive

---

[4]*Metaphysics* IV, 5. 1010a13

[a]*sunt per essentiam suam in anima*: the paraphrase conveys the sense, which is a contrast with things that are 'virtually', *per effectum*, in the soul by means of effects produced in it through the body.

[b]*scientia*, Greek *epistēmē*: the ideal knowledge according to Plato, and to Aristotle's *Posterior Analytics*, the certain and evident knowledge through 'causes' (see below note *m*), derived syllogistically from self-evident, true, better-known premises in such a way as to guarantee the truth of the conclusion. Since this ideal is generally denied today except for abstract logic and mathematics, the argument falls rather flat; it takes for granted that natural science, to be 'science' in this strict sense, must be demonstratively certain. *Scientia*, standing alone, cannot be translated as 'science' without misleading the modern reader—hence the translation 'demonstrative knowledge'. On the other hand, anything other than 'natural science' for *scientia naturalis* would also be misleading.

[c]The Greek Pre-Socratics. The schematic historical approach, such as follows, is often used in the *Summa* to bring out the Aristotelean position. See Appendix 6 for St Thomas's place in the history of theories of knowledge.

[d]This view of Heraclitus, though hallowed by centuries of tradition, has recently

really exist in the soul.[a] But material things are not of this kind. Therefore the soul cannot know them through the intellect.

2. Again, as sense knowledge is to intelligible objects, so is intellectual knowledge to sensible objects. But the soul, by means of sense knowledge, can in no way know spiritual realities, and intelligible objects are of this kind. Neither therefore can the soul in any way know material things by means of the intellect, since such things belong to the order of sensible objects.

3. Again, the objects of intellectual knowledge are necessary and always the same. But all material realities are changeable and not always the same. Therefore the soul through the intellect cannot know material things.

ON THE OTHER HAND, there is the fact that demonstrative knowledge[b] is found in the intellect. Had the intellect no knowledge of material things, it could not have demonstrative knowledge of them. Thus there would be no natural science dealing with changeable material beings.

REPLY: For evidence on this question we should note that the earliest philosophers[c] who inquired into the nature of things thought there was nothing in the world except material reality. Since they recognized that all material things are changeable and thought of them as being in continual flux, they concluded that we can have no certainty about the truth of things. For what is in continual flux cannot be known with certainty—it will have disappeared before the mind can discern it. Heraclitus[d] said, *It is impossible to step twice into the same river*, so Aristotle reports.[4]

Coming after these men, Plato, trying to save the fact that we can have certitude in knowing the truth, maintained that there were, in addition to the material things around us,[e] another class[f] of beings, separate[g] from

---

been challenged; cf G. S. Kirk and J. E˙ Raven: *The Pre-Socratic Philosophers*. Cambridge, 1957.

[e]A circumlocution standing for St Thomas's use of *ista* ('these') and its counterpart *illa* ('those', which will be translated 'somewhere else'—not necessarily in a place apart, but separate from material, sensible things in some sense; see note *h*).

[f]A modernism, but preferable to the transliteration 'genus'. Though 'class' is often used in a nominalist sense opposed to Aristotelean *genus*, its official meaning is neutral, and it better expresses the meaning in the present context .(See below, art. 2, note *o*.)

[g]*separatum*: a technical term which is difficult to translate. It means 'apart from' though not necessarily in the sense of 'in a place apart'. It sometimes means simply 'in a state different from' something else, as the immaterial differs from the material. 'Separate' (*not* 'separated') will serve as well as any other English term if it is understood in this technical sense. However, wherever the context will allow, 'immaterial' will be used rather than 'separate'.

deas, per quarum participationem unumquodque istorum singularium et sensibilium dicitur vel homo vel equus vel aliquid hujusmodi. Sic ergo dicebat scientias et definitiones et quidquid ad actum intellectus pertinet non referri ad ista corpora sensibilia, sed ad illa immaterialia et separata; ut sic anima non intelligat ista corporalia, sed intelligat horum corporalium species separatas.

Sed hoc dupliciter apparet falsum. Primo quidem quia, cum illæ species sint immateriales et immobiles, excluderetur a scientiis cognitio motus et materiæ (quod est proprium scientiæ naturalis), et demonstratio per causas moventes et materiales.

Secundo autem,* quia derisibile videtur ut, dum rerum quæ nobis manifestæ sunt notitiam quærimus, alia entia in medium afferamus, quæ non possunt esse earum† substantiæ, cum ab eis differant secundum esse: et sic, illis substantiis separatis cognitis, non propter hoc de istis sensibilibus iudicare possemus.

Videtur autem in hoc Plato deviasse‡ a veritate, quia, cum æstimaret omnem cognitionem per modum alicujus similitudinis esse, credidit quod forma cogniti ex necessitate sit in cognoscente eo modo quo est in cognito. Consideravit autem quod forma rei intellectæ est in intellectu universaliter et immaterialiter et immobiliter: quod ex ipsa operatione intellectus apparet, qui intelligit universaliter et per modum necessitatis cujusdam; modus enim actionis est secundum modum formæ agentis. Et ideo existimavit quod oporteret res intellectas hoc modo in seipsis subsistere, scilicet immaterialiter et immobiliter.

Hoc autem necessarium non est. Quia etiam in ipsis sensibilibus videmus quod forma alio modo est in uno sensibilium quam in altero: puta cum in uno est albedo intensior, in alio remissior, et§ in uno est albedo cum dulcedine, in alio sine dulcedine. Et per hunc etiam modum forma sensibilis alio modo est in re quæ est extra animam, et alio modo in sensu, qui suscipit formas sensibilium absque materia, sicut colorem auri sine auro. Et similiter intellectus species corporum, quæ sunt materiales et

---

*Piana omits *autem*
‡Piana: *deviare*
†Piana: *eorum*
§Piana adds *cum*

ʰGreek *idea* and *eidos* are rather well transliterated into Latin by *idea* and *species*, but it has become customary in English to refer to Platonic Ideas and Forms (capitalized).

¹A technical term in Plato's philosophy, the meaning of which is disputed. Aristotle (*Metaphysics* 1, 6 and 9. 987b13, 991a20, 992a25) says that Plato never clarified its meaning. None the less, St Thomas uses the term and gives something of the sense in which he does so in art. 4.

ʲA technical term, contrasted with 'universal'. Ideas are universal, material beings singular.

ᵏ*causas*, but to translate as 'causes'—something very often done—is misleading.

matter and change, which he called Ideas or Forms.[h] By participation[i] in these, all singular,[j] sensible objects around us get their designation as 'man', 'horse', etc. Accordingly, Plato held that demonstrative knowledge, definitions, and everything else pertaining to the activity of the intellect has reference, not to sensible material things around us, but to separate immaterial objects somewhere else. Thus the soul would understand, not the material things around us, but their immaterial Forms.

This may be shown to be false for two reasons. Because first, since the Ideas are immaterial and unchanging, demonstrative knowledge of change and matter (such as is characteristic of natural science) would be ruled out, as would any demonstration in terms of material or changeable explanatory principles.[k]

Because secondly it would seem ludicrous, in seeking knowledge of things that are evident to us, to bring in as a means other realities which could not be of the essence of these evident things since they are of an essentially different order. Thus even if these immaterial substances were known, we would not thereby be able to know[l] anything about the sensible things around us.

It would seem that, in this matter, Plato strayed from the truth because —aware that all knowledge comes by way of likenesses—he believed the form of the thing known must necessarily be in the knower exactly as it is in the thing known. Now he recognized that the form of a thing understood is in the intellect in a universal, immaterial, and unchanging way. This is apparent from the mode of operation of the intellect, which must understand in terms of universality and at least some sort of necessity; for ways of acting correspond to the form of the agent. Thus Plato concluded that the things understood must exist in themselves in this same way, namely, in an immaterial and unchanging way.

But there is no necessity for this. Even in sensible things we observe that the same form can be in different sensible objects in different ways; for instance, whiteness can be more intense in one thing than another, and whiteness can be associated with sweetness in one thing but not in another. Furthermore, the same is true of the form of a sensible object: it exists in a different way in the thing outside than it does in sense knowledge, which receives sensible forms without their matter—for instance, the colour of gold without the gold itself. Similarly, the intellect receives material and changeable species of material things in an immaterial and unchanging

---

'Explanation' would be the most accurate translation, but there are reasons why it could also be misleading. Hence the use of the generic 'principle' (*causæ* are a kind of principle, according to Aristotle and St Thomas), with a qualifying adjective. [l]*judicare*, to discern intelligently.

mobiles, recipit immaterialiter et immobiliter, secundum modum suum: nam receptum est in recipiente per modum recipientis.

Dicendum est ergo quod anima per intellectum cognoscit corpora cognitione immateriali, universali et necessaria.

1. Ad primum ergo dicendum quod verbum Augustini est intelligendum quantum ad ea quibus intellectus cognoscit, non autem quantum ad ea quæ* cognoscit. Cognoscit enim corpora intelligendo, sed non per corpora, neque per similitudines materiales et corporeas, sed per species immateriales et intelligibiles, quæ per sui essentiam in anima esse possunt.

2. Ad secundum dicendum quod, sicut Augustinus dicit,[5] non est dicendum quod, sicut sensus cognoscit sola corporalia, ita intellectus cognoscit sola spiritualia: quia sequeretur quod Deus et angeli corporalia non cognoscerent. Hujus autem diversitatis ratio est, quia inferior virtus non se extendit ad ea quæ sunt superioris virtutis; sed virtus superior ea quæ sunt inferioris virtutis excellentiori modo operatur.

3. Ad tertium dicendum quod omnis motus supponit aliquid immobile: cum enim transmutatio fit secundum qualitatem, remanet substantia immobilis; et cum transmutatur forma substantialis, remanet materia immobilis. Rerum etiam mutabilium sunt immobiles habitudines: sicut Socrates etsi non semper sedeat, tamen immobiliter est verum quod quandocumque† sedet in uno loco manet. Et propter hoc nihil prohibet de rebus mobilibus immobilem scientiam habere.

articulus 2. utrum anima per essentiam suam corporalia intelligat

AD SECUNDUM sic proceditur:[1] 1. Videtur quod anima per essentiam suam corporalia intelligat. Dicit enim Augustinus[2] quod anima *imagines corporum convolvit et rapit factas in semetipsa de semetipsa: dat enim eis formandis quiddam substantiæ suæ.* Sed per similitudines corporum corpora intelligit. Ergo per essentiam suam, quam dat formandis talibus similitudinibus, et de qua eas format, cognoscit corporalia.

2. Præterea, Philosophus dicit[3] quod *anima quodammodo est omnia.* Cum ergo simile simili cognoscatur, videtur quod anima per seipsam corporalia cognoscat.

---

*Piana adds *intellectus*
†Piana: *quando*
[5]*De civitate Dei* XXII, 29. PL 41, 800
[1]cf II *Sent.* 3, 2, 2, 1; III *Sent.* 14, 1, 2. *De veritate* VIII, 8. *CG* II, 98.
[2]*De Trinitate* X, 5. PL 42, 977
[3]*De Anima* III, 8. 431b20

way, in accord with its nature; for things are received in a subject according to the nature of the subject.

We must conclude, therefore, that the soul knows material things through the intellect with a knowledge that is immaterial, universal and necessary.

HENCE: 1. Augustine's words must be understood as referring to that by which the intellect knows, not to what it knows. For the intellect does know material things intellectually, but not by means of material things or material and corporeal likenesses of things; rather, by immaterial, intellectual species which can really exist in the soul.

2. As Augustine notes,[5] it is not correct to say, as the senses know only material things, so the intellect knows only spiritual things—the consequence would be that God and the angels could not know material realities. The reason for the difference is that a lower power does not extend as far as a higher, but a greater power can do what belongs to a lesser—and do it better.

3. Every change presupposes something unchanging: in a qualitative change[m] the underlying substance remains unchanged, and in a substantial change primary matter remains the same. Again, even in changeable things there are unchanging relations—for instance, although Socrates is not always seated, whenever he does sit it is unchangeably true that he remains in one place.[n] Thus it follows that there is nothing against having an unchanging demonstrative knowledge of changeable things.

article 2. does the soul know material things through its own essence?

THE FIRST POINT:[1] 1. It would seem that the soul does know material things by means of its own essence. For Augustine says[2] that the soul *collects and lays hold of the images of bodies, which are formed in and out of the soul; for in forming them it gives them something of its own substance.* But the soul understands material things by means of their likenesses. Therefore it knows material things through its own essence—which it gives to these likenesses in forming them, and out of which it forms them.

2. Again, Aristotle says[3] that *the soul is in a way all things.* Thus, since like is known by like, it would seem that the soul knows material things by means of itself.

---

[m] In Aristotelean natural philosophy, one of the three types of 'accidental change'— according to quality, quantity (size, i.e., growth, expansion, diminution), and place (motion in the modern sense).

[n] Though the 'place' might be, for instance, a seat in a moving vehicle; place means the immediately surrounding body or bodies.

3. Præterea, anima est superior corporalibus creaturis. Inferiora autem sunt in superioribus eminentiori modo quam in seipsis, ut Dionysius dicit.[4] Ergo omnes creaturæ corporeæ nobiliori modo existunt in ipsa substantia* animæ quam in seipsis. Per suam ergo substantiam potest creaturas corporeas cognoscere.

SED CONTRA est quod Augustinus dicit[5] quod *mens corporearum rerum notitias per sensus corporis colligit.* Ipsa autem anima non est cognoscibilis per corporis sensus. Non ergo cognoscit corporea per suam substantiam.

RESPONSIO: Dicendum quod antiqui philosophi posuerunt quod anima per suam essentiam cognoscit corpora. Hoc enim animis omnium communiter inditum fuit, quod *simile simili cognoscitur.*[6] Existimabant autem quod forma cogniti sit in cognoscente eo modo quo est in re cognita.

E contrario tamen Platonici posuerunt. Plato enim, quia perspexit intellectualem animam immaterialem esse et immaterialiter cognoscere, posuit formas rerum cognitarum immaterialiter subsistere.

Priores vero Naturales, quia considerabant res cognitas esse corporeas et materiales, posuerunt oportere res cognitas etiam in anima cognoscente materialiter esse. Et ideo, ut animæ attribuerent omnium cognitionem, posuerunt eam habere naturam communem cum omnibus. Et quia natura principiatorum ex principiis constituitur, attribuerunt animæ naturam principii: ita quod qui dixit principium omnium esse ignem, posuit animam esse de natura ignis; et similiter de aëre et aqua. Empedocles autem, qui posuit quatuor elementa materialia et duo moventia, ex his etiam dixit animam esse constitutam. Et ita, cum res materialiter in anima ponerent, posuerunt omnem cognitionem animæ materialem esse, non discernentes inter intellectum et sensum.

Sed hæc opinio improbatur. Primo quidem, quia in materiali principio, de quo loquebantur, non existunt principiata nisi in potentia. Non autem cognoscitur aliquid secundum quod est in potentia, sed solum† secundum

*Piana: *essentia,* essence †Piana omits *solum*
[4]*De cælest. hierarchia* 12, 2. PG 3, 293
[5]op cit IX, 3. PL 42, 963
[6]Aristotle, *De Anima* I, 2. 404b17
[a]i.e., the Pre-Socratics, and especially the Ionians.
[b]Or 'physicists', *phusikoi,* Aristotle's term for the Pre-Socratic Ionians; cf *Physics* I, 4. 187a12.
[c]The Latin *principium* literally means 'beginning'. As St Thomas uses the term here and elsewhere, it can refer to anything at all upon which something else is dependent—as a simple starting-point, as an explanatory principle in knowing or in being (Latin *causa*), or especially as an 'efficient cause', a productive or moving agent (English 'cause').

3. Again, the soul is superior to material creatures. But lower things are contained in those of a higher order in a better way than in themselves, as Dionysius says.[4] Therefore all material creatures exist in a nobler way in the substance of the soul than in themselves. Thus the soul is capable of knowing material creatures by means of its own substance.

ON THE OTHER HAND, there is what Augustine says,[5] that *the mind gathers the knowledge of corporeal things through the senses of the body.* But the soul cannot know itself by means of these bodily senses. Therefore it does not know material things by way of its own substance.

REPLY: It was the position of the ancient philosophers[a] that the soul knows material things through its own essence—for it was a commonplace in their minds that *like is known by like.*[6] Further, they thought that the form of the object known should be in the knower exactly as it is in the thing known.

Plato's followers, on the other hand, held the contrary. For Plato, aware that the intellectual soul is immaterial and knows in an immaterial way, had held that the forms of things known subsist immaterially.

The earlier 'natural philosophers',[b] however, recognizing that the things known by the soul are material or corporeal, maintained that they must necessarily also exist in the soul in a material way. Thus, in order to attribute to the soul knowledge of everything, they held that it has a nature in common with everything. Further, because the nature of things that have principles is derived from those principles,[c] they attributed to the soul the nature of their principles: the philosopher[d] who said that fire is the principle of all things held that the soul has the nature of fire, and so on for air[e] and water.[f] Even Empedocles, who postulated four material elements and two motive principles,[g] held that the soul is made up of these principles. They supposed that things were in the soul in a material way; they maintained as a result that all the soul's knowledge is material, and thus did not discern intellectual from sense knowledge.

This opinion can be disproved. First, because the things that have as principles the elements of which these men spoke exist only potentially in such principles. A thing is not known, however, as potential, but only

---

[d]Heraclitus, according to Aristotle, *Metaphysics* I, 3. 984a5.
[e]Anaximenes.
[f]Thales.
[g]Fire, air, water, and earth; love and strife (*Metaphysics* I, 3 & 4. 984a7, 985a2–9). It should not be too easily supposed that these thinkers meant air, water, friendship, etc., as these are commonly experienced. They had in mind something 'purer' (though analogous to the realities of everyday experience).

quod est actu, ut patet in *Meta.*[7] Unde nec ipsa potentia cognoscitur nisi per actum. Sic igitur non sufficeret attribuere animæ principiorum naturam ad hoc quod omnia cognosceret, nisi inessent ei naturæ et formæ singulorum effectuum, puta ossis et carnis et aliorum hujusmodi; ut Aristoteles contra Empedoclem argumentatur.[8]

Secundo quia, si oporteret rem cognitam materialiter in cognoscente existere, nulla ratio esset quare res quæ materialiter extra animam subsistunt, cognitione carerent:* puta, si anima igne cognoscit ignem, et ignis etiam qui est extra animam, ignem cognosceret.

Relinquitur ergo quod oportet materialia cognita in cognoscente existere non materialiter, sed magis immaterialiter. Et hujus ratio est, quia actus cognitionis se extendit ad ea quæ sunt extra cognoscentem: cognoscimus enim etiam ea quæ extra nos sunt. Per materiam autem determinatur forma rei ad aliquid unum. Unde manifestum est quod ratio cognitionis ex opposito se habet ad rationem materialitatis. Et ideo quæ non recipiunt formas nisi materialiter, nullo modo sunt cognoscitiva, sicut plantæ.[9]

Quanto autem aliquid immaterialius habet formam rei cognitæ, tanto perfectius cognoscit. Unde et intellectus, qui abstrahit speciem non solum a materia sed etiam a materialibus conditionibus individuantibus, perfectius cognoscit quam sensus, qui accipit formam rei cognitæ sine materia quidem, sed cum materialibus conditionibus. Et inter ipsos sensus, visus est magis cognoscitivus, quia est minus materialis, ut supra dictum est.[10] Et inter ipsos intellectus, tanto quilibet est perfectior, quanto immaterialior.

Ex his ergo patet quod, si aliquis intellectus est qui per essentiam suam cognoscit omnia, oportet quod essentia ejus habeat in se immaterialiter† omnia; sicut antiqui posuerunt essentiam animæ actu componi ex principiis omnium materialium, ut cognosceret omnia.

Hoc autem est proprium Dei, ut sua essentia sit immaterialiter comprehensiva omnium prout effectus virtute præexistunt in causa. Solus igitur

---

*Piana: *carent*   †Piana: *materialiter*

[7]*Metaphysics* IX 9. 1051a29   [8]*De Anima* I, 5. 409b28-32
[9]ibid II, 12. 424a30   [10]1a. 78, 3
[h]*ratio*, definition or essential meaning.
[1]A clumsy term in English, but one that has now become standard epistemological terminology in widely disparate schools of thought. The term is loaded with overtones that can be seriously misleading. For an explanation of St Thomas's use, cf 1a. 85, 1.
[j]Technical terminology. The objects of our knowledge, in the Aristotelean understanding of things, include two kinds of material elements: those that make things material in the first place, and those that make them to be these particular material objects, here and now. The intellect abstracts from the here and now, the senses do not.
[k]Literally, 'is more of a knower'. In a sense the translation is anachronistic, but it

in so far as it is actual, as Aristotle makes evident.[7] (Thus even potentiality itself can be known only through its actualizations.) For the soul, then, to know everything, it is not enough to attribute to it the nature of the principles in this way, unless we further admit in the soul the natures and forms of individual effects, for instance, their flesh and bones, etc. (Aristotle argues in just this way against Empedocles.[8])

Secondly, because, were it necessary for a thing known to be in the soul materially, there would be no reason why things which exist materially outside the soul would not have knowledge. For instance, if it is by means of fire that the soul knows fire, then fire existing outside the soul would also know fire.

We are left with the conclusion, therefore, that material things when known must exist in the knower not materially but immaterially. And the reason for this is that the act of knowing goes out to things outside the knower—for we do also know things which are outside ourselves. But the form of a thing is limited by its matter to one thing. Therefore it is evident that the nature[h] of knowledge is opposite to the nature of materiality. Thus things that receive forms only in a material way are non-knowers, for instance, plants.[9]

Furthermore, the more immaterial a thing's way of having the forms of things known, the more perfect is its knowledge. Thus the intellect, which abstracts[i] species not only from matter but even from individuating material conditions,[j] has more perfect knowledge than the senses, which, while they receive the forms of things known without matter, do not do so without these material conditions. And among the senses, sight, which is least material, has the widest range of knowledge,[k] as was said before.[10] Again, among intellects, the more perfect are the more immaterial.[l]

Thus from all this it becomes evident that for an intellect to know everything by means of its own essence it would have to be such that its essence would contain everything in itself in an immaterial way. This was the sense in which the ancient philosophers held that the essence of the soul contains, in an actual way,[m] the principles of all material things so that it can know everything.

It is, however, characteristic of God alone that his essence comprehends all things in an immaterial way—in so far as effects have a

---

does give the flavour of what St Thomas intended. The sense in which sight is 'least material' is that it is dependent on fewer 'individuating material conditions'; it is more 'ethereal' than the other senses.
[l]The contrast is not between intellectual capabilities of different men, but between human, angelic, and divine intellects.
[m]As opposed to the potential way in which a knower has objects in itself, virtually and by way of images.

Deus per essentiam suam omnia intelligit; non autem anima humana, neque etiam angelus.

1. Ad primum ergo dicendum quod Augustinus ibi loquitur de visione imaginaria, quæ fit per imagines corporum. Quibus imaginibus formandis dat anima aliquid suæ substantiæ, sicut subjectum datur ut informetur per aliquam formam. Et sic de seipsa facit hujusmodi imagines: non quod anima vel aliquid animæ convertatur, ut sit hæc vel illa imago, sed sicut dicitur de corpore fieri aliquid coloratum, prout informatur colore. Et hic sensus apparet ex his quæ sequuntur. Dicit enim quod *servat aliquid*, scilicet non formatum tali imagine, *quod libere de specie talium imaginum judicet:* et hoc dicit esse *mentem* vel *intellectum.* Partem autem quæ informatur hujusmodi imaginibus, scilicet imaginativam, dicit esse *communem nobis et bestiis.*[11]

2. Ad secundum dicendum quod Aristoteles non posuit animam esse actu compositam ex omnibus, sicut antiqui Naturales; sed dixit *quodammodo animam esse omnia*, inquantum est in potentia ad omnia; per sensum quidem ad sensibilia, per intellectum vero ad intelligibilia.

3. Ad tertium dicendum quod quælibet creatura habet esse finitum et determinatum. Unde essentia superioris creaturæ, etsi habeat quandam similitudinem inferioris creaturæ prout communicant in aliquo genere, non tamen complete habet similitudinem illius, quia determinatur ad aliquam speciem, præter quam est species inferioris creaturæ. Sed essentia Dei est perfecta similitudo omnium quantum ad omnia quæ in rebus inveniuntur, sicut universale principium omnium.

articulus 3. utrum anima intelligat omnia per species sibi naturaliter inditas

AD TERTIUM sic proceditur:[1] 1. Videtur quod anima intelligat omnia per species sibi naturaliter inditas. Dicit enim Gregorius[2] quod *homo habet commune cum angelis intelligere.* Sed angeli intelligunt omnia* per formas

*Piana: *omnia naturaliter per formas inditas*
[11]*De Trinitate* x, 5. PL 42, 977
[1]cf *De veritate* x, 6; xi, 1; xviii, 7; xix, 1. *CG* ii, 83. Disputations *De anima* 15
[2]*Homilies on the Gospel* ii, 29. PL 76, 1214
nTechnical terminology derived from the Aristotelean conception of qualities (and other characteristics incidental to a thing, or *accidentia*) as forms received in either 'first' or 'second matter'—the latter then being called 'subjects' of the forms.
oOn *genus* as 'class', cf art. 1, note f: (logical) *species*, then, in the next sentence, will be rendered 'sub-class' (though *species* alone, in an obviously logical context, can also be translated as 'class').

pre-existence, virtually, in their cause. God alone, therefore, understands everything by means of his own essence—not so the human soul or even an angel.

Hence: 1. Augustine is there speaking of knowledge in the imagination, which uses material images. And to these images, in forming them, the soul does give of its own substance in the sense that a subject is given to a form, when it is informed by it.[n] Thus it makes these images out of itself, not in the sense that the soul or anything belonging to it is changed into this or that image, but in the sense that a body is said to become coloured when it is informed by a colour.

This reading of the passage is justified by what follows. For Augustine goes on to say that the soul *preserves something* not informed by such images *which freely judges of the nature of such images*, and this he calls *mind* or *intellect*. The part of the soul, on the other hand, which is informed by such images, namely the imagination, he refers to as *common to us and brute animals.*[11]

2. Aristotle was not of the opinion, held by the ancient natural philosophers, that the soul is actually made up of all things. Rather he said that *the soul is 'in a way' all things;* it is in a state of potentiality with respect to all things—to sensible things by means of the senses, to intelligible objects by means of the intellect.

3. Every creature has a limited, determined existence. Hence the essence of a higher creature, although it has some likeness to a lower creature in so far as they both belong to a particular class,[o] does not, even so, have a likeness to it in the complete sense. For it is limited to a particular sub-class, which is not the same as the sub-class of the lower creature.

The essence of God, on the other hand, is a perfect likeness of all things and of every aspect found in all things, as the universal cause[p] of all.

---

article 3. *does the soul understand everything by means of innate species*[a] *natural to it?*

THE FIRST POINT:[1] 1. It would seem that the soul understands everything by means of innate species that it has naturally. For Gregory says[2] that *man has understanding in common with the angels.* But angels understand

---

[p]Literally 'principle', but here obviously used in the third sense listed in note *c* above.
[a]The article is concerned with the problem of 'innate ideas', but the same term *species* is used throughout. It would be possible to translate *species* as 'idea' in this one article, but it seems preferable to be consistent with the usage in other articles and simply note that, in spite of the peculiarity in terminology, St Thomas is entering into a standard discussion of innate ideas.

naturaliter inditas: unde in libro *de Causis*[3] dicitur quod *omnis intelligentia est plena formis*. Ergo et anima habet species rerum naturaliter* inditas, quibus corporalia intelligit.

2. Præterea, anima intellectiva est nobilior quam materia prima corporalis. Sed materia prima est creata a Deo sub formis ad quas est in potentia. Ergo multo magis anima intellectiva est creata a Deo sub speciebus intelligibilibus. Et sic anima intelligit corporalia per species sibi naturaliter inditas.

3. Præterea, nullus potest verum respondere nisi de eo quod scit. Sed aliquis etiam idiota, non habens scientiam acquisitam, respondet verum de singulis, si tamen ordinate interrogetur, ut narratur in *Menone*[4] Platonis de quodam. Ergo antequam aliquis acquirat scientiam, habet rerum cognitionem. Quod non esset nisi anima haberet species naturaliter inditas. Intelligit igitur anima res corporeas per species naturaliter inditas.

SED CONTRA est quod Philosophus dicit,[5] de intellectu loquens, quod est *sicut tabula in qua nihil est scriptum*.

RESPONSIO: Dicendum quod, cum forma sit principium actionis, oportet ut eo modo se habeat aliquid ad formam quæ est actionis principium quo se habet ad actionem illam: sicut si moveri sursum est ex levitate, oportet quod in potentia tantum sursum fertur esse leve solum in potentia, quod autem actu sursum fertur, esse leve in actu.

Videmus autem quod homo est quandoque cognoscens in potentia tantum, tam secundum sensum quam secundum intellectum; et de tali potentia in actum reducitur, ut sentiat quidem, per actiones sensibilium in sensum, ut intelligat autem, per disciplinam aut inventionem. Unde oportet dicere quod anima cognoscitiva sit in potentia tam ad similitudines quæ sunt principia sentiendi, quam ad similitudines quæ sunt principia intelligendi.

Et propter hoc Aristoteles posuit quod intellectus, quo anima intelligit, non habet aliquas species naturaliter inditas, sed est in principio in potentia ad hujusmodi species omnes.

---

*Piana: *naturalium*
[3]Proposition 10   [4]82A
[5]*De Anima* III, 4. 430a1
[b]On this capitalization, see below, art. 4, note *f*.
[c]According to Aristotelean physics there is an intrinsic principle of 'levity' in light bodies just as there is an intrinsic principle of gravity in heavy bodies.
[d]The argument is obscured by the complex way in which it is expressed. It can be reduced to simpler terms: With respect to a form and the activity of which it is a principle, a thing's status—actual or potential—must be the same. But experience

everything by means of innate forms that they have by nature—thus the *De Causis* notes[3] that *every Intelligence*[b] *is full of forms*. Therefore the soul also should have naturally innate species of things by means of which it understands material beings.

2. Again, the intellectual soul is nobler than the primary matter of material beings. But primary matter is created by God as already joined to the forms to which it is potential. Therefore *a fortiori* the intellectual soul should be created by God as already informed with species. Thus the soul understands material beings by means of innate species which it has naturally.

3. Again, no one can give a true answer except about something he knows. But even an ignorant person without any acquired knowledge will give true responses about individual things if the questions are well ordered—as is shown by an individual mentioned in Plato's *Meno*.[4] Therefore a person, before getting any acquired knowledge, does have some knowledge of things, which could not be so unless the soul had naturally innate species. Thus the soul understands material things by means of naturally innate species.

ON THE OTHER HAND, Aristotle, in speaking of the intellect, says[5] that it is like *a writing-tablet on which as yet nothing is written*.

REPLY: Since forms are principles of activities, a thing must have the same relation to a form which is the principle of an activity that it has to the activity itself. (Thus if upward motion comes from lightness[c] as a principle, whatever is only in potentiality to being moved upwards must be only potential with respect to being light, and what is actually moving upwards must be actual with respect to being light.)

Now we recognize that men are sometimes only potentially knowing, both in sense and in intellectual knowledge, and they are brought from this state of potentiality to the actuality of sensation by the action of sensible objects on the senses, and to the actuality of understanding by teaching or discovery. We must therefore conclude that the soul as knower is in a state of potentiality with respect both to the likenesses that are the principles of sensation and to the likenesses that are the principles of understanding.[d]

For this reason Aristotle held that the intellect, by means of which the soul understands, has no naturally innate species but is initially in a state of potentiality with respect to all these species.

---

shows that the soul is sometimes only potential with respect to the activities of sensation and understanding. Therefore there are times when it is potential with respect to the image-forms that are principles of these activities.

Sed quia id quod habet actu formam interdum non potest agere secundum formam propter aliquod impedimentum, sicut leve si impediatur sursum ferri; propter hoc Plato posuit quod intellectus hominis naturaliter est plenus omnibus speciebus intelligibilibus, sed per unionem corporis impeditur ne possit in actum exire.

Sed hoc non videtur convenienter dictum. Primo quidem quia, si habet anima naturalem notitiam omnium, non videtur esse possibile quod hujus naturalis notitiæ tantam oblivionem capiat, quod nesciat se hujusmodi scientiam habere: nullus enim homo obliviscitur ea quae naturaliter cognoscit, sicut quod omne totum sit majus sua parte, et alia hujusmodi. Præcipue autem hoc videtur esse* inconveniens, si ponatur esse animæ naturale corpori uniri, ut supra habitum est:⁶ inconveniens enim est quod naturalis operatio alicujus rei totaliter impediatur per id quod est sibi secundum naturam.

Secundo, manifeste apparet hujus positionis falsitas ex hoc quod, deficiente aliquo sensu, deficit scientia eorum quæ apprehenduntur secundum illum sensum; sicut cæcus natus nullam potest habere notitiam de coloribus. Quod non esset, si† animæ essent naturaliter inditæ omnium intelligibilium rationes.

Et ideo dicendum est quod anima non cognoscit corporalia per species naturaliter inditas.

1. Ad primum ergo dicendum quod homo quidem convenit cum angelis in intelligendo, deficit tamen ab eminentia intellectus eorum: sicut et corpora inferiora, quæ tantum existunt secundum Gregorium, deficiunt ab existentia superiorum corporum.

Nam materia inferiorum corporum non est completa totaliter per formam, sed est in potentia ad formas quas non habet: materia autem cælestium corporum est totaliter completa per formam, ita quod non est in potentia ad aliam formam, ut supra habitum est.⁷ Et similiter intellectus angeli est perfectus per species intelligibiles secundum suam naturam: intellectus autem humanus est in potentia ad hujusmodi species.

2. Ad secundum dicendum quod materia prima habet esse substantiale per formam, et ideo oportuit quod crearetur sub aliqua forma: alioquin non esset in actu. Sub una tamen forma existens, est in potentia ad alias.

Yet because a thing having a form actually can at times be unable to act in accord with that form because of some impediment (a light object, for instance, can be impeded from moving upwards), Plato was led to the opinion[e] that the intellect, while it contains all species, is impeded from coming to a state of actuality by being united with the body.

This, however, does not seem to fit the facts. First, because, if the soul does have a natural knowledge of everything, it would seem impossible for it to be so forgetful of this natural knowledge that it would not know that it had such knowledge. For no one forgets things that are naturally known[f]—such as the axiom that the whole is greater than any of its parts, and so on. And this seems especially inappropriate if one holds that it is natural for the soul to be united to the body (as was held earlier[6]), since it would be inappropriate for a natural operation of a thing to be totally impeded by something belonging to the thing naturally.

Secondly, the falsity of this position is manifestly apparent from the fact that, if any of the senses is lacking, knowledge of what is apprehended by that sense is also lacking—for instance, a man born blind can have no acquaintance with colours. This would not be so if the natures of all intelligible objects were naturally innate in the soul.

We should therefore conclude that the soul does not know material things by means of naturally innate species.

Hence: 1. Man does have understanding in common with the angels, but it lacks the eminence of theirs. Similarly, inferior material beings—which, also according to Gregory, have existence alone—have a deficient existence in comparison with material things of a superior order.

For the matter of lower material beings is not fulfilled by their forms but is in potentiality with respect to forms it does not have, whereas the matter of the heavenly bodies is totally fulfilled by their forms, so that it has no potentiality to other forms, as was mentioned earlier.[7] So also the intellect of an angel has its complement of species naturally, whereas the human intellect is in a state of potentiality with respect to them.

2. Primary matter gets its substantial existence[g] from forms; it must, then, necessarily be created in conjunction with some form. Otherwise it could not actually exist. Once joined to a form, however, it is potential

---

[f]According to a realist epistemology, certain very general features of the world are said to be 'naturally known'. The sense is not that we have inborn ideas—explicitly argued against here—but that these general features, which either are or can be expressed in general axioms, are so evident that they cannot be denied once they are perceived. It is traditionally held that, although thinkers do at times (verbally) deny the axioms, their very denial is an implicit reaffirmation of the very axioms they profess to deny.

[g]Technical terminology; the meaning is 'gets its very existence'.

Intellectus autem non habet esse substantiale per speciem intelligibilem. Et ideo non est simile.

3. Ad tertium dicendum quod ordinata interrogatio procedit ex principiis communibus per se notis ad propria. Per talem autem processum scientia causatur in anima addiscentis. Unde cum verum respondet de his de quibus secundo interrogatur, hoc non est quia prius ea noverit, sed quia tunc ea de novo addiscit. Nihil enim refert utrum ille qui docet proponendo vel interrogando procedat de principiis communibus ad conclusiones; utrobique enim animus audientis certificatur de posterioribus per priora.

articulus 4. utrum species i ntelligibiles effluant in animam ab aliquibus formis separatis

AD QUARTUM sic proceditur:[1] 1. Videtur quod species intelligibiles effluant in animam ab aliquibus formis separatis. Omne enim quod per participationem est tale, causatur ab eo quod est per essentiam tale; sicut quod est ignitum reducitur sicut in causam in ignem. Sed anima intellectiva, secundum quod est actu intelligens, participat ipsa intelligibilia: intellectus enim in actu quodammodo est intellectum in actu. Ergo ea quæ secundum se et per essentiam suam sunt intellecta in actu sunt causæ animæ intellectivæ quod actu intelligat. Intellecta autem in actu per essentiam suam sunt formæ sine materia existentes. Species igitur intelligibiles quibus anima intelligit, causantur a formis aliquibus separatis.

2. Præterea, intelligibilia se habent ad intellectum sicut sensibilia ad sensum. Sed sensibilia quæ sunt in actu extra animam sunt causæ specierum* sensibilium quæ sunt in sensu, quibus sentimus. Ergo species intelligibiles quibus intellectus noster intelligit causantur ab aliquibus actu intelligibilibus extra animam existentibus. Hujusmodi autem non sunt nisi formæ a materia separatæ. Formæ igitur intelligibiles intellectus nostri effluunt ab aliquibus substantiis separatis.

3. Præterea, omne quod est in potentia reducitur in actum per id quod est actu. Si ergo intellectus noster, prius in potentia existens, postmodum actu intelligat, oportet quod hoc causetur ab aliquo intellectu qui semper

---

*Piana: *ipsorum*, of (the sensible objects) themselves
[1]cf *De veritate* x, 6; xi, 1. Disputations *De anima* 15
a*formis separatis*; cf art. 1, note *g*.
bThe Latin says literally that ideas 'flow into the soul from immaterial substances'— a metaphor, perhaps based on an analogy with a 'flood' of light. Since it is doubtful that anyone ever held for a flow in the literal sense, the translation seeks to be fair to the sense without carrying over the Latin metaphor. (Later on St Thomas himself uses the circumlocution, 'through the influence of', cf note *j*, below.) This, along with the following article and question 88, is as close as he ever comes to an explicit treatment of the so-called 'illumination theories' popular in his day.

with respect to others. The intellect, on the contrary, does not get its substantial existence from species. Thus the analogy does not hold.

3. Orderly inquiry goes from general, self-evident principles to particulars, and it is by such a process that knowledge is caused in the soul of a learner. Thus when the latter gives a true response to a later question, it is not because he has prior knowledge of the things involved in the answer; rather, he learns them for the first time then and there. For it makes no difference whether the teacher uses a doctrinal or a questioning method; in either case as long as he goes from general principles to conclusions, the mind of the learner will get its certainty about what follows from what has preceded.

article 4. do species come to the soul through the influence of subsistent immaterial[a] forms?

THE FIRST POINT:[1] 1. It would seem that species do come to the soul by the influence of[b] subsistent immaterial forms. For whatever has a characteristic by participation is caused[c] by what has that characteristic essentially[d] —for instance, the cause of something's being on fire must ultimately be fire itself. The intellectual soul, however, when actually understanding, possesses intelligible objects by participation—for the intellect in act is, in a sense, identified with the object actually understood. Therefore those things which are in themselves and essentially always actually understood are the cause of the intellectual soul's actual understanding. But these things that are essentially always actually understood are forms existing without matter. Thus the species by means of which the soul understands are caused by immaterial forms.

2. Again, the relation of intelligible objects to the intellect is the same as that of sensible objects to the senses. But sensible objects having an actual existence outside the soul are the causes of the sensible images in the senses by means of which sensation takes place. Therefore the species by means of which our intellect understands are caused by actually intelligible objects outside the soul. But these can only be forms separate from matter. Therefore the intellectual forms in our intellects come from immaterial substances.

3. Again, whatever is in a potential state is brought to actuality by something actual. Thus if our intellect, after being in a potential state, actually begins to understand, this must be by the causality of an intellect

[c]Not necessarily by way of efficient causality, but that seems the more natural sense in this article.
[d]Essentially and by participation; technical terms in a common contrast. A paraphrase might be: Whatever has something *as borrowed* (or derived) must get it from something that has it *as its own*.

est in actu. Hic autem est intellectus separatus. Ergo ab aliquibus substantiis separatis causantur species intelligibiles quibus actu intelligimus.

SED CONTRA est quia secundum hoc sensibus non indigeremus ad intelligendum. Quod patet esse falsum ex hoc præcipue quod qui caret uno sensu, nullo modo potest habere scientiam de sensibilibus illius sensus.

RESPONSIO: Dicendum quod quidam posuerunt species intelligibiles nostri intellectus procedere ab aliquibus formis vel substantiis separatis. Et hoc dupliciter.

Plato enim, sicut dictum est,[2] posuit formas rerum sensibilium per se sine materia subsistentes; sicut formam hominis, quam nominabat *per se hominem*, et formam vel ideam equi, quam nominabat *per se equum*, et sic de aliis. Has ergo formas separatas ponebat participari et ab anima nostra, et a materia corporali; ab anima quidem nostra ad cognoscendum, a materia vero corporali ad essendum; ut sicut materia corporalis per hoc quod participat ideam lapidis fit hic lapis, ita intellectus noster per hoc quod participat ideam lapidis fit intelligens lapidem. Participatio autem ideæ fit per aliquam similitudinem ipsius ideæ in participante ipsam, per modum quo exemplar participatur ab exemplato. Sicut igitur ponebat formas sensibiles quæ sunt in materia corporali effluere ab ideis sicut quasdam earum similitudines, ita ponebat species intelligibiles nostri intellectus esse similitudines quasdam idearum ab eis effluentes. Et propter hoc, ut supra dictum est,[3] scientias et definitiones ad ideas referebat.

Sed quia contra rationem rerum sensibilium est quod earum formæ subsistant absque materiis, ut Aristoteles multipliciter probat,[4] ideo Avicenna, hac positione remota, posuit omnium rerum sensibilium intelligibiles species, non quidem per se subsistere absque materia, sed præexistere immaterialiter in intellectibus separatis; a quorum primo derivantur hujusmodi species in sequentem, et sic de aliis usque ad ultimum intellectum separatum, quem nominat *intellectum agentem*; a quo, ut ipse dicit, effluunt species intelligibiles in animas nostras, et formæ sensibiles in materiam corporalem.

Et sic in hoc Avicenna cum Platone concordat, quod species intelligibiles

---

[2]art. 1   [3]art. 1

[4]For instance, *Metaphysics* VII, 14. 1039a24

[e]Or perhaps 'man as such', but not 'the *per se* man' or 'man himself' as *per se homo* is often translated. Cf Paul Friedländer: *Plato: An Introduction* (New York: Pantheon, 1958), p. 22.

[f]Here capitalized because personified, as with Plato's Forms and Ideas. The usage is uncommon in English, yet can serve a useful purpose. (See the next note.)

[g]A number of English translations of this term as it applies to a faculty of the soul

always in a state of actuality. Such are subsistent intellects. Therefore the species by means of which we understand are caused by immaterial substances.

ON THE OTHER HAND, if this position were true, we would not need the senses in order to understand. But this is false, as is especially evident from the fact that a man who lacks one of the senses can nowise know the objects corresponding to it.

REPLY: Some have held that the species in our intellects come from immaterial forms or substances. And this in two versions.

Plato, as has been noted,[2] held for self-subsistent immaterial Forms of sensible things—for instance, the Form of a man, which he called 'the man',[e] and the Form or Idea of a horse, which he called 'the horse', etc. Accordingly, he held that these Forms are possessed by participation both in the soul and in corporeal matter, in our soul for purposes of knowing, in corporeal matter to give existence to material beings. Thus as corporeal matter becomes this particular stone through participating in the Idea of stone, so also our intellect comes to know a particular stone through participating in the Idea of stone. (Having an Idea by participation means that there is a likeness of the Idea in the thing that has it so, rather as the original model is in a copy.) Therefore, just as he held that sensible forms come from the Ideas, as their likenesses, Plato also held that the species in our intellects are likenesses of, and come from, the Ideas. And for this reason, as was indicated earlier,[3] he said that demonstrations and definitions have reference to the Ideas.

However, as Aristotle shows in many ways,[4] that the forms of sensible things should exist without matter contradicts their very nature. Thus Avicenna, rejecting Plato's position, held that the species of all sensible things, while they do not subsist of themselves, have an immaterial pre-existence in subsistent Intellects,[f] such species in the second of the Intellects being derived from the first, and so on until they come to the last of these Intellects, which he called the Agent Intellect.[g] Finally, he says, species come from the Agent Intellect into our souls, and sensible forms into corporeal matter.

Thus to an extent Avicenna agrees with Plato, that the species in our

---

have been tried, not altogether successfully. One of the advantages of capitalizing Avicenna's Intellects is that a developmental flavour can then be given by using 'Agent Intellect' and 'Possible Intellect' when these refer to the personified versions of Avicenna and Averroes, and 'agent' and 'possible intellect' when the reference is to faculties of the soul (with names obviously derived from the other usage). This is similar to the usual practice with Platonic 'Ideas' and 'ideas'.

nostri intellectus effluunt a quibusdam formis separatis: quas tamen Plato dicit per se subsistere, Avicenna vero ponit eas in intelligentia agente. Differunt etiam quantum ad hoc, quod Avicenna ponit species intelligibiles non remanere in intellectu nostro postquam desinit actu intelligere; sed indiget ut iterato se convertat ad recipiendum de novo. Unde non ponit scientiam animae naturaliter inditam, sicut Plato, qui ponit participationes idearum immobiliter in anima permanere.

Sed secundum hanc positionem sufficiens ratio assignari non posset quare anima nostra corpori uniretur. Non enim potest dici quod anima intellectiva corpori uniatur propter corpus: quia nec forma est propter materiam, nec motor propter mobile, sed potius e converso. Maxime autem videtur corpus esse necessarium animæ intellectivæ ad ejus propriam operationem, quæ est intelligere: quia secundum esse suum a corpore non dependet. Si autem anima species intelligibiles secundum suam naturam apta nata esset recipere per influentiam aliquorum separatorum principiorum tantum, et non acciperet eas ex sensibus, non indigeret corpore ad intelligendum: unde frustra corpori uniretur.

Si autem dicatur quod indiget anima nostra sensibus ad intelligendum, quibus quodammodo excitetur ad consideranda ea quorum species intelligibiles a principiis separatis recipit; hoc non videtur sufficere. Quia hujusmodi excitatio non videtur necessaria animæ nisi inquantum est consopita, secundum Platonicos, quodammodo et obliviosa propter unionem ad corpus. Et sic sensus non proficerent animæ intellectivæ nisi ad tollendum impedimentum quod animæ provenit ex corporis unione. Remanet igitur quærendum quæ sit causa unionis animæ ad corpus.

Si autem dicatur, secundum Avicennam, quod sensus sunt animæ necessarii, quia per eos excitatur ut convertat se ad intelligentiam agentem, a qua recipit species; hoc quidem non sufficit. Quia si in natura animæ est ut intelligat per species ab intelligentia agente effluxas, sequeretur quod quandoque anima possit se convertere ad intelligentiam agentem ex inclinatione

---

ʰAccording to either version.
¹This should not be misunderstood, as if soul and body were separately existing substantial beings; cf 1a. 75.
ʲcf note *b*, above.
ᵏIn simple terms the argument says: Since the body is *not* necessary for the existence of the soul (which continues to exist after death), it *is* necessary for the activity most natural to the soul—otherwise it would be totally unnecessary, joined to the body to no purpose.
There is a difficulty here, however: Question 75 has proved that the human soul is subsistent (and consequently immortal) from the fact that its *operation* is *independent* of the body. Now St Thomas turns around and uses the soul's subsistence to show that its *operation* must be *dependent* on the body.
A way out of the difficulty is to recognize that there are different senses of de-

intellects come from subsistent immaterial forms. However, Plato says that Ideas are self-subsistent, Avicenna that they exist in the Agent Intelligence. Again, they differ with respect to Avicenna's opinion that species do not remain in our intellect after it ceases to understand; rather, the intellect needs to return and receive them all over again. Hence he does not hold for naturally innate knowledge in the soul, as Plato did in saying that the participations of the Ideas remain in the soul in an unchangeable way.

In this view,[h] however, no satisfactory reason can be given why our soul is united to the body. On the one hand, it cannot be said that the intellectual soul is united to the body for the sake of the body, because, first, form is not for the sake of matter, nor, second, is the mover for the thing moved—just the reverse. On the other hand, since the soul's existence does not depend upon the body,[1] the body would seem to be especially necessary for the intellectual soul in its characteristic operation, which is understanding. But if the soul were by nature such that it could receive species through the influence of[j] certain immaterial principles alone, and not from the senses, it would not need the body to understand. Thus it would be united to the body to no purpose.[k]

If one should reply that our soul needs the senses in order to understand, in the sense that by them it is awakened somehow to consider the things whose species it is then receiving from the immaterial principles, this does not seem an adequate response. For this awakening would not seem necessary unless the soul were somehow asleep—according to the Platonists— or forgetful because of its union with the body. Thus the senses would only profit the intellectual soul in overcoming an obstacle that befalls it only on account of its union with the body.[1] A question would therefore still remain as to why there should be a union of soul and body in the first place.

If one replies with Avicenna, on the other hand, that the senses are necessary for the soul because it is aroused by them to turn to the Agent Intelligence from which it receives species, neither will this suffice. For if it were in the nature of the soul to understand by way of species coming from an Agent Intelligence, it would follow that the soul could sometimes

---

pendence and independence, and in the Thomist view the soul is in fact *dependent* on the body *both* for existence (it must begin to exist in the body before it can survive after death) and for understanding (in the sense outlined in the present article). However, it is also independent in the spiritual aspect of both its existence and its intellectual operation. It is perhaps unfortunate that St Thomas does not untangle these senses here, but the argument remains valid.

[1]That is, the senses—which belong to the body—would be needed only in order to undo the damage done by the body.

suæ naturæ, vel etiam excitata per alium sensum ut convertat se ad intelligentiam agentem, ad recipiendum species sensibilium quorum sensum aliquis non habet. Et sic cæcus natus posset habere scientiam de coloribus: quod est manifeste falsum. Unde dicendum est quod species intelligibiles quibus anima nostra intelligit, non effluunt a formis separatis.

1. Ad primum ergo dicendum quod species intelligibiles quas participat noster intellectus, reducuntur sicut in primam causam in aliquod principium per suam essentiam intelligibile, scilicet in Deum. Sed ab illo principio procedunt mediantibus formis rerum sensibilium et materialium, a quibus scientiam colligimus, ut Dionysius dicit.[5]

2. Ad secundum dicendum quod res materiales, secundum esse quod habent extra animam, possunt esse sensibiles actu; non autem actu intelligibiles. Unde non est simile de sensu et intellectu.

3. Ad tertium dicendum quod intellectus noster possibilis reducitur de potentia ad actum per aliquod ens actu, idest per intellectum agentem, qui est virtus quædam animæ nostræ, ut dictum est;[6] non autem per aliquem intellectum separatum sicut per causam* proximam, sed forte sicut per causam remotam.

articulus 5. utrum anima intellectiva cognoscat res materiales in rationibus æternis

AD QUINTUM sic proceditur:[1] 1. Videtur quod anima intellectiva non cognoscat res materiales† in rationibus aeternis. Id enim in quo aliquid cognoscitur ipsum magis et per prius cognoscitur. Sed anima intellectiva hominis, in statu præsentis vitæ, non cognoscit rationes æternas: quia non cognoscit ipsum Deum, in quo rationes æternæ existunt, sed *ei sicut ignoto conjungitur*, ut Dionysius dicit.[2] Ergo anima non cognoscit omnia in rationibus æternis.

2. Præterea, dicitur[3] quod *invisibilia Dei per ea quæ facta sunt, conspiciuntur*. Sed inter invisibilia Dei numerantur rationes æternæ. Ergo rationes æternæ per creaturas materiales cognoscuntur, et non e converso.

3. Præterea, rationes æternæ nihil aliud sunt quam ideæ: dicit enim Augustinus[4] quod *ideæ sunt rationes stabiles rerum in mente divina existentes*. Si ergo dicatur quod anima intellectiva cognoscit omnia in rationibus

---

*Piana adds *propriam*, proper   †Piana: *res immateriales*, spiritual things
[5]*De divinis nominibus* 7. PG 3, 886 *lect.* 2.
[6]Ia. 79, 4
[1]cf Ia. 12, 11 ad 3
[2]*De mystic. theol.* 3. PG 3, 1001

turn to the Agent Intelligence by natural inclination—or else, aroused by one sense to turn to the Agent Intelligence—to receive species of the objects of a sense which a person did not have. In this case a man born blind could have knowledge of colours—which is obviously false.

Thus we should conclude that the species by which our soul understands do not come from subsistent immaterial forms.

Hence: 1. The species our intellect has by participation come ultimately from a first cause which is a principle essentially intelligible, namely God. But they proceed from that principle through the medium of sensible, material things, from which, as Dionysius says,[5] we gather our knowledge.

2. Material things, with respect to the existence they have outside the soul, can be actually sensible but not actually intelligible. Hence the analogy does not hold between sense and intellect.

3. Our possible intellect[m] is brought from potentiality to actuality by some being that is actual, namely by the agent intellect—which is a faculty belonging to our soul, as has been said[6]—and not by a separate Intellect as proximate cause, though it might be a remote cause.

article 5. does the intellectual soul know material things in the divine ideas?

THE FIRST POINT:[1] 1. It would seem that the intellectual soul does not know material things in the divine ideas. For there must be prior and better knowledge of that in which a thing is known. Now the intellectual soul of man, in his earthly life, does not know the divine ideas—for it does not know God, in whom these ideas exist, but is, according to Dionysius,[2] *united to him as to the unknown.* Therefore the soul does not know everything in the divine ideas.

2. Again, in Scripture[3] it is said that *the invisible things of God are there for the mind to see in the things he has made.* But among the invisible things of God are the divine ideas. Thus these divine ideas are known through material created things and not the other way around.

3. Again, the divine ideas are precisely that—ideas. For Augustine says,[4] that *ideas are the patterns of things existing unchanged in the divine mind.* Therefore if we say that the intellectual soul knows everything in

---

[3]*Romans* 1, 20
[4]*Lib.* 83 *quæst.* 46. PL 40, 30
[m]This transliteration, though a barbarism, seems better than most substitutes that have been tried. In addition, it can give the same historical flavour as the 'Agent Intellect–agent intellect' pairing, see note *g* above: 'possible intellect' would thus describe the faculty, 'Possible Intellect' the substantialized version of Averroes. On the Possible Intellect in Averroes, cf E. Gilson: *History of Christian Philosophy in the Middle Ages* (New York, 1955), p. 225.

æternis, redibit opinio Platonis, qui posuit omnem scientiam ab ideis derivari.

SED CONTRA est quod dicit Augustinus:[5] *Si ambo videmus verum esse quod dicis, et ambo videmus verum esse quod dico, ubi quæso id videmus? Nec ego utique in te, nec tu in me: sed ambo in ipsa, quæ supra mentes nostras est, incommutabili veritate.* Veritas autem incommutabilis in æternis rationibus continetur. Ergo anima intellectiva omnia vera cognoscit in rationibus æternis.

RESPONSIO: Dicendum quod, sicut Augustinus dicit,[6] *Qui philosophi* vocantur, si qua forte vera et fidei nostræ accommoda dixerunt, ab eis tanquam ab injustis possessoribus in usum nostrum vindicanda sunt. Habent enim doctrinæ gentilium quædam simulata et superstitiosa figmenta, quæ unusquisque nostrum de societate gentilium exiens, debet evitare.*

Et ideo Augustinus, qui doctrinis Platonicorum imbutus fuerat, si qua invenit fidei accommoda in eorum dictis, assumpsit, quæ vero invenit fidei nostræ adversa, in melius commutavit.

Posuit autem Plato, sicut supra dictum est, formas rerum per se subsistere a materia separatas, quas *ideas* vocabat, per quarum participationem dicebat intellectum nostrum omnia cognoscere; ut sicut materia corporalis per participationem ideæ lapidis fit lapis, ita intellectus noster per participationem ejusdem ideæ cognosceret lapidem. Sed quia videtur esse alienum a fide quod formæ rerum extra res per se subsistant absque materia, sicut Platonici posuerunt, dicentes *per se vitam* aut *per se sapientiam* esse quasdam substantias creatrices, ut Dionysius dicit,[7] ideo Augustinus posuit[8] loco harum idearum quas Plato ponebat, rationes omnium creaturarum in mente divina existere, secundum quas omnia formantur, et secundum quas etiam anima humana omnia cognoscit.

Cum ergo quæritur utrum anima humana in rationibus aeternis omnia cognoscat, dicendum est quod aliquid in aliquo dicitur cognosci dupliciter. Uno modo, sicut in objecto cognito; sicut aliquis videt in speculo ea quorum imagines in speculo resultant. Et hoc modo anima, in statu præsentis vitæ, non potest videre omnia in rationibus æternis; sed sic in rationibus æternis cognoscunt omnia beati, qui Deum vident et omnia in ipso. Alio modo dicitur aliquid cognosci in aliquo sicut in cognitionis principio; sicut si dicamus quod in sole videntur ea quae videntur per solem. Et sic necesse est dicere quod anima humana omnia cognoscat in rationibus

---

*Leonine: *Philosophi qui*
[5]*Confessions* XII, 25. PL 32, 840
[6]*De doctrina christiana* II, 40. PL 34, 63

the divine ideas, we revive the opinion of Plato who held that all knowledge is derived from Ideas.

ON THE OTHER HAND, there is Augustine's saying,[5] *If we both see that what you say is true, and if we both see that what I say is true, where, I ask, do we see it? Certainly I do not see it in you, nor you in me, but both in the unchangeable truth itself, which is above our minds.* But the unchangeable truth is contained in the divine ideas. Therefore the intellectual soul knows all truths in the divine ideas.

REPLY: As Augustine says,[6] *If those who are called philosophers said by chance anything that was true and consistent with our faith, we must claim it from them as from unjust possessors. For some of the doctrines of the pagans are spurious imitations or superstitious inventions, which we must be careful to avoid when we renounce the society of the pagans.* Accordingly Augustine, who was steeped in the doctrines of the Platonists, whenever he found anything in their statements consistent with the Faith he accepted it, but amended what he found hostile.

Now Plato, as was said above, held that the forms of things subsist of themselves separate from matter. He called these Ideas and said that our intellects know everything by participation in them; thus, as corporeal matter becomes stone by participation in the Idea of stone, so, by participation in the same Idea, our intellects know stone. However, since it seems alien to the Faith that the forms of things should subsist of themselves, outside things and without matter—as the Platonists held, saying that 'life as such' and 'wisdom as such' are creative substances (according to Dionysius[7])—Augustine substituted[8] in place of these Ideas which Plato posited the ideas of all creatures existing in the divine mind. All things are formed according to these, and in addition the human soul knows everything according to them.

Thus when the question is asked: Does the human soul know everything in the divine ideas?, the reply must be that one thing can be spoken of as known in another in two ways: first, as in an object itself known, for instance, when one may see in a mirror things whose images are reflected there. In this sense the soul, in its earthly state of life, cannot see everything in the divine ideas; on the other hand, the blessed who see God and everything else in God do thus know everything in the divine ideas. Secondly, a thing is spoken of as known in another as in a principle of knowledge; for instance, we might say that things seen by sunlight are seen in the sun. In this sense we must say that the human soul knows everything in the divine

---

[7]*De divinis nominibus* 11. PG 3, 956. *lect.* 6.   [8]*Lib.* 83 *quæst.* 46. PL 40, 30

æternis, per quarum participationem omnia cognoscimus. Ipsum enim lumen intellectuale quod est in nobis nihil est aliud quam quædam participata similitudo luminis increati, in quo continentur rationes æternæ.

Unde dicitur,[9] *Multi dicunt, Quis ostendit nobis bona?* cui quæstioni Psalmista respondet, dicens, *Signatum est super nos lumen vultus tui, Domine.* quasi dicat, Per ipsam sigillationem divini luminis in nobis, omnia nobis* demonstrantur.

Quia tamen præter lumen intellectuale in nobis, exiguntur species intelligibiles a rebus acceptæ ad scientiam de rebus materialibus habendam; ideo non per solam participationem rationum æternarum de rebus materialibus notitiam habemus, sicut Platonici posuerunt quod sola idearum participatio sufficit ad scientiam habendam. Unde Augustinus dicit,[10] *Numquid quia philosophi documentis certissimis persuadent æternis rationibus omnia temporalia fieri, propterea potuerunt in ipsis rationibus perspicere, vel ex ipsis colligere quot sint†animalium genera, quæ semina singulorum? Nonne ista omnia per locorum ac temporum historiam quæsierunt?*

Quod autem Augustinus non sic intellexerit omnia cognosci *in rationibus æternis,* vel *in incommutabili veritate,* quasi ipsæ rationes æternæ videantur, patet per hoc quod ipse dicit,[11] quod *rationalis anima non omnis et quælibet,‡ sed quæ sancta et pura fuerit, asseritur illi visioni,* scilicet rationum æternarum, *esse idonea;* sicut sunt animæ beatorum.§

Et per hæc patet responsio ad objecta.

articulus 6. utrum intellectiva cognitio accipiatur a rebus sensibilibus

AD SEXTUM sic proceditur:[1] 1. Videtur quod intellectiva cognitio non accipiatur a rebus sensibilibus. Dicit enim Augustinus,[2] quod *non est expectanda sinceritas veritatis a corporis sensibus.* Et hoc probat dupliciter. Uno modo, per hoc quod *omne quod corporeus sensus attingit sine ulla intermissione temporis commutatur; quod autem non manet percipi non potest.* Alio modo, per hoc quod *omnia quæ per corpus sentimus, etiam cum non adsunt sensibus, imagines tamen eorum patimur, ut in somno vel furore; non autem sensibus discernere valemus utrum ipsa sensibilia, vel imagines eorum falsas sentiamus. Nihil autem percipi potest quod a falso non discernitur.*

Et sic concludit quod non est expectanda veritas a sensibus. Sed cognitio intellectualis est apprehensiva veritatis. Non ergo cognitio intellectualis est expectanda a sensibus.

---

*Piana omits *nobis*
‡Piana: *quæcumque*
[9]*Psalms* 4, 6–7
[10]*De Trinitate* IV, 16. PL 42, 902

†Piana: *sunt*
§Piana: *bonorum,* of the good

[11]*Lib.* 83 *quæst.* 46. PL 40, 30

ideas, and that by participation in them we know everything. For the intellectual light in us is nothing more than a participating likeness of the uncreated light in which the divine ideas are contained.

Many say: Who will give us sight of happiness?[9] and the Psalmist replies to the question, *The light of your face, Lord, is signed upon us,* as if to say, by the seal of the divine light in us everything is made known to us.

Nevertheless, since besides the intellectual light which is in us, species taken from things are required for our knowledge of material things, we do not have this merely by participation in the divine ideas in the way in which Platonists held that mere participation in the Ideas sufficed for knowledge. And so Augustine asks,[10] *For pray, because philosophers dispute most truly, and persuade us by most certain proofs, that all things temporal are made after ideas that are eternal, are they therefore able to see clearly in these ideas, or to collect from them, how many kinds of animals there are, what are the seeds of each in their beginnings? Have they not sought out all these things through the actual history of places and times?*

Moreover, that Augustine did not understand everything to be known *in the divine ideas* or *in the unchangeable truth* in the sense that the divine ideas themselves were seen is clear from what he writes,[11] *Not any and every rational soul can be called worthy of that vision,* namely of the divine ideas, *but only one that is pure and holy*—such as are the souls of the blessed.

From all this the replies to the objections are evident.

article 6. is intellectual knowledge taken from sensible things?

THE FIRST POINT:[1] 1. It would seem that intellectual knowledge is not taken from sensible things. For Augustine says[2] that *we cannot expect to acquire the pure truth from the corporeal senses,* and he proves this in two ways. First, from the fact that *whatever a corporeal sense attains is changing, and this without any lapse of time; but if something does not remain the same, it cannot be perceived.* Secondly, from the fact that *everything that we sense by means of the body we also receive in images, even when the things are not present to the senses* (as for instance in sleep or in a rage). *Yet we cannot distinguish by means of the senses whether we are perceiving the sensible things themselves or false images, and nothing can be perceived which is indistinguishable from what is false.*

He thus concludes that truth cannot be expected from the senses. But intellectual knowledge does apprehend the truth. Therefore intellectual knowledge should not be looked for from the senses.

---

[1]cf *De veritate* x, 6. *Quodl.* VIII, 2, 1. *Compend. Theol.* 81
[2]*Lib.* 83 *quæst.* 9. PL 40, 13

2. Præterea, Augustinus dicit,[3] *Non est putandum facere aliquid corpus in spiritum, tanquam spiritus corpori facienti materiæ vice subdatur: omni enim modo præstantior est qui facit, ea re de qua aliquid facit.* Unde concludit quod *imaginem corporis non corpus in spiritu, sed ipse spiritus in seipso facit.* Non ergo intellectualis cognitio a sensibilibus* derivatur.

3. Præterea, effectus non se extendit ultra virtutem suæ causæ. Sed intellectualis cognitio se extendit ultra sensibilia: intelligimus enim quædam quæ sensu percipi non possunt. Intellectualis ergo cognitio non derivatur a rebus sensibilibus.

SED CONTRA est quod Philosophus probat,[4] quod principium nostræ cognitionis est a sensu.

RESPONSIO: Dicendum quod circa istam quæstionem triplex fuit philosophorum opinio. Democritus enim posuit quod *nulla est alia causa cujuslibet nostræ cognitionis, nisi cum ab his corporibus quæ cogitamus, veniunt atque intrant imagines in animas nostras;* ut Augustinus dicit.[5] Et Aristoteles etiam dicit[6] quod Democritus posuit cognitionem fieri *per idola et defluxiones.*

Et hujus positionis ratio fuit, quia tam ipse Democritus quam alii antiqui naturales non ponebant intellectum differre a sensu, ut Aristoteles dicit.[7] Et ideo, quia sensus immutatur a sensibili, arbitrabantur omnem nostram cognitionem fieri per solam immutationem a sensibilibus. Quam quidem immutationem Democritus asserebat fieri per imaginum defluxiones.

Plato vero e contrario posuit intellectum differre a sensu; et intellectum quidem esse virtutem immaterialem organo corporeo non utentem in suo actu. Et quia incorporeum non potest immutari a corporeo, posuit quod cognitio intellectualis non fit per immutationem intellectus a sensibilibus, sed per participationem formarum intelligibilium separatarum, ut dictum est. Sensum etiam posuit virtutem quamdam per se operantem. Unde nec ipse sensus, cum sit quædam vis spiritualis, immutatur a sensibilibus: sed organa sensuum a sensibilibus immutantur, ex qua immutatione anima quodammodo excitatur ut in se species sensibilium formet.

Et hanc opinionem tangere videtur Augustinus,[8] ubi dicit quod *corpus non sentit, sed anima per corpus, quo velut nuntio utitur ad formandum in seipsa quod extrinsecus nuntiatur.*

---

*Piana: *sensibus,* from the senses
[3]*De Genesi ad litteram* XII, 16. PL 34, 467
[4]*Metaphysics* I, 1. 981a2; *Posterior Analytics* II, 15. 100a3
[5]*Epist.* 118, *ad Dioscurum* 4. PL 33, 446   [6]*De divinatione per somnum* 2. 464a5

2. Again, Augustine says,[3] *We must not think that the body can make an impression on the spirit, as though the spirit were to be subject, like matter, to the body's action; for that which acts is in every way more excellent than that on which it acts.* From which he concludes that *the body does not cause its image in the spirit, but the spirit causes it in itself.* Therefore intellectual knowledge is not derived from sensible things.

3. Again, an effect does not go beyond the reach of its cause. But, since we understand some things which cannot be perceived by the senses, intellectual knowledge does go beyond sensible things. Therefore intellectual knowledge is not derived from sensible things.

ON THE OTHER HAND, Aristotle proves[4] that the beginning of our knowledge is in the senses.

REPLY: On this question there were among the philosophers three opinions. Democritus held that *there is no other cause, for any of our knowledge, than the fact that images come into our souls from the bodies of which we think,* according to Augustine.[5] Aristotle also remarks[6] that Democritus held that knowledge comes about *by means of images and emanations.*

The reason for this position was that neither Democritus nor the other ancient natural philosophers distinguished between intellect and sense, according to Aristotle.[7] Thus, since a change is effected in the senses by the sensible object, they thought that all our knowledge comes about merely by such a change effected by sensible objects. And it was this change that Democritus claimed is brought about by emanations of images.

Plato, on the other hand, held that the intellect is distinct from the senses, and indeed that it is an immaterial faculty which does not use a corporeal organ when it acts. Now since the incorporeal cannot be affected by the corporeal, Plato also held that intellectual knowledge does not come about by a change effected in the intellect by sensible things, but rather by participation in separate intelligible forms, as mentioned earlier. He further held that the senses are independently operating faculties: thus even the senses themselves—since they are spiritual faculties—are not affected by sensible objects. Instead, the organs of the senses are affected by sensible things, and the soul is somehow awakened by this change to form within itself the images of sensible objects.

Augustine seems to touch on this opinion when he says[8] that *the body does not feel, but the soul by means of the body, which it makes use of as a kind of messenger to reproduce within itself what is announced from without.*

---

[7]*De Anima* III, 3. 427a17
[8]*De Genesi ad litteram* XII, 24. PL 34, 475

35

Sic igitur secundum Platonis opinionem, neque intellectualis cognitio a sensibili procedit, neque etiam sensibilis totaliter a sensibilibus rebus; sed sensibilia excitant animam sensibilem ad sentiendum, et similiter sensus excitant animam intellectivam ad intelligendum.

Aristoteles autem media via processit. Posuit enim cum Platone intellectum differre a sensu. Sed sensum posuit propriam operationem non habere sine communicatione corporis;[9] ita quod sentire non sit actus animæ tantum, sed conjuncti. Et similiter posuit de omnibus operationibus sensitivæ partis. Quia igitur non est inconveniens quod sensibilia quæ sunt extra animam causent aliquid in conjunctum, in hoc Aristoteles cum Democrito concordavit, quod operationes sensitivæ partis causentur per impressionem sensibilium in sensum: non per modum defluxionis, ut Democritus posuit, sed per quandam operationem. Nam et Democritus omnem actionem fieri posuit per influxionem atomorum.[10]

Intellectum vero posuit Aristoteles habere operationem absque communicatione corporis.[11] Nihil autem corporeum imprimere potest in rem incorpoream. Et ideo ad causandam intellectualem operationem, secundum Aristotelem, non sufficit sola impressio sensibilium corporum, sed requiritur aliquid nobilius, quia *agens est honorabilius patiente*, ut ipse dicit.[12]

Non tamen ita quod intellectualis operatio causetur in nobis* ex sola impressione aliquarum rerum superiorum, ut Plato posuit: sed illud superius et nobilius agens quod vocat intellectum agentem, de quo jam supra diximus,[13] facit phantasmata a sensibus accepta intelligibilia in actu, per modum abstractionis cujusdam.

Secundum hoc ergo, ex parte phantasmatum intellectualis operatio a sensu causatur. Sed quia phantasmata non sufficiunt immutare intellectum possibilem, sed oportet quod fiant intelligibilia actu per intellectum agentem; non potest dici quod sensibilis cognitio sit totalis et perfecta causa intellectualis cognitionis, sed magis quodammodo est materia causæ.

1. Ad primum ergo dicendum quod per verba illa Augustini datur intelligi quod veritas non sit totaliter a sensibus expectanda. Requiritur enim lumen intellectus agentis, per quod immutabiliter veritatem in rebus mutabilibus cognoscamus, et discernamus ipsas res a similitudinibus rerum.

2. Ad secundum dicendum quod Augustinus ibi† non loquitur de

---

*Piana omits *in nobis,* in us
†Piana omits *ibi,* here
[9]cf *De somno* 454a7
[10]Aristotle, *De generatione* I, 8. 324b5
[11]*De Anima* III, 4. 429a24
[12]ibid III, 5. 430a18

Thus, according to the opinion of Plato, intellectual knowledge does not start from sensible knowledge, nor does sensible knowledge itself proceed totally from sensible things. Rather, sensible objects awaken the sensible soul to sense and, similarly, the senses awaken the intellectual soul to understand.

Aristotle, finally, proceeded along a middle course. With Plato he agreed in holding that the intellect is distinct from the senses, but he did not hold that the senses have a proper activity without communication with the body.[9] Thus for him sensation is not an activity of the soul alone but of the body-soul composite, and the same is true of all the activities of the sensible part of man. Accordingly, since there is no difficulty in the fact that sensible objects outside the soul should have an effect on the composite, Aristotle was in agreement with Democritus to this extent: the activities of the sensible part are brought about by an impression made on the senses by sensible objects—not by means of an emanation, as Democritus held, but by some kind of activity. (Democritus, indeed, held that every action is produced by an influx of atoms.[10])

On the other hand, Aristotle held that the intellect does have an activity in which the body does not communicate.[11] But nothing corporeal can make an impression on an incorporeal thing. Therefore, to cause an intellectual activity, according to Aristotle, a mere impression made by sensible bodies is not enough—something of a higher order is required because *the active is superior to the passive factor*, as he says.[12]

Nevertheless, this does not imply that our intellectual activity is caused merely by an impression from things of a higher order as Plato held. That higher, superior agent which Aristotle calls the agent intellect—spoken of earlier[13]—by a process of abstraction makes images received from the senses actually intelligible.

According to this, then, intellectual activity is caused by the senses by way of these images. However, since these images are not capable of effecting a change in the possible intellect but must be made actually intelligible by the agent intellect, it is not right to say that sensible knowledge is the total and complete cause of intellectual knowledge—better to say it is somehow the material of the cause.

Hence: 1. Augustine's words there should be understood in the sense that truth is not to be looked for entirely from the senses. For the light of the agent intellect is required for us to know the truth found in changeable things in an unchanging way, and to distinguish real things from likenesses of things.

2. Augustine is not there speaking of intellectual knowledge, but of

[13]Ia. 79, 3-4

intellectuali cognitione, sed de imaginaria. Et quia, secundum Platonis opinionem, vis imaginaria habet operationem quæ est animæ solius; eadem ratione usus est Augustinus ad ostendendum quod corpora non imprimunt suas similitudines in vim imaginariam, sed hoc facit ipsa anima, qua utitur Aristoteles[14] ad probandum intellectum agentem esse aliquid separatum, quia scilicet *agens est honorabilius patiente*.

Et procul dubio oportet, secundum hanc positionem, in vi imaginativa ponere non solum potentiam passivam, sed etiam activam. Sed si ponamus, secundum opinionem Aristotelis,[15] quod actio virtutis imaginativæ sit conjuncti, nulla sequitur difficultas: quia corpus sensibile est nobilius organo animalis, secundum hoc quod comparatur ad ipsum ut ens in actu ad ens in potentia, sicut coloratum in actu ad pupillam, quæ colorata est in potentia.

Posset tamen dici quod, quamvis prima immutatio virtutis imaginariæ sit per motum sensibilium, quia *phantasia est motus factus secundum sensum*,[16] tamen est quædam operatio animæ in homine quæ dividendo et componendo format diversas rerum imagines, etiam quæ non sunt a sensibus acceptæ. Et quantum ad hoc possunt accipi verba Augustini.

3. Ad tertium dicendum quod sensitiva cognitio non est tota causa intellectualis cognitionis. Et ideo non est mirum si intellectualis cognitio ultra sensitivam se extendit.

articulus 7. utrum intellectus possit actu intelligere per species
intelligibiles quas penes se habet non convertendo se ad phantasmata

AD SEPTIMUM sic proceditur:[1] 1. Videtur quod intellectus possit actu intelligere per species intelligibiles quas penes se habet, non convertendo se ad phantasmata. Intellectus enim fit in actu per speciem intelligibilem qua informatur. Sed intellectum esse in actu est ipsum intelligere. Ergo species intelligibiles sufficiunt ad hoc quod intellectus actu intelligat, absque hoc quod ad phantasmata se convertat.

2. Præterea, magis dependet imaginatio a sensu, quam intellectus ab imaginatione. Sed imaginatio potest imaginari actu, absentibus sensibilibus. Ergo multo magis intellectus potest intelligere actu, non convertendo se ad phantasmata.

3. Præterea, incorporalium non sunt aliqua phantasmata: quia imaginatio

---

[14]*De Anima* III, 5. 430a18
[15]ibid I, 1. 430a5
[16]ibid III, 3. 429a1
[1]cf II *Sent.* 20, 2, 2 ad 3. *De veritate* x, 2 ad 7. *In De memor.* 3
[a]This article has been called the touchstone of Aristotelean–Thomistic realism—and rightly so. The most important aspect of the doctrine is found in the sentence,

knowledge in the imagination. And since according to Plato's view the faculty of imagination has an activity belonging to the soul alone, Augustine uses the same argument to show that bodies do not impress their likenesses on the imagination (the soul does this itself) that Aristotle uses[14] to prove that the agent intellect is immaterial—namely, that *the active is superior to the passive factor*.

Without doubt we must suppose, according to this view, not only a passive, but also an active capacity in the imagination. However, if we hold, according to the view of Aristotle,[15] that the activity of the imagination belongs to the composite, there is no difficulty. For a sensible body is 'superior' to an organ of an animal to the extent that in comparison with the organ, it is a being actual relative to a being potential, even as a coloured object is with respect to the potentially coloured pupil of the eye.

It could nevertheless be said that, although the primary change in the imagination is produced by changes coming from sensible objects— *imagination is a movement resulting from an actual exercise of a sense faculty*[16] —still there is an activity of the soul in man which, by separating and joining, forms different images of things (even of things not received from the senses), and Augustine's words can be taken as referring to this.

3. Sense knowledge is not the whole cause of intellectual knowledge, and it is thus no cause for wonder if intellectual knowledge goes beyond sense knowledge.

article 7. can the intellect, using only the species it has and not turning to sense images, actually understand?[a]

THE FIRST POINT:[1] 1. It would seem that the intellect could actually understand by means of the species it has, without turning to sense images. For the intellect is placed in a state of actuality by an informing species. But for the intellect, being in a state of actuality is precisely the act of understanding. Therefore species suffice to make the intellect actually understood, without any turning to sense images.

2. Again, the imagination is more dependent on the senses than is the intellect upon imagination. But the faculty of imagination can exercise its act in the absence of sensible objects. Therefore *a fortiori* the intellect can actually understand without turning to sense images.

3. Again, there are no sense images of incorporeal beings since the

---

'Hence it is obvious that for the intellect actually to understand (not only in acquiring new knowledge but also *in using knowledge already* acquired) acts of the imagination and the other faculties are necessary.'

Convertendo se: this technical terminology is clarified in 1a. 89, 1 & 2, which contrasts the way the separated soul 'turns itself to' objects with the way the soul joined to the body 'turns itself to sense images'.

tempus et continuum non transcendit. Si ergo intellectus noster non posset aliquid intelligere in actu nisi converteretur ad phantasmata, sequeretur quod non posset intelligere incorporeum aliquid. Quod patet esse falsum: intelligimus enim veritatem ipsam, et Deum et angelos.

SED CONTRA est quod Philosophus dicit,[2] *nihil sine phantasmate intelligit anima.*

RESPONSIO: Dicendum quod impossibile est intellectum nostrum,* secundum præsentis vitæ statum quo passibili corpori conjungitur, aliquid intelligere in actu, nisi convertendo se ad phantasmata. Et hoc duobus indiciis apparet. Primo quidem quia, cum intellectus sit vis quædam non utens corporali organo, nullo modo impediretur in suo actu per læsionem alicuius corporalis organi, si non requireretur ad eius actum actus alicujus potentiæ utentis organo corporali. Utuntur autem organo corporali sensus et imaginatio et aliæ vires pertinentes ad partem sensitivam. Unde manifestum est quod ad hoc quod intellectus actu intelligat, non solum accipiendo scientiam de novo, sed etiam utendo scientia iam acquisita, requiritur actus imaginationis et ceterarum virtutum.

Videmus enim quod, impedito actu virtutis imaginativæ per læsionem organi, ut in phreneticis, et similiter impedito actu memorativæ virtutis, ut in lethargicis, impeditur homo ab intelligendo in actu etiam ea quorum scientiam præaccepit.

Secundo, quia hoc quilibet in seipso experiri potest, quod quando aliquis conatur aliquid intelligere, format aliqua phantasmata sibi per modum exemplorum, in quibus quasi inspiciat quod intelligere studet. Et inde est etiam quod quando alium† volumus facere aliquid intelligere, proponimus ei exempla, ex quibus sibi phantasmata formare possit ad intelligendum.

Hujus autem ratio est, quia potentia cognoscitiva proportionatur cognoscibili. Unde intellectus angelici,‡ qui est totaliter a corpore separatus, objectum proprium est substantia intelligibilis a corpore separata; et per hujusmodi intelligibilia materialia cognoscit. Intellectus autem humani, qui est conjunctus corpori, proprium objectum est quidditas sive natura in materia corporali existens; et per hujusmodi naturas visibilium rerum etiam in invisibilium rerum aliqualem cognitionem ascendit. De ratione autem hujus naturæ est, quod in aliquo individuo existat, quod non est absque materia corporali: sicut de ratione naturæ lapidis est quod sit in hoc lapide, et de ratione naturæ equi§ quod sit in hoc equo, et sic de aliis. Unde

*Piana omits *nostrum,* our
‡Piana: *angeli*
[2]*De Anima* III, 7. 431a16

†Piana: *aliquem,* someone
§Piana adds *est,* is

imagination does not transcend the world of time and extension. If, therefore, our intellect could not actually understand a thing without turning to sense images, it would follow that it could not understand anything incorporeal. But this is clearly false since we understand truth itself, as well as God and the angels.

ON THE OTHER HAND, Aristotle claims[2] that *the soul never thinks without an image.*

REPLY: It is impossible for our intellect, in its present state of being joined to a body capable of receiving impressions, actually to understand anything without turning to sense images. This is evident on two counts. First, because, since it is a faculty which does not use a corporeal organ, the intellect would be in no sense impeded by an injury to a corporeal organ if for its act another act of a faculty that does use a corporeal organ were not required. But the senses, the imagination, and the other faculties of the sense part of man do use corporeal organs. Hence it is obvious that, for the intellect actually to understand (not only in acquiring new knowledge but also in using knowledge already acquired), acts of the imagination and the other faculties are necessary.

We see, in fact, that if acts of the imagination are impeded by an injury to its organ—for instance, in a seizure—or, similarly, if acts of sense memory are impeded—for instance, in coma—a man is impeded from actually understanding even things which he had known before.

The second count is this. As anyone can experience for himself, if he attempts to understand anything, he will form images for himself which serve as examples in which he can, as it were, look at what he is attempting to understand. This is the reason, indeed, why, when we want to help someone understand something, we propose examples to him so that he can form images for himself in order to understand.

The reason for all this is that cognitive faculties are proportioned to their objects. For instance, an angel's intellect, which is totally separate from corporeal reality, has as its proper object intelligible substances separate from corporeal reality, and it is by means of these intelligible objects that it knows material realities. The proper object of the human intellect, on the other hand, since it is joined to a body, is a nature or 'whatness'[b] found in corporeal matter—the intellect, in fact, rises to the limited knowledge it has of invisible things by way of the nature of visible things. But by definition a nature of this kind exists in an individual which has corporeal matter, for instance, it is of the nature of stone that it should

---

[b] *quidditas*, essence, what a thing is; see Appendix 2.

natura lapidis, vel cujuscumque materialis rei, cognosci non potest complete et vere, nisi secundum quod cognoscitur ut in particulari existens. Particulare autem apprehendimus per sensum et imaginationem. Et ideo necesse est ad hoc quod intellectus actu* intelligat suum objectum proprium, quod convertat se ad phantasmata, ut speculetur naturam universalem in particulari existentem.

Si autem proprium objectum intellectus nostri esset forma separata, vel si naturæ† rerum sensibilium subsisterent non in particularibus, secundum Platonicos, non oporteret quod intellectus noster semper intelligendo converteret se ad phantasmata.

1. Ad primum ergo dicendum quod species conservatæ in intellectu possibili, in eo existunt habitualiter quando actu non intelligit, sicut supra dictum est.[3] Unde ad hoc quod intelligamus in actu non sufficit ipsa conservatio specierum, sed oportet quod eis utamur secundum quod convenit rebus quarum sunt species, quæ sunt naturæ in particularibus existentes.

2. Ad secundum dicendum quod etiam ipsum phantasma est similitudo rei particularis: unde non indiget imaginatio aliqua alia similitudine particularis,‡ sicut indiget intellectus.

3. Ad tertium dicendum quod incorporea, quorum non sunt phantasmata, cognoscuntur a nobis per comparationem ad corpora sensibilia, quorum sunt phantasmata. Sicut veritatem intelligimus ex consideratione rei circa quam veritatem speculamur; Deum autem, ut Dionysius dicit,[4] cognoscimus ut causam, et per excessum et per remotionem; alias etiam incorporeas substantias, in statu præsentis vitæ, cognoscere non possumus nisi per remotionem, vel aliquam comparationem ad corporalia. Et ideo cum de hujusmodi aliquid intelligimus, necesse habemus converti ad phantasmata corporum, licet ipsorum non sint phantasmata.

articulus 8. utrum judicium intellectus impediatur per ligamentum sensus

AD OCTAVUM sic proceditur:[1] 1. Videtur quod judicium intellectus non impediatur per ligamentum sensus. Superius enim non dependet ab

---

*Piana omits *actu*, actually
†Piana: *formæ*, forms
‡Piana: *particulari*

[3]1a. 79, 6
[4]*De divinis nominibus* I, 5. PG 3, 593
[1]cf 2a2æ. 154, 5. *De veritate* XII, 3 ad 1 sqq.
[c]For our analogical knowledge of God and the spiritual world, and its two ways of 'eminence' (*per excessum*) and 'negation' (*per remotionem*) see 1a. 12 & 13. Vol. 3 of this series. Introduction (2).
[a]*Judicium intellectus*, the judgment of the intellect. The phrase is ambiguous and

exist in this or that particular stone, or of the nature of horse that it should exist in this or that particular horse, etc. Thus the nature of stone or any other material reality cannot be known truly and completely except in so far as it exists in a particular thing. Now we apprehend the particular through the senses and imagination. Therefore if it is actually to understand its proper object, then the intellect must needs turn to sense images in order to look at universal natures existing in particular things.

Whereas if the proper object of our intellect were an immaterial form, or if the natures of sensible things subsisted apart from particulars, as the Platonists think, it would not be necessary for our intellect when understanding always to be turning to sense images.

Hence: 1. Species stored up in the possible intellect remain there in a habitual way when the intellect is not actually understanding, as was said above.[3] Thus, in order for us actually to understand, a mere storing of species is not sufficient; we must also use them, and indeed in accord with the things of which they are images, which are natures existing in particulars.

2. Since the sense image is itself a likeness of a particular thing, the imagination does not need a further likeness of a particular, as does the intellect.

3. We know incorporeal realities, which have no sense images, by analogy with sensible bodies, which do have images, just as we understand truth in the abstract by a consideration of things in which we see truth. God we know, according to Dionysius,[4] as cause about which we ascribe the utmost perfection and negate any limit.[c] Furthermore, we cannot, in our present state, know other incorporeal substances except negatively and by analogy with corporeal realities. Thus when we understand anything of these beings, we necessarily have to turn to images of sensible bodies even though they do not themselves have such images.

article 8. is intellectual discernment[a] *hindered when the senses are bound?*

THE FIRST POINT:[1] 1. It would seem that intellectual discernment is not hindered when the senses are bound. For the higher is not dependent on

---

elliptical. In one sense it is the equivalent of the English 'discrimination', or 'discernment', cf 1a. 78, 4 ad 2 (with reference to the senses, internal and external), and 1a. 85, 6 (with reference to the simple apprehension of an essence or 'whatness'). In an extended sense, however, St Thomas will also use *judicium* where we would use 'judgment'—in this case a judgment based on a prior 'discernment', e.g., of one of the senses; cf 1a. 85, 2. In either case the basic etymological sense is preserved, i.e., a distinguishing by comparison with a standard; cf *De veritate* x, 9.

inferiori. Sed judicium intellectus est supra sensum. Ergo judicium intellectus non impeditur per ligamentum sensus.

2. Præterea, syllogizare est actus intellectus. In somno autem ligatur sensus;[2] contingit tamen quandoque quod aliquis dormiens syllogizat. Ergo non impeditur judicium intellectus per ligamentum sensus.

SED CONTRA est quod in dormiendo ea quæ contra licitos mores contingunt, non imputantur ad peccatum; ut Augustinus dicit.[3] Hoc autem non esset si homo in dormiendo liberum usum rationis et intellectus haberet. Ergo impeditur rationis usus per ligamentum sensus.

RESPONSIO: Dicendum quod, sicut dictum est, proprium objectum intellectui nostro proportionatum est natura rei sensibilis. Judicium autem perfectum de re aliqua dari non potest, nisi ea omnia quæ ad rem pertinent cognoscantur; et præcipue si ignoretur* id quod est terminus et finis judicii. Dicit autem Philosophus[4] quod *sicut finis factivæ scientiæ est opus, ita naturalis scientiæ finis est quod videtur principaliter secundum sensum:* faber enim non quærit cognitionem cultelli nisi propter opus, ut operetur hunc particularem cultellum; et similiter naturalis non quærit cognoscere naturam lapidis et equi, nisi ut sciat rationes eorum quæ videntur secundum sensum. Manifestum est autem quod non posset esse perfectum judicium fabri de cultello si opus ignoraret: et similiter non potest esse perfectum judicium scientiæ naturalis de rebus naturalibus si sensibilia ignorentur.

Omnia autem quæ in præsenti statu intelligimus, cognoscuntur a nobis per comparationem ad res sensibiles naturales. Unde impossibile est quod sit in nobis judicium intellectus perfectum, cum ligamento sensus, per quem res sensibiles cognoscimus.

1. Ad primum ergo dicendum quod, quamvis intellectus sit superior sensu, accipit tamen aliquo modo a sensu, et ejus objecta prima et principalia in sensibilibus fundantur. Et ideo necesse est quod impediatur judicium intellectus ex ligamento sensus.

---

*Piana: *ignoraretur*

[2]Aristotle, *De somno* 454b11: 'Sleep is an affection of the organ of sense-perception —a sort of tie or inhibition of function.'

[3]*De Genesi ad litteram* XII, 15. PL 34, 466

[4]*De cælo* III, 7. 306a16

[b]*perfectum* and *perfecte*, perfect, perfectly: St Thomas will use these terms repeatedly throughout the treatise in a technical sense. That sense is here defined in the remainder of the sentence: Complete (or perfect) knowledge of a thing is had

the lower. But intellectual discernment is above sensation. Therefore intellectual discernment is not hindered when the senses are bound.

2. Again, syllogizing is an act of the intellect. But, though in sleep sensing is suspended,[2] it can at times happen that a person syllogizes in his sleep. Therefore the discernment of the intellect is not impeded through suspension of the senses.

ON THE OTHER HAND, if things happen in sleep that are against good morals, they are not counted as sins, according to Augustine.[3] But this would not be true if while asleep a man had free use of reason and understanding. Therefore the use of reason is impeded by a binding of the senses.

REPLY: As mentioned, the proper object proportioned to our intellect is the nature of sensible things. Now complete[b] insight into a thing cannot be had unless all that belongs to it is known, especially if what is unknown is the term or goal of the insight. But Aristotle says[4] that the term, *which in the case of productive knowledge is the work itself, in the knowledge of nature is the unimpeachable evidence of the senses.* A smith, for instance, seeks only to know about blades because of his job, which is to forge a good one. Likewise, the philosopher seeks only to know the nature of stone or horse in order to have an explanation of things which are seen with the senses. It is evident, however, that the smith's judgment about a blade would not be complete if he was ignorant of what it was for, and, likewise, the judgment of natural science with respect to natural things if sensible things themselves were not known.

Now everything we understand in the present life we know in relation to[c] natural, sensible realities. Therefore it is impossible for us to have complete intellectual discernment when the senses through which we know sensible realities are bound.

Hence: 1. Although the intellect is superior to the senses, it does in a manner also receive from them; its primary and principal objects have their foundation in sensible objects. Thus intellectual discernment is necessarily hindered when the senses are bound.

---

when *everything* about it is known, down to the last detail and including its ultimate material conditions.

[c] *per comparationem ad*: this is difficult to translate literally since we can only properly compare things known. What is meant is that we can be given a clue to the existence of something, then attribute to it, or deny of it, qualities found in what first gave the hint. Thus the idea is more that of 'knowing in relation to' than of 'knowing by comparison with'.

2. Ad secundum dicendum quod sensus ligatur in dormientibus propter evaporationes quasdam et fumositates resolutas.[5] Et ideo secundum dispositionem hujusmodi evaporationum contingit esse ligamentum sensus maius vel minus.

Quando enim multus fuerit motus vaporum, ligatur non solum sensus, sed etiam imaginatio, ita ut nulla appareant phantasmata; sicut præcipue accidit cum aliquis incipit dormire post multum cibum et potum. Si vero motus vaporum aliquantulum fuerit remissior, apparent phantasmata, sed distorta et inordinata; sicut accidit in febricitantibus. Si vero adhuc magis motus sedetur, apparent phantasmata ordinata; sicut maxime solet contingere in fine dormitionis, et in hominibus sobriis et habentibus fortem imaginationem. Si autem motus vaporum fuerit modicus, non solum imaginatio remanet libera, sed etiam ipse sensus communis ex parte solvitur; ita quod homo judicat interdum in dormiendo ea quæ videt somnia esse, quasi dijudicans inter res et rerum similitudines. Sed tamen ex aliqua parte remanet sensus communis ligatus; et ideo, licet aliquas similitudines discernat a rebus, tamen semper in aliquibus decipitur.

Sic igitur per modum quo sensus solvitur et imaginatio in dormiendo, liberatur et* judicium intellectus, non tamen ex toto. Unde illi qui dormiendo syllogizant, cum excitantur, semper recognoscunt se in aliquo defecisse.

---

*Piana omits *et*, also

[5]Aristotle, *De somno* 456b17: 'Sleep is not co-extensive with any and every impotence of the perceptive faculty, but this affection is one which arises from the evaporation attendant upon the process of nutrition.'

2. In sleepers the senses are bound because of vapours or gases that are released during digestion,[5] and proportionately to their amount.

Thus when there is a good bit of movement of the vapours, both the senses and the imagination are bound and no sense images appear—as happens especially when someone falls asleep after taking a large amount of food and drink. If, second, the movement of the vapours is a little less, then images appear, though distorted and disorganized, as in the case of high fever. If, further, the movement quietens down still more, then orderly images appear, as normally happens especially towards the end of sleep and in men who are sober or gifted with strong imagination. If, finally, the movement of vapours is very slight, not only does the imagination remain free, but even the *sensus communis* is partly freed, so that a man can sometimes recognize while still asleep that what he sees are dreams, discerning, as it were, between things and likenesses of things. Nevertheless, the *sensus communis* remains partly bound, so that, although it discriminates between some likenesses and the reality, it is always deceived in others.

Thus to the extent that the senses and imagination are free in sleep intellectual discernment is also unfettered, but not totally. Therefore those who syllogize in their sleep, when awakened, will invariably recognize a flaw in some respect.

Quæstio 85. de modo et ordine intelligendi

DEINDE CONSIDERANDUM EST de modo et ordine intelligendi, et circa hoc quæruntur octo:

1. utrum intellectus noster intelligat abstrahendo species a phantasmatibus;
2. utrum species intelligibiles abstractæ a phantasmatibus, se habeant ad intellectum nostrum ut quod intelligitur, vel sicut id quo intelligitur;
3. utrum intellectus noster naturaliter intelligat prius magis universale;
4. utrum intellectus noster possit multa simul intelligere;
5. utrum intellectus noster intelligat componendo et dividendo;
6. utrum intellectus possit errare;
7. utrum unus possit eamdem rem melius intelligere quam alius;
8. utrum intellectus noster per prius cognoscat indivisibile quam divisibile.

articulus I. utrum intellectus noster intelligat res corporeas et
materiales per abstractionem a phantasmatibus

AD PRIMUM sic proceditur:[1] 1. Videtur quod intellectus noster non intelligat res corporeas et materiales per abstractionem a phantasmatibus. Quicumque enim intellectus intelligit rem aliter quam sit est falsus. Formæ autem rerum materialium non sunt abstractæ a particularibus, quorum similitudines sunt phantasmata. Si ergo intelligamus res materiales per abstractionem specierum a phantasmatibus, erit falsitas in intellectu nostro.

2. Præterea, res materiales sunt res naturales, in quarum definitione cadit materia. Sed nihil potest intelligi sine eo quod cadit in definitione eius. Ergo res materiales non possunt intelligi sine materia. Sed materia est individuationis principium. Ergo res materiales non possunt intelligi per abstractionem universalis a particulari, quod est abstrahere species intelligibiles a phantasmatibus.

3. Præterea, dicitur[2] quod phantasmata se habent ad animam intel-

---

[1]cf Ia. 12, 4, *CG* II, 77. *In Meta.* II, lect. I
[2]*De Anima* III, 7. 431a14
[a]Abstraction and abstractionism have long been debated in philosophy. Elaborate treatises have been written on positive and negative abstraction, on 'separation' as a distinct form of abstraction, etc. All this is interesting and important, but com-

Question 85. the mode and order of understanding

NEXT TO BE CONSIDERED are the mode and order of understanding, and with respect to these there are eight issues for discussion:

1. whether our intellect understands by abstracting species from sense images;
2. whether the species abstracted from images are related to our intellect as *what* is understood or as *that whereby* things are understood;
3. whether our intellect naturally understands first the more universal;
4. whether our intellect can understand more than one thing at a time;
5. whether our intellect understands by combining and separating;
6. whether the intellect can be in error;
7. whether, with respect to the same reality, one can have a better understanding than another;
8. whether our intellect knows the indivisible before the divisible.

article 1. does our intellect understand material, corporeal realities by abstraction from sense images?

THE FIRST POINT:[1] 1. It would seem that our intellect does not understand material and corporeal realities by abstraction from sense images.[a] For if one understands an object otherwise than as it really is then he is in error. But the forms of material things are not abstract, set apart from the particulars represented by sense images. Therefore if we understand in abstraction species from sense images, our intellect will be in error.

2. Again, material things are natural things, requiring matter in their definition. Now nothing can be understood without something which is required for its definition. Hence material things cannot be understood without matter. But matter is the principle of individuation. Therefore material things cannot be understood by abstracting the universal from the particular, which is the same as abstracting species from sense images.

3. Again, Aristotle says[2] that sense images have the same relation to the

plicated, sometimes needlessly. There is thus an advantage in presenting St Thomas's own view in an uncluttered way, exactly as he presents it in this article. He follows Aristotle's general lead, yet his treatment is original: Aristotle himself is unclear on the nature of abstraction. See Appendix 2, on the simple understanding of essence or *quidditas*, 'whatness .

lectivam sicut colores ad visum. Sed visio non fit per abstractionem aliquarum specierum a coloribus, sed per hoc quod colores imprimunt in visum. Ergo nec intelligere contingit per hoc quod aliquid abstrahatur a phantasmatibus, sed per hoc quod phantasmata imprimunt in intellectum.

4. Præterea, ut dicitur,[3] in intellectiva anima sunt duo, scilicet intellectus possibilis et agens. Sed abstrahere a phantasmatibus species intelligibiles non pertinet ad intellectum possibilem, sed recipere species jam abstractas. Sed nec etiam videtur pertinere ad intellectum agentem, qui se habet ad phantasmata sicut lumen ad colores, quod non abstrahit aliquid a coloribus, sed magis eis influit. Ergo nullo modo intelligimus abstrahendo a phantasmatibus.

5. Præterea, Philosophus dicit[4] quod *intellectus intelligit species in phantasmatibus*; non ergo eas abstrahendo.

SED CONTRA est quod dicitur,[5] *sicut res sunt separabiles a materia, sic circa intellectum sunt.* Ergo oportet quod materialia intelligantur inquantum a materia abstrahuntur, et a similitudinibus materialibus, quæ sunt phantasmata.

RESPONSIO: Dicendum quod, sicut supra dictum est,[6] objectum cognoscibile proportionatur virtuti cognoscitivæ. Est autem triplex gradus cognoscitivæ virtutis. Quædam enim cognoscitiva virtus est actus organi corporalis, scilicet sensus. Et ideo objectum cujuslibet sensitivæ potentiæ est forma prout in materia corporali existit. Et quia hujusmodi materia est individuationis principium, ideo omnis potentia sensitivæ partis est cognoscitiva particularium tantum.

Quædam autem virtus cognoscitiva est quæ neque est actus organi corporalis, neque est aliquo modo corporali materiæ conjuncta, sicut intellectus angelicus. Et ideo hujus virtutis cognoscitivæ objectum est forma sine materia subsistens: etsi enim materialia cognoscant, non tamen nisi in immaterialibus ea intuentur, scilicet* vel in seipsis vel in Deo.

Intellectus autem humanus medio modo se habet: non enim est actus alicujus organi, sed tamen est quædam virtus animæ, quæ est forma corporis, ut ex supra dictis patet.[7] Et ideo proprium ejus est cognoscere formam in materia quidem corporali individualiter existentem, non tamen prout est in tali materia. Cognoscere vero id quod est in materia individuali, non prout est in tali materia, est abstrahere formam a materia individuali,

*Piana omits *scilicet*
[3]*De Anima* III, 5. 430a14
[4]ibid III, 7. 431b2
[5]ibid III, 4. 429b21

intellectual soul that colour has to sight. But seeing does not take place by abstracting images from colours, but by colours being impressed on the sight. Neither, therefore, does understanding happen by way of something being abstracted from sense images, but by an impression made on the intellect by sense images.

4. Again, as Aristotle says,[3] in the intellectual soul there are two faculties: namely, the possible and the agent intellects. But the function of the possible intellect is not that of abstracting species from images but of receiving species already abstracted. Neither, however, does it seem to be the function of the agent intellect: it has the same relation to sense images that light has to colours, which is not that of abstracting anything from colours but rather of streaming out to them. Therefore in no way do we understand by abstracting from sense images.

5. Again, Aristotle says[4] that the intellect *thinks the forms in the images*. Not therefore, by abstracting them.

ON THE OTHER HAND, Aristotle says[5] that *as realities are separable from matter, so is it with their being understood*. Therefore material realities must be understood precisely as abstracted or set apart from matter and from material likenesses such as sense images.

REPLY: As was said earlier,[6] knowable objects are proportioned to knowing faculties, and there are three levels of such faculties. First, one kind of cognitive faculty is the form of a corporeal organ: such is sense. Accordingly, the object of every sense faculty is a form existing in corporeal matter, and so, since this sort of matter is the principle of individuation, all the faculties of the sense part of man only know particulars.

A second kind of cognitive faculty is neither the form of a corporeal organ nor in any way joined to corporeal matter; such is an angel's intellect. Accordingly, its object is a form subsisting without matter, for although angels can know material things, they see them only in something immaterial, namely either in themselves or in God.

The human intellect stands in the middle. It is not the form of an organ, although it is a faculty of the soul which is the form of a body, as is clear from what was said earlier.[7] Accordingly, it is proper for it to know forms which, in fact, exist individually in corporeal matter, yet not precisely as existing in such or such individual matter. Now to know something which in fact exists in individuated matter, but not as existing in such or such matter is to abstract a form from individual matter, represented by

quam repræsentant phantasmata. Et ideo necesse est dicere quod intellectus noster intelligit materialia abstrahendo a phantasmatibus.

Et per materialia sic considerata in immaterialium aliqualem cognitionem devenimus, sicut e contra angeli per immaterialia materialia cognoscunt.

Plato vero, attendens solum ad* immaterialitatem intellectus humani, non autem ad hoc quod est corpori quodammodo unitus, posuit objectum intellectus ideas separatas; et quod intelligimus, non quidem abstrahendo, sed magis abstracta participando, ut supra dictum est.[8]

1. Ad primum ergo dicendum quod abstrahere contingit dupliciter. Uno modo, per modum compositionis et divisionis; sicut cum intelligimus aliquid non esse in alio, vel esse separatum ab eo. Alio modo, per modum simplicis et absolutæ considerationis;† sicut cum intelligimus unum, nihil considerando de alio.

Abstrahere igitur per intellectum ea quæ secundum rem non sunt abstracta, secundum primum modum abstrahendi non est absque falsitate. Sed secundo modo abstrahere per intellectum quæ non sunt abstracta secundum rem, non habet falsitatem; ut in sensibilibus manifeste‡ apparet. Si enim intelligamus vel§ dicamus colorem non inesse corpori colorato, vel esse separatum ab eo, erit falsitas in opinione vel in oratione. Si vero consideremus colorem et proprietates‖ ejus, nihil considerantes de pomo colorato, vel quod sic¶ intelligimus, etiam§ voce exprimamus; erit absque falsitate opinionis et orationis. Pomum enim non est de ratione coloris; et ideo nihil prohibet colorem intelligi, nihil intelligendo de pomo.

Similiter dico quod ea quæ pertinent ad rationem speciei cujuslibet rei materialis, puta lapidis aut hominis aut equi, possunt considerari sine principiis individualibus, quæ non sunt de ratione speciei. Et hoc est abstrahere universale a particulari, vel speciem intelligibilem a phantasmatibus, considerare scilicet naturam speciei absque consideratione individualium principiorum, quæ per phantasmata repræsentantur.

Cum ergo dicitur quod intellectus est falsus qui intelligit rem aliter quam sit, verum est si ly 'aliter' referatur ad rem intellectam. Tunc enim intellectus est falsus, quando intelligit rem esse aliter quam sit. Unde falsus esset intellectus, si sic abstraheret speciem lapidis a materia, ut intelligeret eam non esse in materia, ut Plato posuit.

Non est autem verum quod proponitur, si ly 'aliter' accipiatur ex parte

---

*Piana omits *ad*
†Piana: *simplicitatis* (instead of *simplicis et absolutæ considerationis*)
‡Piana: *ut in sensu* (instead of *ut in sensibilibus manifeste*)
§Piana omits *intelligamus vel*, understand or
‖Piana: *proprietatem*

sense images. Thus we have to say that our intellect understands material things by abstraction from sense images.

Through material things known in this way we come to a limited knowledge of immaterial realities, just as, in the contrary way, angels know material realities by way of the immaterial.

Now Plato, paying attention only to the immateriality of the human intellect and not to the fact that it is somehow joined to a body, held that the object of the intellect is immaterial Ideas, and that we understand, as we have mentioned,[8] not by abstraction, but by participation in abstract entities.

Hence: 1. Abstraction occurs in two ways: one, by way of combining and separating, as when we understand one not to be in another or to be separate from it; two, by way of a simple and absolute consideration, as when we understand one without considering the other at all.

And so although for the intellect in the first way to abstract objects which in reality are not abstract is not without falsehood, it is not in the second way, as clearly appears with sensible realities. For example, were we to understand or say that colour does not exist in a coloured body, or that it exists apart from it, there would be falsehood in the opinion or statement. Whereas were we to consider colour and its properties, without any consideration of the apple which has colour, and go on to express verbally what we thus understand, the opinion or statement would be without falsehood. For being an apple is not part of the definition of colour, and thus nothing prevents colour from being understood apart from the apple being understood.

I claim likewise that whatever pertains to the definition of any species of material reality, for instance stone or man or horse, can be considered without individuating conditions which are no part of the definition of the species. And this is what I mean by abstracting the universal from the particular, the idea from sense images, to consider the nature of a species without considering individuating conditions represented by sense images.

Therefore when it is said that that understanding is false which understands a thing other than as it is, the statement is true if 'other than' refers to the thing understood. For the understanding is false whenever one understands a thing to be other than it is; hence the understanding would be false if one should so abstract the species of stone from matter that he would understand it to exist apart from matter, as Plato held.

The proposition, however, would not be true if 'other than' were taken

---

¶Piana: *sic quod*
§Piana omits *etiam*, even

[8]1a. 84, 1

intelligentis. Est enim absque falsitate ut alius sit modus intelligentis in intelligendo, quam modus rei in existendo: quia intellectum est in intelligente immaterialiter, per modum intellectus; non autem materialiter, per modum rei materialis.

2. Ad secundum dicendum quod quidam putaverunt quod species rei naturalis sit forma solum, et quod materia non sit pars speciei. Sed secundum hoc, in definitionibus rerum naturalium non poneretur materia.

Et ideo aliter dicendum est, quod materia est duplex, scilicet communis, et signata vel individualis: communis quidem, ut caro et os; individualis autem, ut hæ carnes et hæc ossa. Intellectus igitur abstrahit speciem rei naturalis a materia sensibili individuali, non autem a materia sensibili communi. Sicut speciem hominis abstrahit ab his carnibus et his ossibus, quæ non sunt de ratione speciei, sed sunt* partes individui, ut dicitur;[9] et ideo sine eis considerari potest. Sed species hominis non potest abstrahi per intellectum a carnibus et ossibus.

Species autem mathematicæ possunt abstrahi per intellectum a materia sensibili non solum individuali, sed etiam communi; non tamen a materia intelligibili communi, sed solum individuali. Materia enim sensibilis dicitur materia corporalis secundum quod subjacet qualitatibus sensibilibus, scilicet calido et frigido, duro et molli, et hujusmodi. Materia vero intelligibilis dicitur substantia secundum quod subjacet quantitati. Manifestum est autem quod quantitas prius inest substantiæ quam qualitates sensibiles. Unde quantitates, ut numeri et dimensiones et figuræ, quæ sunt terminationes quantitatum, possunt considerari absque qualitatibus sensibilibus, quod est eas abstrahi a materia sensibili: non tamen possunt considerari sine intellectu substantiæ quantitati subjectæ, quod esset eas abstrahi a materia intelligibili communi. Possunt tamen considerari sine hac vel illa substantia; quod est eas abstrahi a materia intelligibili individuali.

Quædam vero sunt quæ possunt abstrahi etiam a materia intelligibili communi, sicut ens, unum, potentia et actus, et alia hujusmodi, quæ etiam esse possunt absque omni materia, ut patet in substantiis immaterialibus.

Et quia Plato non consideravit quod dictum est de duplici modo abstractionis, omnia quæ diximus abstrahi per intellectum, posuit abstracta esse secundum rem.

---

*Piana omits *sunt*

[9]*Metaphysics* VI, 10. 1035b28

[b]This response gets its force from a Latin ambiguity that is difficult to carry over into English. *Species (intelligibilis)*, the form that is principle of understanding, I have been translating as 'species'; when, on the other hand, *species* means the nature in reality mirrored (in a universal way) by the species, I translate it as 'specific nature'. I will continue to do so here, even though some of the force of the argument is lost. (Incidentally it should be noted that this careful ambiguity

as referring to the one understanding. For there is no falsity if the mode of understanding in the one who understands is different from the mode of existing in the thing—a thing understood is in the one who understands in an immaterial way, according to the mode of the intellect, and not in a material way, according to the mode of a material reality.

2. Some have thought that the species[b] of a natural thing is all form, that matter is not a part of the species; but if this were so, matter would not be included in definitions of natural things.

Another way of speaking is thus required, distinguishing between two kinds of matter, *common* and *designated* or *individual: common* would be, for instance, flesh and bones, and *individual* this flesh and these bones. The intellect abstracts the species of a natural thing from individual sensible matter, but not from common sensible matter. Thus it abstracts the species of man from this flesh and these bones which do not pertain to the definition of the specific nature—they are, rather, as Aristotle says,[9] parts of the individual. The specific nature therefore can be considered without them. However, the species of man cannot be abstracted by the intellect from flesh and bones as such.

Mathematical species, on the other hand, can be abstracted by the intellect from both individual and common *sensible matter*—though not from common (but only individual) *intelligible matter.* For *sensible matter* means corporeal matter as underlying sensible qualities—hot and cold, hard and soft, etc.—whereas *intelligible matter* means substance as underlying quantity. Now it is obvious that quantity inheres in substance,[c] before sensible qualities do. Hence quantities—numbers, dimensions, shapes (which are boundaries of quantities)—can be considered apart from sensible qualities, and this is precisely to abstract them from sensible matter. They cannot, however, be considered apart from an understanding of *some* substance as underlying quantity—which would be to abstract them from common intelligible matter—though they can be considered apart from this or that substance—which is to abstract them from individual intelligible matter.

Finally, some things—such as being, oneness, potentiality and actuality, etc.—can be abstracted even from common intelligible matter, as is evident in immaterial substances.

Plato, however, since he gave no consideration to the two modes of abstraction mentioned above, held that all the things we have spoken of as abstracted by the intellect exist in reality as abstract entities.

---

between the two senses of the Latin *species* is a clue to what *species intelligibilis* means for St Thomas; cf Appendix 2.)
[c]As an incidental characteristic, an *accidens* or 'accident'.

3. Ad tertium dicendum quod colores habent eundem modum existendi prout sunt in materia corporali individuali, sicut et* potentia visiva: et ideo possunt imprimere suam similitudinem in visum. Sed phantasmata, cum sint similitudines individuorum, et existant in organis corporeis,† non habent eundem modum existendi quem habet intellectus humanus, ut ex dictis patet: et ideo non possunt sua virtute imprimere in intellectum possibilem.

Sed virtute intellectus agentis resultat quædam similitudo in intellectu possibili ex conversione intellectus agentis supra phantasmata, quæ quidem est repræsentativa eorum quorum sunt phantasmata, solum quantum ad naturam speciei. Et per hunc modum dicitur abstrahi species intelligibilis a phantasmatibus: non quod aliqua eadem numero forma, quæ prius fuit in phantasmatibus postmodum fiat in intellectu possibili, ad modum quo corpus accipitur ab uno loco et transfertur ad alterum.

4. Ad quartum dicendum quod phantasmata et illuminantur ab intellectu agente, et iterum ab eis, per virtutem intellectus agentis, species intelligibiles abstrahuntur. Illuminantur quidem, quia, sicut pars sensitiva ex conjunctione ad intellectivam‡ efficitur virtuosior, ita phantasmata ex virtute intellectus agentis redduntur habilia ut ab eis intentiones intelligibiles abstrahantur. Abstrahit autem intellectus agens species intelligibiles a phantasmatibus, inquantum per virtutem intellectus agentis accipere possumus in nostra consideratione naturas specierum sine individualibus conditionibus, secundum quarum similitudines intellectus possibilis informatur.

5. Ad quintum dicendum quod intellectus noster et abstrahit species intelligibiles a phantasmatibus, inquantum considerat naturas rerum in universali; et tamen intelligit eas in phantasmatibus, quia non potest intelligere etiam§ ea quorum species abstrahit, nisi convertendo se ad phantasmata, ut supra dictum est.[10]

articulus 2. utrum species intelligibiles a phantasmatibus abstractæ se habeant ad intellectum nostrum sicut id quod intelligitur

AD SECUNDUM sic proceditur:[1] 1. Videtur quod species intelligibiles a phantasmatibus abstractæ se habeant ad intellectum nostrum sicut id quod

---

*Piana: *in*, in   †Piana: *corporis*, of the body
‡Piana: *ad intellectum*, to the intellect   §Piana omits *etiam*, even
[10]Ia. 84, 7   [1]cf *De veritate* x, 9, *CG* IV, 11. *In De anima* III, *lect.* 8
d*intentio*: here used as a synonym of *species intelligibilis*; normally (as noted in Appendix 1), when taken in a cognitive, not volitional sense, *intentio* is a synonym of *ratio* or *conceptio*, which Thomists ordinarily limit to the *species expressa*. 'Intentionality' has, in recent philosophy, become an important epistemological term, expressing the relationship of knower to thing known.

3. Colours, as existing in individual corporeal matter, have the same mode of existence as the faculty of sight. Consequently, they can impress their likeness on sight. Sense images, on the contrary, since they are likenesses of individuals and exist in corporeal organs, do not have the same mode of existence as the human intellect—as is obvious from what has been said. Consequently, they cannot, of their own power, make an impression on the possible intellect.

However, in virtue of the agent intellect and by its turning to sense images (which, in turn, represent the realities of which they are images), a likeness is effected in the possible intellect, but only with respect to the specific nature. And it is thus that species are said to be abstracted from sense images, and not as though a form, numerically the same as the one that existed before in the sense images, should now come to exist in the possible intellect in the way in which a body is taken from one place and transferred to another.

4. Sense images are illuminated by the agent intellect and further, by its power, species are abstracted from them. They are illuminated because sense images, by the power of the agent intellect, are rendered apt to have intellectual intentions[d] or species abstracted from them, just as man's sense part receives heightened power from being joined to his intellectual part. The agent intellect, moreover, abstracts species from images, in that by its power we can consider specific natures without individuating conditions, and it is by likenesses of these natures that the possible intellect is informed.

5. Our intellect both abstracts species from sense images—in so far as it considers the natures of things as universal—and yet, at the same time, understands these in sense images, since it cannot understand even the things from which it abstracts species without turning to sense images, as mentioned before.[10]

article 2. do species abstracted from sense images stand in relation to our intellect as what is understood?[a]

THE FIRST POINT:[1] 1. It would seem that species abstracted from sense images do stand in relation to our intellect as *that which* is understood. For

---

[a] St Thomas is now turning to a consideration of 'representationalism'—the theory that the objects of our knowledge are ideas or images impressed on the mind of the knower. He implicitly attributes the idea to the 'ancients', a term usually reserved for the Pre-Socratics, and to a lesser extent (and only in a very limited way) to Plato. Since these historical attributions are very uncertain, however, it seems likely that the article is to be explained historically in one of two ways. Either the opinion was held by some of St Thomas's contemporaries, otherwise unidentified; or else he raises the question as a possibility to be derived from other doctrines that were being held.

intelligitur. Intellectum enim in actu est in intelligente; quia intellectum in actu est ipse intellectus in actu. Sed nihil de re intellecta est in intellectu actu intelligente, nisi species intelligibilis abstracta. Ergo hujusmodi species est ipsum intellectum in actu.

2. Præterea, intellectum in actu oportet in aliquo esse: alioquin nihil esset. Sed non est in re quæ est extra animam: quia, cum res* extra animam sit materialis, nihil quod est in ea, potest esse intellectum in actu. Relinquitur ergo quod intellectum in actu sit in intellectu. Et ita nihil est aliud quam species intelligibilis prædicta.

3. Præterea, Philosophus dicit[2] quod *voces sunt notæ earum quæ sunt in anima passionum.* Sed voces significant res intellectas: id enim voce significamus quod intelligimus. Ergo ipsæ passiones animæ, scilicet species intelligibiles, sunt ea quæ intelliguntur in actu.

SED CONTRA, species intelligibilis se habet ad intellectum sicut species sensibilis ad sensum. Sed species sensibilis non est illud quod sentitur, sed magis id quo sensus sentit. Ergo species intelligibilis non est quod intelligitur,† sed id quo intelligit intellectus.

RESPONSIO: Dicendum quod quidam posuerunt quod vires cognoscitivæ quæ sunt in nobis‡ nihil cognoscunt nisi proprias passiones; puta quod sensus non sentit nisi passionem sui organi. Et secundum hoc, intellectus nihil intelligit nisi suam passionem, idest§ speciem intelligibilem in se receptam. Et secundum hoc, species hujusmodi est ipsum quod intelligitur.‖

Sed hæc opinio manifeste apparet falsa ex duobus. Primo quidem, quia eadem sunt quæ intelligimus, et de quibus sunt scientiæ. Si igitur ea quæ intelligimus essent solum species quæ sunt in anima, sequeretur quod scientiæ omnes non essent de rebus quæ sunt extra animam, sed solum de speciebus intelligibilibus quæ sunt in anima; sicut secundum Platonicos omnes scientiæ sunt de ideis, quas ponebant esse intellecta in actu.

Secundo, quia sequeretur error antiquorum dicentium quod *omne quod videtur est verum;*[3] et sic¶ quod contradictoriæ essent simul veræ. Si enim potentia non cognoscit nisi propriam passionem, de ea solum judicat. Sic autem videtur aliquid secundum quod potentia cognoscitiva afficitur. Semper ergo judicium potentiæ cognoscitivæ erit de eo quod judicat,

---

*Piana adds *quæ est,* which is
†Leonine adds *actu,* actually
‡Piana: *vires quæ sunt in nobis cognoscitivæ* (different word order)
§Piana: *scilicet,* namely
‖Piana omits *Et secundum hoc species hujusmodi est ipsum quod intelligitur,* Again according to this opinion species of this sort are what is understood
¶Piana: *similiter,* similarly

what is actually understood exists in the one who understands; it is, in fact, identical with the intellect as actualized. But of the thing understood there is nothing in the intellect which understands except the abstracted species. Therefore this species is what is actually understood.

2. Again, what is actually understood must exist in something, or else it would simply not exist. But it does not exist in anything outside the soul, for, since things outside the soul are material, nothing in them can be what is actually understood. Therefore it follows by exclusion that what is actually understood is in the intellect, and thus that it is nothing other than the species mentioned.

3. Again, Aristotle says[2] that *spoken words are the symbols of things experienced in the soul.* But words signify things understood, since we use words precisely to signify what we understand. Therefore things experienced in the soul, namely species, are the things actually understood.

ON THE OTHER HAND, a species has the same relation to the intellect as a sensible image to the senses. But sensible images are not *what* is sensed; they are rather *that by which* sensation takes place. Therefore the species is not *what* is understood, but *that by which* the intellect understands.

REPLY: Some have held that our cognitive faculties know only what is experienced within them, for instance, that the senses perceive only the impressions made on their organs. According to this opinion the intellect understands only what is experienced within it, i.e., the species received in it. Thus, again according to this opinion, these species are *what* is understood.

The opinion, however, is obviously false for two reasons. First, because the things we understand are the same as the objects of science. Therefore, if the things we understand were only species existing in the soul, it would follow that none of the sciences would be concerned with things existing outside the soul, but only with species existing in the soul. (It may be recalled how the Platonists held that all the sciences are concerned with Ideas, which they said were things actually understood.)

Second, because a consequence would be the error of the ancient philosophers who said that *all appearances are true,*[3] implying that contradictory opinions could at the same time be true. For if a faculty knows only what is experienced within it, that only is what it can discern. Now a thing 'appears' in accord with the way a cognitive faculty is affected. Therefore the discernment of a cognitive faculty will always judge a thing to be what

---

[2]*Peri Hermeneias* I, I. 16a3
[3]Aristotle, *Metaphysics* III, 5. 1009a8

scilicet de propria passione, secundum quod est; et ita omne judicium erit verum.

Puta si gustus non sentit nisi propriam passionem, cum aliquis habens sanum gustum judicat mel esse dulce, vere judicabit; et similiter si ille qui habet gustum infectum, judicet mel esse amarum, vere judicabit: uterque enim judicat* secundum quod gustus ejus afficitur. Et sic sequitur quod omnis opinio æqualiter erit vera, et universaliter omnis acceptio.

Et ideo dicendum est quod species intelligibilis se habet ad intellectum ut quo intelligit intellectus. Quod sic patet. Cum enim sit duplex actio,[4] una quæ manet in agente, ut videre et intelligere,† altera quæ transit in rem exteriorem, ut calefacere et secare; utraque fit secundum aliquam formam. Et sicut forma secundum quam provenit actio tendens in rem exteriorem est similitudo objecti actionis, ut calor calefacientis‡ est similitudo calefacti; similiter forma secundum quam provenit actio manens in agente est similitudo objecti. Unde similitudo rei visibilis est secundum quam visus videt; et similitudo rei intellectæ, quæ est species intelligibilis, est forma secundum quam intellectus intelligit.

Sed quia intellectus supra seipsum reflectitur, secundum eandem reflexionem intelligit et suum intelligere et speciem qua intelligit. Et sic species intellectiva§ secundario est id quod intelligitur. Sed id quod intelligitur primo est res cujus species intelligibilis est similitudo.

Et hoc etiam patet ex antiquorum opinione, qui ponebant *simile simili cognosci*.[5] Ponebant enim quod anima per terram quæ in ipsa erat, cognosceret terram quæ extra ipsam erat; et sic de aliis. Si ergo accipiamus speciem terræ loco terræ, secundum doctrinam Aristotelis, qui dicit[6] quod *lapis non est in anima, sed species lapidis*, sequetur quod anima per species intelligibiles cognoscat res quæ sunt extra animam.

1. Ad primum ergo dicendum quod intellectum‖ est in intelligente per suam similitudinem. Et per hunc modum dicitur quod intellectum in actu est intellectus in actu, inquantum similitudo rei intellectæ est forma

---

*Piana: *judicabit*, will judge   †Piana adds *et*, and
‡Piana: *calefaciens*, heating   §Piana: *intellecta*, understood
‖Piana: *intellectus*, the intellect

[4]Aristotle, *Metaphysics* VIII, 8. 1050a23
[5]Aristotle, *De Anima* I, 2 & 5. 404b17; 409b25   [6]ibid III, 8. 431b29
[b]See below Ia. 87, 1.
[c]*terra*; 'earth', was one of the four elements of ancient and medieval science. As noted earlier (84, 2, note *g*), it should not be too easily assumed that the 'earth', 'dirt', etc., of common experience was intended. It can be safely assumed that air, earth, and water, as elements, had roughly the same meaning for the ancients as the solid, liquid, and gaseous states for us. Their element of 'fire' is more difficult to find a parallel for, but in many contexts what they meant was something like the modern

it discerns, namely, what is experienced within it, and accordingly every judgment will be true.

For instance, if the sense of taste perceives only what is experienced within it, then when a man whose sense of taste is healthy discerns that honey is sweet, his judgment will be true. Similarly, if a sick man, whose sense of taste is affected, experiences honey as bitter, his judgment will be true. For each makes his judgment as his sense of taste is affected. It will thus follow that every opinion—and indeed every perception of any kind —has an equal claim to truth.

We must say, therefore, that species stand in relation to the intellect as *that by which* the intellect understands. To make the matter clear: although there are two kinds of activity[4]—one that remains within the agent (e.g., seeing or understanding), and one that passes over into a thing outside (e.g., heating or cutting)—nevertheless each is produced in accord with a form. Now just as the form from which an activity extending to a thing outside proceeds is like the object of the activity (for instance, the heat of a heater is like that of the thing heated), so also, in a similar way, the form from which an activity remaining within an agent proceeds is a likeness of the object. Thus it is according to a likeness of a visible thing that the faculty of sight sees, and likewise a likeness of a thing understood, i.e., a species, is the form according to which the intellect understands.

However, since the intellect reflects upon itself, by such reflection it understands both its own understanding and the species by which it understands. Thus species are secondarily that which is understood.[b] But what is understood first is the reality of which a particular species is a likeness.

This is, in fact, already evident in the opinion of the ancient philosophers who held that *like is known by like*.[5] For they held that the soul would know solids[c] that are outside it by means of solids within it, etc. Thus if we understand the species of a solid instead of actual solid materials—according to Aristotle's teaching,[6] *it is not the stone which is present in the soul but its form* —it will follow that by means of species the soul knows things which are outside the soul.

Hence: 1. What is understood is in the one who understands by means of its likeness. This is the meaning of the saying that what is actually understood is identical with the intellect as actualized, in so far as a likeness of the thing understood is the form of the intellect,[d] just as a likeness of a

---

concept of energy. Be warned, however, of a major difference. The ancient elements were crude, commonsense characterizations; their modern counterparts are carefully worked-out concepts of physics and chemistry, with many more experimentally verified properties than the ancients dreamed of.

[d]i.e., it is the form that actualizes the intellect as potential; see Appendix 1.

intellectus; sicut similitudo rei sensibilis est forma sensus in actu. Unde non sequitur quod species intelligibilis abstracta sit id quod actu intelligitur, sed quod sit similitudo ejus.

2. Ad secundum dicendum quod, cum dicitur *intellectum in actu*, duo importantur, scilicet res quæ intelligitur, et hoc quod est ipsum intelligi. Et similiter cum dicitur *universale abstractum*, duo intelliguntur, scilicet ipsa natura rei, et abstractio seu universalitas. Ipsa igitur natura cui accidit vel intelligi vel abstrahi, vel intentio universalitatis, non est nisi in singularibus; sed hoc ipsum quod est intelligi vel abstrahi, vel intentio universalitatis, est in intellectu. Et hoc possumus videre per simile in sensu. Visus enim videt colorem pomi sine ejus odore. Si ergo quæratur ubi sit color qui videtur sine odore, manifestum est quod color qui videtur non est nisi in pomo; sed quod sit sine odore perceptus, hoc accidit ei ex parte visus, inquantum in visu est similitudo coloris et non odoris.

Similiter humanitas quæ intelligitur, non est nisi in hoc vel in illo homine: sed quod humanitas apprehendatur sine individualibus conditionibus, quod est ipsam abstrahi* ad quod sequitur intentio universalitatis, accidit humanitati secundum quod percipitur ab intellectu, in quo est similitudo naturæ speciei, et non individualium principiorum.

3. Ad tertium dicendum quod in parte sensitiva invenitur duplex operatio. Una secundum solam immutationem: et sic perficitur operatio sensus per hoc quod immutatur a sensibili. Alia operatio est formatio, secundum quod vis imaginativa format sibi aliquod idolum rei absentis, vel etiam nunquam visæ. Et utraque hæc operatio conjungitur in intellectu. Nam primo quidem consideratur passio intellectus possibilis secundum quod informatur specie intelligibili. Qua quidem formatus, format secundo vel definitionem vel divisionem vel compositionem, quæ per vocem significatur. Unde ratio quam significat nomen est definitio, et enuntiatio significat compositionem et divisionem intellectus. Non ergo voces significant ipsas species intelligibiles; sed ea quæ intellectus sibi format ad judicandum de rebus exterioribus.

---

*Piana: *quod est ipsum abstrahi*, which is (the state of) being abstracted

ᵉThe so-called 'second intention', i.e., the universal as universal, which can only be known reflexively, in the knowing of something else (as indicated in the body of the article).

ᶠThis is as close as the author comes, in the present treatise, to an explicit distinction between *species impressa* and *species expressa*; cf Appendix 1.

ᵍSee articles 4–5 below and Appendix 3 for a clarification of this terminology.

sensible reality is the form of a sense when actualized. Hence it does not follow that an abstracted species is what is actually understood, but only that it is a likeness of it.

2. The phrase 'what is actually understood' involves two points: namely, the thing which is understood and the being understood. And likewise in the term 'abstracted universal' there are two, namely, the nature of a thing and its state of abstraction or universality. Thus the nature, to which 'being understood' and 'being abstracted' (or the intention[e] of universality) are applied, exists only in individuals, whereas 'being understood' and 'being abstracted' (or the intention of universality) exist in the intellect.

We can more easily see this by comparison with the senses. For instance, the sense of sight sees the colour of an apple but not its characteristic scent. Thus if one asks: Where does this colour, which is seen apart from the scent, exist?, it is obvious, on one hand, that the colour seen exists only in the apple, but on the other that being perceived without the scent can be attributed to it only with respect to sight, in so far as in the sense of sight there is a likeness of the one but not of the other.

Similarly, humanity, when understood, exists only in this or that human being, but its being apprehended without individuating conditions (i.e., its 'being abstracted' and the consequent intention of universality) can be attributed to humanity only as perceived by the intellect where there is a likeness of the specific nature, but not of individuating conditions.

3. In the sense part of man there are two kinds of activity. One takes place by way of a change effected from outside, thus the activity of the senses is fully carried out through a change effected by sensible objects. The other activity is a 'formation' by which the faculty of imagination formulates for itself a model of something absent or even of something never seen.

Now both of these activities are joined in the intellect. For, first, there is indeed an effect produced in the possible intellect in so far as it is informed by a species; and then, secondly, when it is thus informed, it formulates[f] either a definition or else an affirmative or negative statement, which is then signified by words. Thus the meaning which a name signifies is a definition, and an enunciation or proposition[g] signifies the intellect's combining or separating. Therefore words do not signify the effects produced in the possible intellect but those things which the intellect formulates for itself in order to understand[h] things outside.

---

[h]*judicandum*, judge; 84, 8, note *a*.

articulus 3. *utrum magis universalia sint priora in nostra cognitione intellectuali*

AD TERTIUM sic proceditur:[1] 1. Videtur quod magis universalia non sint priora in nostra cognitione intellectuali. Quia ea quæ sunt priora et notiora secundum naturam sunt posteriora et minus nota secundum nos. Sed universalia sunt priora secundum naturam: quia *prius est a quo non convertitur subsistendi consequentia.*[2] Ergo universalia sunt posteriora in cognitione nostri intellectus.

2. Præterea, composita sunt priora quoad nos quam simplicia. Sed universalia sunt simpliciora. Ergo sunt posterius nota quoad nos.

3. Præterea, Philosophus dicit,[3] quod definitum prius cadit in cognitione nostra quam partes definitionis. Sed universaliora sunt partes definitionis minus universalium, sicut *animal* est pars definitionis hominis. Ergo universalia sunt posterius nota quoad nos.

4. Præterea, per effectus devenimus in causas et principia. Sed universalia sunt quædam principia. Ergo universalia sunt posterius nota quoad nos.

SED CONTRA est quod dicitur:[4] *ex universalibus in singularia oportet devenire.*

RESPONSIO: Dicendum quod in cognitione nostri intellectus duo oportet considerare. Primo quidem, quod cognitio intellectiva aliquo modo a sensitiva primordium sumit. Et quia sensus est singularium, intellectus autem universalium; necesse est quod cognitio singularium, quoad nos, prior sit quam universalium cognitio.

Secundo oportet considerare quod intellectus noster de potentia in actum procedit. Omne autem quod procedit de potentia in actum prius pervenit ad actum incompletum, qui est medius inter potentiam et actum, quam ad actum perfectum. Actus autem perfectus ad quem pervenit intellectus, est scientia completa, per quam distincte et determinate res cognoscuntur. Actus autem incompletus est scientia imperfecta, per quam sciuntur res indistincte sub quadam confusione: quod enim sic cognoscitur, secundum quid cognoscitur in actu, et quodammodo in potentia. Unde Philosophus dicit[5] quod *sunt primo nobis manifesta et certa confusa magis; posterius autem cognoscimus distinguendo distincte principia et elementa.*

---

[1]cf *In Physic.* I, *lect.* 1; *In Poster.* I, *lect.* 4   [2]Aristotle, *Categories* 12, 14a29
[3]*Physics* I, *lect.* 1. 184b11   [4]*Physics* I, *lect.* 1. 184a24   [5]*Physics* I, *lect.* 1. 184a21
[a]*magis universalia*: the most correct English equivalent, strictly speaking, would be 'universals with greater extension', i.e., universals applicable to more individuals. However, since the objections (which, we should remember, St Thomas himself edited) assume the existence of subsistent universal *entities*, it seems necessary to translate *magis universalia* or *universaliora* as '*things* that are more universal', leaving it ambiguous whether these are concepts or realities. It should be noted

article 3. do things that are more universal[a] have priority in our intellectual knowledge?

THE FIRST POINT.[1] 1. It would seem that things which are more universal do not have priority in our intellectual knowledge. For things which are first known and better known by nature are known later and less well by us. But universal entities by nature have priority, since *one thing is said to be 'prior' to another when the sequence of their being cannot be reversed.*[2] Therefore universal entities come later in our intellect's knowledge.

2. Again, with respect to ourselves, complex realities have priority over simple realities. But universal entities are more simple. Therefore in us their knowledge comes later.

3. Again, Aristotle says[3] that we know the thing defined before we know the elements of a definition. But things with greater universality are elements in the definition of the less universal; for instance, *animal* is an element in the definition of man. Therefore in us the knowledge of the more universal comes later.

4. Again, we come to principles and causes by way of effects. But universal entities are among these principles.[b] Therefore universal entities are known later by us.

ON THE OTHER HAND, Aristotle says[4] that *we must advance from generalities to particulars.*

REPLY: Two points must be considered with respect to our intellect's knowledge. The first, that intellectual knowledge has its origin partially in sense knowledge. Thus, since singulars are the object of the senses, universals of the intellect, our knowledge of singular things must come before our knowledge of things as universal.

The second, that we should recall how the intellect goes from potentiality to actuality. But anything that goes from potentiality to actuality arrives at incomplete actuality (midway between potentiality and actuality) before it arrives at complete actuality. Now the complete actuality at which the intellect arrives is complete knowledge, in which things are known definitely and distinctly, whereas its incomplete actuality is imperfect knowledge, where things are known indistinctly and confusedly. (For what is known in this way is partly actually known, partly only potentially known.) Thus Aristotle says[5] that *what is to us plain and obvious at first is rather confused masses, the elements and principles of which become known to us later by analysis.*

---

none the less, that the responses to the objections (with one minor exception) insist on treating *universaliora* as concepts and not realities.
[b]See 84, 1, note *k*.

Manifestum est autem quod cognoscere aliquid in quo plura continentur, sine hoc quod habeatur propria notitia uniuscujusque eorum quæ continentur in illo, est cognoscere aliquid sub confusione quadam. Sic autem potest cognosci tam totum universale, in quo partes continentur in potentia, quam etiam totum integrale: utrumque enim totum potest cognosci in quadam confusione, sine hoc quod partes distincte cognoscantur. Cognoscere autem distincte id quod continetur in toto universali est habere cognitionem de re minus communi. Sicut cognoscere animal indistincte est cognoscere animal inquantum est animal; cognoscere autem animal distincte, est cognoscere animal inquantum est animal rationale vel irrationale, quod est cognoscere hominem vel leonem.

Prius igitur occurrit intellectui nostro cognoscere animal quam cognoscere hominem: et eadem ratio est si comparemus quodcumque magis universale ad minus universale.

Et quia sensus exit de potentia in actum sicut et intellectus, idem etiam ordo cognitionis apparet in sensu. Nam prius secundum sensum dijudicamus magis commune quam minus commune, et secundum locum et secundum tempus. Secundum locum quidem, sicut, cum aliquid videtur a remotis, prius deprehenditur esse corpus, quam deprehendatur esse animal; et prius deprehenditur esse animal, quam deprehendatur esse homo; et prius homo, quam Socrates vel Plato. Secundum tempus autem, quia puer a principio prius distinguit hominem a non homine, quam distinguat hunc hominem ab alio homine; et ideo *pueri a principio appellant omnes viros patres, posterius autem determinant unumquemque,* ut dicitur.[6]

Et hujus ratio manifesta est. Quia qui scit aliquid indistincte, adhuc est in potentia ut sciat distinctionis principium; sicut qui scit genus est in potentia ut sciat differentiam. Et sic patet quod cognitio indistincta media est inter potentiam et actum.

Est ergo dicendum quod cognitio singularium est prior quoad nos quam cognitio universalium, sicut cognitio sensitiva quam cognitio intellectiva. Sed tam secundum sensum quam secundum intellectum, cognitio magis communis est prior quam cognitio minus communis.

1. Ad primum ergo dicendum quod universale dupliciter potest considerari. Uno modo, secundum quod natura universalis consideratur simul cum intentione universalitatis. Et cum intentio universalitatis, ut scilicet unum et idem habeat habitudinem ad multa, proveniat ex abstractione

---

[6]*Physics* 1, *lect.* 1. 184b11

[c]*totum universale,* a universal considered as a whole having parts, the particulars 'contained' in or under it; to be contrasted, as containing its parts potentially or virtually, with the *totum integrale,* a whole in the normal sense, containing its parts actually.

[d]*secundum locum:* St Thomas uses the Aristotelean reference frame, 'place', where

Now it is evident that knowing something which contains many aspects without having a precise knowledge of each of them is a rather confused knowledge of the thing. But both a 'universal whole'ᶜ (which contains its 'parts' or particulars virtually) and an 'integral whole' can be known in this way—each can be known in a confused way, without the parts being known distinctly. On the other hand, to have distinct knowledge of what is contained in a universal whole is to have knowledge of something less universal. For instance, knowing animals indistinctly means knowing the class 'animal', whereas knowing animals distinctly means knowing animals as rational or non-rational—it means knowing, for instance, man or lion.

Therefore knowing 'animal' comes within the scope of our intellect before knowing the class 'man', and the same is true in any comparison of something more universal with something less universal.

Since the senses, like the intellect, go from potentiality to actuality, the same order of knowledge is also apparent in them. For we discern, with the senses, the more before the less general, both with respect to spaceᵈ and with respect to time. With respect to space, for instance, when a thing is seen from a distance, it is recognized as a body before it is recognized as an animal, as an animal before being recognized as a man, and as a man before Socrates or Plato. So also with respect to time, thus a child in the beginning distinguishes man from non-man before he distinguishes this man from that one; as Aristotle says,[6] *a child starts by calling all men 'father', but later on distinguishes between each of them.*

The reason for this is evident. For anyone who knows something indistinctly is in a state of potentiality with respect to knowing the principle of distinction—for instance, one who knows a class is in a state of potentiality with respect to knowing a specific difference.ᵉ Thus it is evident that indistinct knowledge is midway between potentiality and actuality.

In conclusion then, we must say that in us the knowledge of singulars precedes the knowledge of universals in so far as sense knowledge precedes intellectual knowledge. But both in the senses and in the intellect more general precedes less general knowledge.

Hence: 1. The universal can be considered in two ways. First, a universal nature can be considered together with the intention of universality. Now since the intention of universality—i.e., the fact that one and the same thing has a relation to many particulars—comes from the intellect's abstraction, in this consideration the universal must be posterior. Thus

---

we use the term, 'space'; the latter is preferred here as conveying the sense in a more obvious way.
ᵉ*differentiam (specificam)*: i.e., the characteristic distinguishing one sub-class from another within a class.

intellectus, oportet quod secundum hunc modum universale sit posterius. Unde dicitur[7] quod *animal universale aut nihil est, aut posterius est.*

Sed secundum Platonem, qui posuit universalia subsistentia, secundum hanc considerationem universale esset prius quam particularia, quæ secundum eum non sunt nisi per participationem universalium subsistentium, quæ dicuntur ideæ.

Alio modo potest considerari quantum ad ipsam naturam, scilicet animalitatis vel humanitatis, prout invenitur in particularibus. Et sic dicendum est quod duplex est ordo naturæ. Unus secundum viam generationis et temporis: secundum quam viam, ea quæ sunt imperfecta et in potentia, sunt priora. Et hoc modo magis commune est prius secundum naturam: quod apparet manifeste in generatione hominis et animalis; nam *prius generatur animal quam homo.*[8] Alius est ordo perfectionis, sive intentionis naturæ; sicut actus simpliciter est prius secundum naturam quam potentia, et perfectum prius quam imperfectum. Et per hunc modum, minus commune est prius secundum naturam quam magis commune, ut homo quam animal: naturæ enim intentio non sistit in generatione animalis, sed intendit generare hominem.

2. Ad secundum dicendum quod universale magis commune comparatur ad minus commune ut totum et ut pars. Ut totum quidem, secundum quod in magis universali non solum continetur in potentia minus universale, sed etiam alia; ut sub *animali* non solum *homo,* sed etiam *equus.* Ut pars autem, secundum quod minus commune continet in sui ratione non solum magis commune, sed etiam alia; ut *homo* non solum *animal,* sed etiam *rationale.*

Sic igitur animal consideratum in se, prius est in nostra cognitione quam homo; sed homo est prius in nostra cognitione quam quod animal sit pars rationis ejus.

3. Ad tertium dicendum quod pars aliqua dupliciter potest cognosci. Uno modo absolute, secundum quod in se est: et sic nihil prohibet prius cognoscere partes quam totum, ut lapides quam domum. Alio modo, secundum quod sunt partes hujus totius: et sic necesse est quod prius cognoscamus totum quam partes; prius enim cognoscimus domum quadam confusa cognitione, quam distinguamus singulas partes ejus.

Sic igitur dicendum est quod definientia, absolute considerata, sunt prius nota quam definitum: alioquin non notificaretur definitum per ea. Sed secundum quod sunt partes definitionis, sic sunt posterius nota: prius

[7]*De Anima* I, I. 402b8
[8]*De generatione animal.* II, 3. 736a36–b3: 'That they [the male seed and the embryo in the female] possess the nutritive soul is plain. As they develop they also acquire the sensitive soul in virtue of which an animal is an animal; e.g., an animal does not become at the same time an animal and a man.'

Aristotle says[7] that *the universal, 'animal', must be treated either as nothing at all or as a later product.*[ƒ]

According to Plato, however, who maintained that universals were subsistent, the universal would come before particulars in this consideration. For according to him particulars only exist by participation in subsistent universals, called Ideas.

Secondly, a universal can be considered with respect to the nature itself (e.g., of animality or humanity) as found in particulars. In this sense we must say that the order of nature is of two kinds. One is the way of generation or time according to which things that are imperfect and potential come first. In this sense the more general is by nature first, as is apparent in an obvious way in the generation of a human *via* an animal, for in the uterus there is first generated an animal and then a human being.[8] The second is the order of perfection, of 'nature's intention', in which actuality is by nature prior, simply speaking, to potentiality, and the perfect to the imperfect. In this sense the less general is by nature prior to the more general—man to animal, for instance; for the intention of nature, in the process mentioned, is not to stop with the generation of an animal, but to go on to the generation of man.

2. A more general universal is related to the less general both as whole and as part. As whole, in so far as the more universal virtually contains both the less universal and other things—for instance, *animal* contains not only *man* but also *horse*. As part, on the other hand, in so far as the less general contains in its definition both the more general and other things; for instance, *man* contains not only *animal* but also *rational*.

Thus, in our knowledge, 'animal' considered in itself comes before 'man'; but our knowledge of man precedes our knowledge of the fact that 'animal' is an element in the definition of man.

3. A part can be known in two ways. First, absolutely, as it is in itself; and in this sense nothing prevents our knowing parts before we know the whole (e.g., stones before knowing a house). Secondly, as parts of this particular whole; and in this sense we must know the whole before the parts. For instance, we know a house in a confused way before we distinguish its individual parts.

Accordingly we have to say that the elements in a definition, the defining factors, considered absolutely, are known before the thing defined, otherwise this would not be clarified by using them. However, as parts of the definition they are known later; for instance, we know man in a confused

---

[ƒ]i.e., as presupposing the various sorts of animals instead of being presupposed by them.

enim cognoscimus hominem quadam confusa cognitione, quam sciamus distinguere omnia quæ sunt de hominis ratione.

4. Ad quartum dicendum quod universale, secundum quod accipitur cum intentione universalitatis, est quidem quodammodo principium cognoscendi, prout intentio universalitatis consequitur modum intelligendi qui est per abstractionem. Non autem est necesse quod omne quod est principium cognoscendi, sit principium essendi, ut Plato existimavit: cum quandoque cognoscamus causam per effectum, et substantiam per accidentia. Unde universale sic acceptum, secundum sententiam Aristotelis, non est principium essendi, neque substantia.[9]

Si autem consideremus ipsam naturam generis et speciei prout est in singularibus, sic quodammodo habet rationem principii formalis respectu singularium: nam singulare est propter materiam, ratio autem speciei sumitur ex forma.

Sed natura generis comparatur ad naturam speciei magis per modum materialis principii: quia natura generis sumitur ab eo quod est materiale in re, ratio vero speciei ab eo quod est formale; sicut ratio animalis a sensitivo, ratio vero hominis ab intellectivo. Et inde est quod ultima* naturæ intentio est ad speciem, non autem ad individuum, neque ad genus: quia forma est finis generationis, materia vero est propter formam.

Non autem oportet quod cujuslibet causæ vel principii cognitio sit posterior quoad nos: cum quandoque cognoscamus per causas sensibiles, effectus ignotos; quandoque autem e converso.

articulus 4. utrum possimus multa simul intelligere

AD QUARTUM sic proceditur:[1] 1. Videtur quod possimus multa simul intelligere. Intellectus enim est supra tempus. Sed prius et posterius ad tempus pertinent. Ergo intellectus non intelligit diversa secundum prius et posterius, sed simul.

2. Præterea, nihil prohibet diversas formas non oppositas simul eidem actu inesse, sicut odorem et colorem pomo. Sed species intelligibiles non sunt oppositæ. Ergo nihil prohibet intellectum unum simul fieri in actu secundum diversas species intelligibiles. Et sic potest multa simul intelligere.

*Piana: *ultimæ*, of ultimate (nature)
[9]*Metaphysics* VI, 13. 1038
[1]cf Ia. 12, 10; 58, 2. II *Sent.* 3, 3, 4. *De veritate* VIII, 14; *CG* I, 55; *Quodl.* VII, 1, 2
[g]The response seems somewhat odd when compared with the objection raised. Where the objection seemed to take *universalia* as (efficient) causes of physical realities, the response simply by-passes this idea and concentrates on a delineation of the several ways in which universal concepts can be spoken of as 'principles' of the individual.

way before we know how to distinguish all the elements in the definition of man.

4. The universal,[g] when taken together with the intention of universality, is admittedly a *principle of knowledge*, in the sense namely that the intention of universality is a consequence of the fact that our intellect understands by way of abstraction. However, there is no necessary reason why every principle of knowledge should also be a *principle of being* (as Plato thought), since we sometimes know causes through their effects and substances by way of accidents.[h] Therefore the universal, taken in this sense (and according to the opinion of Aristotle), is neither a principle of being nor a substance.[9]

On the other hand, if we consider the natures corresponding to class and sub-class as these are found in individuals, then in a sense they stand in relation to the individuals as their *formal principle*, since singularity is accounted for by matter, the specific nature by form.

Note however that within this formal principle the class aspect is related to the sub-class aspect as *material principle*, for the class-nature is taken from what is material in a thing, the sub-class-nature from what is formal—for instance, 'animal' from the sense part of man, 'human' from the intellectual. Consequently the ultimate 'intention of nature' is concerned with the specific nature, not with the individual or class, since form is the goal of generation (matter entering in as required by the form).

Finally, it is not necessary that the knowledge of every principle and cause be posterior in us: sometimes we come to know unknown effects through causes that are sensible, sometimes the reverse is true.

article 4. can we understand more than one thing at a time?[a]

THE FIRST POINT:[1] 1. It would seem that we can understand more than one thing at a time. For the intellect is above time. But before and after belong to time. Therefore the intellect does not understand different things one after another but at the same time.

2. Again, nothing prevents different forms, if they are not opposites, from being in the same subject actually and at the same time; for instance, colour and odour in an apple. But species are not opposed to one another. Therefore nothing prevents a single intellect from being actualized at the same time by different species. It can thus understand several things at a time.

---

[h]*accidentia*: generally in the translation 'incidental characteristics' has been preferred, but the terms 'substance' and 'accident' are common enough to be clear in this case.
[a]On the relation between this article and the next, see Appendix 3.

3. Præterea, intellectus simul intelligit aliquod totum, ut hominem vel domum. Sed in quolibet toto continentur multæ partes. Ergo intellectus simul multa intelligit.

4. Præterea, non potest cognosci differentia unius ad alterum, nisi simul utrumque apprehendatur,[2] et eadem ratio est de quacumque alia comparatione. Sed intellectus noster cognoscit differentiam et comparationem* unius ad alterum. Ergo cognoscit multa simul.

SED CONTRA est quod dicitur,[3] *intelligere est unum solum, scire vero multa.*

RESPONSIO: Dicendum quod intellectus quidem potest multa intelligere per modum unius, non autem multa per modum multorum: dico autem per modum unius vel multorum, per unam vel plures species intelligibiles. Nam modus cujusque actionis consequitur formam quæ est actionis principium. Quæcumque ergo intellectus potest intelligere sub una specie, simul intelligere potest: et inde est quod Deus omnia simul videt, quia omnia videt† per unum, quod est essentia sua. Quæcumque vero intellectus per diversas species intelligit, non simul intelligit.

Et hujus ratio est, quia impossibile est idem subjectum perfici simul pluribus formis unius generis et diversarum specierum: sicut impossibile est quod idem corpus secundum idem simul coloretur diversis coloribus, vel figuretur diversis figuris. Omnes autem species intelligibiles sunt unius generis, quia sunt perfectiones unius intellectivæ potentiæ; licet res quarum sunt species sint diversorum generum. Impossibile est ergo quod idem intellectus simul perficiatur diversis speciebus intelligibilibus ad intelligendum diversa in actu.

1. Ad primum ergo dicendum quod intellectus est supra tempus, quod est numerus motus corporalium rerum. Sed ipsa pluralitas specierum intelligibilium causat vicissitudinem quandam intelligibilium operationum, secundum quam una operatio est prior altera. Et hanc vicissitudinem Augustinus nominat tempus, cum dicit[4] quod *Deus movet creaturam spiritualem per tempus.*

2. Ad secundum dicendum quod non solum oppositæ formæ non possunt esse simul‡ in eodem subjecto, sed nec quæcumque formæ ejusdem generis, licet non sint oppositæ: sicut patet per exemplum inductum de coloribus et figuris.

---

*Piana omits *et comparationem*, compares
†Piana omits *quia omnia videt*, because he sees all things
‡Piana omits *simul*, at the same time

[2]Aristotle, *De Anima* III, 2. 426b22
[3]*Topics* II, 10. 114b34
[4]*De Genesi ad litteram* VIII, 20; 22. PL 34, 388; 389

3. Again, the intellect understands a whole—e.g., a man or a house—all at once. But more than one part is contained in any whole. Therefore the intellect knows more than one thing at a time.

4. Again, the difference between one thing and another cannot be known unless the two are known at the same time,[2] and the same is true of any other comparison. But our intellect compares and contrasts things with one another. Therefore it knows more than one thing at a time.

ON THE OTHER HAND, Aristotle says[3] that *it is possible to know many things but not to be thinking of them* at the same time.[b]

REPLY: The intellect can indeed know several things as one but not several as several—by 'as one' and 'as several' I mean by means of one or several species. For the modality of any activity follows the form that is principle of the activity. Therefore whatever an intellect can understand as informed by one species it can understand at one time. (Thus God sees everything at once because he sees all things by means of one thing—his own essence.) On the other hand, whatever an intellect understands by way of different species it does not understand at one time.

The reason for this is that it is impossible for the same subject to be perfected at the same time by several forms differing in kind but belonging to the same class; for instance, it is impossible for the same body, in the same part, at the same time to have different colours or different shapes. But all species belong to one class—they are perfections of a single faculty, the intellect—even though the things of which they are images belong to different classes. Therefore it is impossible for the same intellect to be perfected by different species, allowing it actually to understand different things at one time.

Hence: 1. The intellect is above time taken as the measure of the motion of corporeal realities. But the very plurality of species effects a quasi-temporality of intellectual activities according to which one activity comes after another. Augustine even calls this quasi-temporality time: he says[4] that *God moves spiritual creatures through time.*

2. It is not only opposite forms that cannot at the same time be in one subject—no forms can, if they belong to the same class, even if they are not opposites. This is obvious from the example mentioned, of colours and shapes.

---

[b]The point of the passage is not obvious except in context: Aristotle is suggesting that there is a difference between 'knowing' and 'thinking about' something; St Thomas takes the former as referring to knowledge in a habitual state, the latter as actual here-and-now understanding.

3. Ad tertium dicendum quod partes possunt intelligi dupliciter. Uno modo, sub quadam confusione, prout sunt in toto: et sic cognoscuntur per unam formam totius, et sic simul cognoscuntur. Alio modo, cognitione distincta, secundum quod quælibet cognoscitur per suam speciem: et sic non simul intelliguntur.

4. Ad quartum dicendum quod quando intellectus intelligit differentiam vel comparationem unius ad alterum, cognoscit utrumque differentium vel comparatorum sub ratione ipsius comparationis vel differentiæ; sicut dictum est quod cognoscit partes sub ratione totius.

articulus 5. utrum intellectus noster intelligat componendo et dividendo

AD QUINTUM sic proceditur:[1] 1. Videtur quod intellectus noster non intelligat componendo et dividendo. Compositio enim et divisio non est nisi multorum. Sed intellectus non potest simul multa intelligere. Ergo non potest intelligere componendo et dividendo.

2. Præterea, omni compositioni et divisioni adjungitur tempus præsens, præteritum vel futurum. Sed intellectus abstrahit a tempore, sicut etiam ab aliis particularibus conditionibus. Ergo intellectus non intelligit componendo et dividendo.

3. Præterea, intellectus intelligit per assimilationem ad res. Sed compositio et divisio nihil est in rebus: nihil enim invenitur in rebus nisi res quæ significatur per prædicatum et subjectum, quæ est una et eadem si compositio est vera; homo enim est vere id quod est animal. Ergo intellectus non componit et dividit.

SED CONTRA, voces significant conceptiones intellectus, ut dicit Philosophus.[2] Sed in vocibus est compositio et divisio; ut patet in propositionibus affirmativis et negativis. Ergo intellectus componit et dividit.

RESPONSIO: Dicendum quod intellectus humanus necesse habet intelligere componendo et dividendo. Cum enim intellectus humanus exeat de potentia in actum, similitudinem quamdam habet cum rebus generabilibus,

---

[1]cf 1a. 14, 14; 16, 2; 58, 3; 4
[2]*Peri Hermeneias* I, 1. 16a3
[a]The source of the doctrine here is to be found in Aristotle, *De Anima* III, 6 and *Peri Hermeneias* I, 3, where the terminology ('putting together', 'combination', 'synthesis', and their opposites) seems to be derived from an attempt to make a clear distinction between infallible *simple* understanding and a fallible *complex* act in which truth and falsity are found in the proper sense. St Thomas seems at times to equate 'combining and separating' with the formation of an enunciation or proposition; cf 1a. 14, 14: *per modum compositionis vel divisionis, enuntiationem*

3. Parts can be understood in two ways: first, in a confused way, as they are in the whole; in this way they are known in the single form of the whole and thus at one time; second, in a distinct way, as things are known each by way of its own species; and in this way they are not understood at one time.

4. When the intellect compares or contrasts one with another, it knows the two compared or contrasted under the aspect of that comparison or contrast—in the same way that, as mentioned, it knows parts in the light of the whole.

article 5. does our intellect understand by combining and separating?[a]

THE FIRST POINT:[1] 1. It would seem that our intellect does not understand by combining and separating. For combining and separating can only take place with respect to more than one thing. But the intellect cannot understand more than one thing at a time. Therefore it cannot understand by combining and separating.

2. Again, every combination or separation has attached to it either present, past or future time.[b] But the intellect abstracts from time as from other particular conditions. Therefore the intellect does not understand by combining and separating.

3. Again, the intellect understands by assimilation to things. But combinations and separations are not found in things, for, in things, there is nothing but the reality signified by subject and predicate, and it is one and the same if a combination is a true one.

ON THE OTHER HAND, words signify the intellect's conceptions, according to Aristotle.[2] But there are combinations and separations of words, as appears in affirmative and negative statements.[c] Therefore the intellect combines and separates.

REPLY: The human intellect must understand by combining and separating. For, in so far as the human intellect goes from potentiality to actuality, it has a certain similarity to realities in the world of generation and

---

formando; and 1a. 16, 2: *hoc facit componendo et dividendo*: *nam in omni propositione aliquam formam significatam per prædicatum, vel applicat alicui rei significatæ per subjectum, vel removet ab ea.* But see Appendix 3 for a detailed consideration of the matter.

[b]The primary meaning here corresponds to grammatical tense: every sentence must have a tense, past, present or future. However, Aristotle and St Thomas make the same temporal requirement of the logical proposition signified by a verbal sentence.

[c]Distinguishing between verbal statements and the mental propositions (or enunciations) they signify.

quæ non statim perfectionem suam habent, sed eam successive acquirunt. Et similiter intellectus humanus non statim in prima apprehensione capit perfectam rei cognitionem; sed primo apprehendit aliquid de ipsa, puta quidditatem ipsius rei, quæ est primum et proprium objectum intellectus; et deinde intelligit proprietates et accidentia et habitudines circumstantes rei essentiam. Et secundum hoc, necesse habet unum apprehensum alii componere vel* dividere; et ex una compositione vel divisione ad aliam procedere, quod est ratiocinari.

Intellectus autem angelicus et divinus se habet sicut res incorruptibiles, quæ statim a principio habent suam totam perfectionem. Unde intellectus angelicus et divinus statim perfecte totam rei cognitionem habet. Unde in cognoscendo quidditatem rei, cognoscit de re simul quidquid nos cognoscere possumus componendo et dividendo et ratiocinando.

Et ideo intellectus humanus cognoscit componendo et dividendo, sicut et ratiocinando. Intellectus autem divinus et angelicus cognoscunt quidem compositionem et divisionem et ratiocinationem, non componendo et dividendo et ratiocinando, sed per intellectum simplicis quidditatis.

1. Ad primum ergo dicendum quod compositio et divisio intellectus secundum† quamdam differentiam vel comparationem fit. Unde sic intellectus cognoscit multa componendo et dividendo, sicut cognoscendo differentiam vel comparationem rerum.

2. Ad secundum dicendum quod intellectus et‡ abstrahit a phantasmatibus, et tamen non intelligit actu nisi§ convertendo se ad phantasmata, sicut supra dictum est.[3] Et ex ea parte qua se ad phantasmata convertit, compositioni et divisioni intellectus adjungitur tempus.

3. Ad tertium dicendum quod similitudo rei recipitur in intellectu secundum modum intellectus, et non secundum modum rei. Unde compositioni et divisioni intellectus respondet quidem aliquid ex parte rei; tamen non eodem modo se habet in re sicut in intellectu. Intellectus enim humani proprium objectum est quidditas rei materialis, quæ sub sensu et imaginatione cadit.

Invenitur autem duplex compositio in re materiali. Prima quidem, formæ ad materiam: et huic respondet compositio intellectus qua totum universale de sua parte prædicatur; nam genus sumitur a materia communi, differentia vero completiva speciei a forma, particulare vero a materia individuali. Secunda vero compositio est accidentis ad subjectum:

---

*Piana: *et*, and
‡Piana omits *et*
†Piana: *per* (same meaning)
§Piana: *non*, not
[3]1a. 84, 7
[a]What the thing is, its essence, whether generic or specific; see Appendix 2.
[e]*accidentia*: cf above art. 3, note *h*.

corruption, which are not fully completed from the outset but achieve completeness step by step. So also the human intellect does not immediately, in first apprehending a thing, have complete knowledge; rather, it first apprehends only one aspect of the thing—namely, its whatness,[d] which is the primary and proper object of the intellect—and only then can it understand the properties, accidents[e] and relationships incidental to the thing's essence. Accordingly, it must necessarily either combine one apprehension with another or separate them, or else it must go from one combination or separation to another (which is the process of reasoning).

The intellects of God and the angels, on the other hand, are like incorruptible realities[f] which do have their total perfection immediately and from the outset; thus the intellects of God and the angels have a completely perfect knowledge of a thing from the outset. Therefore, in knowing the whatness of a thing, they know at the same time all the things that we are able to know by combining, separating, and reasoning.

Thus the human intellect knows by combining, separating, and reasoning. The intellects of God and the angels, on the other hand, know combinations, separations, and processes of reasoning by way of a simple understanding of what things are, not by way of combining, separating, and reasoning.

Hence: 1. The intellect's combinations and separations come about by way of a comparison or contrast. The intellect thus knows several objects by combining and separating in the same way that it compares or contrasts things.

2. The intellect, while it does abstract from sense images, nevertheless cannot actually understand except by turning to sense images, as mentioned above.[3] And it is by reason of that aspect in which it turns to images that time is attached to the intellect's combinations and separations.

3. The likeness of a thing is received in the intellect according to the mode of the intellect, not according to the mode of the thing. Thus, although there is something in the thing that corresponds to the combination or separation in the intellect, its state in the thing is not the same as in the intellect. For the human intellect's proper object is the whatness of a material thing, and this whatness is subject to the senses and imagination.

Now there are two kinds of composition in material things. The first, of form and matter—corresponding to this in the intellect is the combination in which a 'universal whole' is attributed to one of its 'parts' or particulars (in so far as the class aspect is taken from a thing's common matter and the specific difference from the form, whereas the particular aspect is taken from individual matter). The second, of subject or substance and accident;

---

[f]Celestial bodies in the cosmology of Aristotle; see Vol. 10 in this series.

et huic reali* compositioni respondet compositio intellectus secundum quam prædicatur accidens de subjecto, ut cum dicitur, homo est albus.

Tamen differt compositio intellectus a compositione rei: nam ea quæ componuntur in re sunt diversa; compositio autem intellectus est signum identitatis eorum quæ componuntur. Non enim intellectus sic componit, ut dicat quod homo est albedo; sed dicit quod homo est albus, idest habens albedinem: idem autem est subjecto quod est homo, et quod est habens albedinem.† Et simile est de compositione formæ et materiæ: nam animal significat id quod habet naturam‡ sensitivam, rationale vero quod habet naturam intellectivam, homo vero quod habet utrumque, Socrates vero quod habet omnia hæc cum materia individuali; et secundum hanc identitatis rationem, intellectus noster unum componit alteri prædicando.

articulus 6. utrum intellectus possit esse falsus

AD SEXTUM sic proceditur:[1] 1. Videtur quod intellectus possit esse falsus. Dicit enim Philosophus[2] quod *verum et falsum sunt in mente.* Mens autem et intellectus idem sunt, ut supra dictum est.[3] Ergo falsitas est in intellectu.

2. Præterea, opinio et ratiocinatio ad intellectum pertinent. Sed in utraque istarum invenitur falsitas. Ergo potest esse falsitas in intellectu.

3. Præterea, peccatum in parte intellectiva est. Sed peccatum cum falsitate est: *errant* enim *qui operantur malum.*[4] Ergo falsitas potest esse in intellectu.

SED CONTRA EST quod dicit Augustinus:[5] *omnis qui fallitur, id in quo fallitur non intelligit.* Et Philosophus dicit[6] quod *intellectus semper est rectus.*

RESPONSIO: Dicendum quod Philosophus[7] comparat, quantum ad hoc, intellectum sensui. Sensus enim circa proprium objectum non decipitur, sicut visus circa colorem; nisi forte per accidens, ex impedimento circa organum contingente, sicut cum gustus febrientium dulcia judicat amara, propter hoc quod lingua malis humoribus est repleta. Circa sensibilia vero communia decipitur sensus, sicut in dijudicando§ de magnitudine vel

---

*Piana omits *reali*, in reality

†Piana omits *idem autem est subjecto quod est homo, et quod est habens albedinem*, and it is the same subject which is man and has whiteness

‡Piana: *materiam*, matter   §Piana: *sicut judicando* (meaning unchanged)

[1]cf Ia. 16, 2; 17, 3; 58, 5. I *Sent.* 19, 5, 1 ad 7. *De veritate* 1, 12; *In De anima* III, 11. *In Periherm.* I, 3. *In Meta.* VI, 4; IX, 11

[2]*Metaphysics* V, 4. 1027b27   [3]Ia. 79, 1

[4]*Proverbs* 14, 22 (Douay)   [5]*Lib.* 83 *quæst.* 32, PL 40, 22

[6]*De Anima* III, 10. 433a26   [7]ibid III, 6. 430b29

ªOn the important question of truth in human knowledge, St Thomas's parallel

corresponding to this composition in reality is the intellectual combination in which an accident is attributed to its subject, as in the sentence, 'Man is white.'

Nevertheless, the intellectual combinations differ from the real compositions, since the things combined in reality are distinct, whereas intellectual combination signifies the identity of the things combined. For the intellect's combination is not such as to say that 'man is whiteness'; rather it says that 'man is white', i.e., 'has whiteness', and it is the same subject which *is* man and *has* whiteness. So also with respect to the composition of form and matter: 'animal' signifies 'that which has sensation'; 'rational', 'that which has an intellectual nature'; 'man', 'that which has both'; 'Socrates', 'that which has all these, together with individual matter'—and it is because of this relation of identity that our intellect attributes one to the other in its combinations.

article 6. can the intellect be in error?[a]

THE FIRST POINT:[1] 1. It would seem that the intellect can be in error. For *falsity and truth are in the mind,* as Aristotle says,[2] not in things. But the mind is the same thing as the intellect, as mentioned before.[3] Therefore falsity is in the intellect.

2. Again, opinion and reasoning belong to the intellect. But falsity is found in both of these. Therefore there can be falsity in the intellect.

3. Again, sin is found in the intellectual part of man. But sin involves falsity—for *they err that work evil.*[4] Therefore falsity can be found in the intellect.

ON THE OTHER HAND, Augustine says[5] that *everyone who is in error fails to understand that about which he is in error.* And Aristotle says[6] that *mind is always right.*

REPLY: In this matter Aristotle[7] compares the intellect with the senses. The senses are not deceived with respect to their proper object—sight, for example, with respect to colour—except, as may happen, in an incidental way when there is an impediment in the organ (for instance when, in a feverish person, the sense of taste experiences sweet things as bitter because the tongue is coated unhealthily[b]). On the other hand, the senses

---

considerations should be consulted; for the present question in particular, see Appendix 2.
[b]Literally: 'is filled with bad humours', in the technical medical sense of 'humours' according to the ancients.

figura; ut cum judicat solem esse pedalem, qui tamen est major terra. Et multo magis decipitur circa sensibilia per accidens; ut cum judicat fel esse mel, propter coloris similitudinem. Et hujus ratio est in evidenti. Quia ad proprium objectum unaquæque potentia per se ordinatur, secundum quod ipsa. Quæ autem sunt hujusmodi, semper eodem modo se habent. Unde manente potentia, non deficit ejus judicium circa proprium objectum. Objectum autem proprium intellectus est quidditas rei. Unde circa quidditatem rei, per se loquendo, intellectus non fallitur. Sed circa ea quæ circumstant rei essentiam vel quidditatem, intellectus potest falli, dum unum ordinat ad aliud, vel componendo vel dividendo vel etiam ratiocinando. Et propter hoc etiam circa illas propositiones errare non potest, quæ statim cognoscuntur cognita terminorum quidditate, sicut accidit circa prima principia: ex quibus etiam accidit infallibilitas veritatis, secundum certitudinem scientiæ, circa conclusiones.

Per accidens tamen contingit intellectum decipi circa *quod quid est* in rebus compositis; non ex parte organi, quia intellectus non est virtus utens organo, sed ex parte compositionis intervenientis circa definitionem, dum vel definitio unius rei est falsa de alia, sicut definitio circuli de triangulo, vel dum aliqua definitio in seipsa est* falsa, implicans compositionem impossibilium, ut si accipiatur hoc ut definitio alicujus rei, *animal rationale alatum.*

Unde in rebus simplicibus, in quarum definitionibus compositio intervenire non potest, non possumus decipi; sed deficimus in totaliter non attingendo, sicut dicitur.[8]

1. Ad primum ergo dicendum quod falsitatem dicit esse Philosophus† in mente secundum compositionem et divisionem. Et similiter dicendum est ad secundum, de opinione et ratiocinatione. Et ad tertium, de errore peccantium, qui consistit in applicatione ad appetibile.

Sed in absoluta consideratione quidditatis rei, et eorum quæ per eam cognoscuntur, intellectus nunquam decipitur. Et sic loquuntur auctoritates in contrarium inductae.

---

*Piana: *est in se* (meaning unchanged)
†Piana: *falsitas dicitur esse*, falsity is said to be
[8]*Metaphysics* VIII, 10. 1052a1
cThings sensed immediately in and with the proper objects of the senses: extension, local motion (and its contrary, rest), shapes and sizes, position relative to other bodies, etc.
dThings not properly sensed at all, but associated with the proper (or common)

can be deceived with respect to the 'common sensibles'[c]—for example in discerning sizes and shapes (as when they perceive the sun as a foot wide, when it is in fact larger than the earth). Finally *a fortiori* they can be deceived still more with respect to the '*per accidens* sensibles'[d]—as when they mistake gall for honey because of the likeness in colour.

The reason for this is obvious, in so far as any faculty, as such, has an essential ordination to its proper object. But things with this sort of ordination must always be the same. Thus, granting the existence of the faculty, its discernment of its proper object cannot fail.

Now the proper object of the intellect is the whatness of things. Hence with respect to the whatness of things, speaking essentially, the intellect makes no mistakes. But with respect to whatever is incidental to the essence or whatness of a thing—when it relates one thing to another, either in combining and separating or else in reasoning—the mind can be mistaken. On this account also it cannot be in error with respect to those propositions which are known immediately when the essences of their terms are known, as happens with first principles (from which a further infallible truth is derived, that of the certain conclusions in demonstrative knowledge).

Nevertheless, the intellect can be deceived about what a thing is,[e] incidentally and with respect to *composite* things. This is not by reason of its organ, since the intellect is not a faculty that uses an organ, but by reason of some combination affecting a definition—for instance, a definition of one thing is false when applied to another (e.g., the definition of a circle applied to a triangle), or a definition can be false in itself if it implies an impossible combination (e.g., if the phrase 'winged rational animal' were taken to be the definition of anything).

Thus with respect to *simple* things, where there are no combinations in their definitions, we cannot be deceived; as Aristotle says, if we fail it is in not attaining them at all.[8]

Hence: 1. Aristotle's statement about falsity in the mind is concerned with combinations and separations. Also the same is true with respect to opinion and reasoning. With respect as well to the error of sinners which consists in a mistaken application in appetitive matters.

On the other hand, in an absolute consideration of the whatness of a thing, or of whatever is known by means of it, the intellect is never deceived. And this is the meaning of the authorities in the counterargument.

---

objects of the senses in perception: e.g., substance with respect to any of the senses, the object of hearing with reference to sight, etc.

[e] *quod quid est*, a synonym for *quidditas*, what a thing is; cf Appendix 2.

articulus 7. utrum unam et eamdem rem unus alio melius intelligere possit

AD SEPTIMUM sic proceditur:[1] 1. Videtur quod unam et eamdem rem unus alio melius intelligere non possit. Dicit enim Augustinus:[2] *Quisquis ullam rem aliter quam est intelligit, non eam intelligit. Quare non est dubitandum esse perfectam intelligentiam, qua præstantior esse non possit; et ideo non* per infinitum ire quod quælibet res intelligitur; nec eam posse alium alio plus intelligere.*

2. Præterea, intellectus intelligendo verus est. Veritas autem, cum sit æqualitas quædam intellectus et rei, non recipit magis et minus: non enim proprie dicitur aliquid magis et minus æquale. Ergo neque magis et minus aliquid intelligi dicitur.

3. Præterea, intellectus est id quod est formalissimum in homine. Sed differentia formæ causat differentiam speciei. Si igitur unus homo magis alio intelligit, videtur quod non sint unius speciei.

SED CONTRA est quod per experimentum inveniuntur aliqui aliis profundius intelligentes; sicut profundius intelligit qui conclusionem aliquam potest reducere in prima principia et causas primas, quam qui potest reducere solum in causas proximas.†

RESPONSIO: Dicendum quod aliquem intelligere unam et eamdem rem magis quam alium, potest intelligi dupliciter. Uno modo, sic quod *ly* 'magis' determinet actum intelligendi ex parte rei intellectæ. Et sic non potest unus eamdem rem magis intelligere quam alius: quia si intelligeret eam aliter esse‡ quam sit, vel melius vel pejus, falleretur, et non intelligeret, ut arguit Augustinus.[3] Alio modo potest intelligi ut determinet actum intelligendi ex parte intelligentis. Et sic unus alio potest eamdem rem melius intelligere, quia est melioris virtutis in intelligendo; sicut melius videt visione corporali rem aliquam qui est perfectioris virtutis, et in quo virtus visiva est perfectior.

Hoc autem circa intellectum contingit dupliciter. Uno quidem modo, ex parte ipsius§ intellectus, qui est perfectior. Manifestum est enim quod

---

*Piana adds *est*, is
‡Piana omits *esse*, to be
†Piana adds *proprias*, proper
§Piana omits *ipsius*, itself

[1] cf *De veritate* 11, 2 ad 11
[3] *Lib. 83 quæst.* 32. PL 40, 22
[2] *LXXXIII quæst.* 32. PL 40, 22

[a] *reducere (in prima principia)*: Properly this should be translated as 'take back, or resolve a conclusion into first principles'. Especially, after Descartes it has become necessary to distinguish Aristotelean *syllogismus* and *demonstratio* from a Cartesian, rationalist 'deduction'. Aristotle and St Thomas do not begin with self-evident principles and derive conclusions therefrom in a rationalist-deductive mode (even though the *Posterior Analytics* is often interpreted this way); rather, they begin with a statement to be justified (it will become the 'conclusion' only in a formal

article 7. with respect to one and the same reality, can one man have a better under-standing than another?

THE FIRST POINT:[1] 1. It would seem that, with respect to one and the same reality, one man could not have a better understanding than another. For Augustine says,[2] *Whoever understands a thing other than as it is, does not understand it at all. Hence it is clear that the understanding is perfect and there can be none better. Therefore there are not infinite degrees in the understanding of a thing, nor can one man understand it better than another.*

2. Again, in understanding, the intellect has truth. But truth, since it is an equating of intellects and things, does not have degrees. (It cannot properly be said that a thing is more or less equal.) Neither, therefore, can anything be spoken of as more or less understood.

3. Again, understanding is man's special characteristic. But differences in form bring about different classes of being. Therefore if one man has a better understanding than another, it would seem that they do not have the same specific nature.

ON THE OTHER HAND, experience shows that some men have a more profound understanding than others—for instance, the man who can justify[a] a conclusion by means of first principles and primary causes has a more profound understanding than one who can do so only through proximate principles.

REPLY: That one man should understand one same reality better than another can be understood in two senses. First, in the sense that the 'better' qualifies the act of understanding *with respect to the thing understood.* In this sense one man cannot understand the same reality better than another because, if he should understand the thing to be other than as it is (whether as better or worse), he would not really be understanding but making a mistake, as Augustine argues.[3] Second, as qualifying the act of understanding *with respect to the person who understands.* In this sense one man can understand the same thing better than another in so far as he has a greater capacity for understanding[b] (as, similarly, one who has greater strength and better vision can, in terms of corporeal sight, see things better.)

In the intellect this can happen in two ways. First, on the part of an intellect which is itself more perfect. For it is evident that the better

---

restatement of the argument) and 'reduce' it back to its ultimate explanatory prin-ciples. Cf Ernst Kapp: *Greek Foundations of Traditional Logic* (New York, 1942).
[b]It would, of course, be an anachronism to translate this as 'has a higher I.Q.', but St Thomas's distinction, between innate capacity for intelligence and the good dispositions required for superior intelligence, would allow for the measurement of intelligence through tests such as are used today.

quanto corpus est melius dispositum, tanto meliorem sortitur animam: quod manifeste apparet in his quæ sunt secundum speciem diversa. Cujus ratio est, quia actus et forma recipitur in materia secundum materiæ capacitatem. Unde cum etiam in hominibus quidam habeant corpus melius dispositum, sortiuntur animam majoris virtutis in intelligendo: unde dicitur[4] quod *molles carne bene aptos mente videmus.* Alio modo contingit hoc ex parte inferiorum virtutum, quibus intellectus indiget ad sui operationem: illi enim in quibus virtus imaginativa et cogitativa et memorativa est melius disposita sunt melius dispositi ad intelligendum.

1 & 2. Ad primum ergo patet solutio ex dictis, et similiter ad secundum: veritas enim intellectus in hoc consistit, quod intelligatur res esse sicuti est.

3. Ad tertium dicendum quod differentia formæ quæ non provenit nisi ex diversa dispositione materiæ non facit diversitatem secundum speciem, sed solum secundum numerum; sunt enim diversorum individuorum diversæ formæ, secundum materiam diversificatæ.

articulus 8. *utrum intellectus per prius cognoscat indivisibile quam divisibile*

AD OCTAVUM sic proceditur[1] 1. Videtur quod intellectus noster per prius cognoscat*indivisibile quam divisibile. Dicit enim Philosophus[2] quod *intelligimus et scimus ex principiorum et elementorum cognitione.* Sed indivisibilia sunt principia et elementa divisibilium. Ergo per prius sunt nobis nota indivisibilia quam divisibilia.

2. Præterea, id quod ponitur in definitione alicujus per prius cognoscitur a nobis: quia definitio est *ex prioribus et notioribus.*[3] Sed indivisibile ponitur in definitione divisibilis, sicut punctum in definitione lineæ: *linea* enim, ut Euclides dicit,[4] *est longitudo sine latitudine, cujus extremitates sunt duo puncta.* Et unitas ponitur in definitione numeri: quia *numerus est multitudo mensurata per unum.*[5] Ergo intellectus noster per prius intelligit indivisibile quam divisibile.

3. Præterea, *simile simili cognoscitur.*[6] Sed indivisibile est magis simile intellectui quam divisible: quia *intellectus est simplex.*[7] Ergo intellectus noster prius cognoscit indivisibile.

SED CONTRA est quod dicitur:[8] *indivisible monstratur sicut privatio.* Sed privatio per posterius cognoscitur. Ergo et indivisibile.

---

*Piana: *intelligat,* understand
[4]*De Anima* II, 9. 421a25
[1]cf 1a. 11, 2 ad 4. *In De anima* III, *lect.* 11
[2]*Physics* I, *lect.* 1. 184a12   [3]Aristotle, *Topics* VI, 4. 141a26
[4]*Elements* I, definitions 2–3   [5]Aristotle, *Metaphysics* IX, 6. 1057a3
[6]Aristotle, *De Anima* I, 2; 5. 404b17; 409b25

disposed a body is the better soul it will have: this is clearly apparent where there is a difference in specific nature. The reason is that forms and actualities are received in matter according to its capacity. Thus since even among different men some have bodies that are better disposed, the same ones will have souls with a greater capacity for understanding; as Aristotle says,[4] *men whose flesh is tender are well endowed with intelligence.* Secondly, on the part of those lesser faculties which the intellect needs for its activity. For those in whom imagination, the cogitative faculty, and sense memory are better disposed are also better disposed for understanding.

Hence: 1 & 2. The solution to the first objection is obvious, and similarly with respect to the second, since truth in the intellect consists in the fact that things are known to be as they are.

3. Differences in form which come only from different dispositions in the matter bring about, not a difference in specific nature, but only a numerical difference. For they are different forms corresponding to different individuals, the diversity being in accord with matter.[c]

article 8. does our intellect know the indivisible before the divisible?

THE FIRST POINT:[1] 1. It would seem that our intellect does know the indivisible before the divisible. For Aristotle says[2] that *it is through acquaintance with principles and elements that knowledge, that is to say scientific knowledge, is attained.* But indivisibles are principles and elements of divisibles. Therefore indivisibles are known by us before divisibles.

2. Again, what is included in the definition of a thing we know beforehand, in so far as definitions are from the *prior and more intelligible.*[3] But the indivisible is included in the definition of the divisible, the point in the definition of a line—for, as Euclid says,[4] *a line is a length without breadth, the extremities of which are two points*—and unity in the definition of number—in so far as *number is plurality measurable by one.*[5] Therefore our intellect understands the indivisible before the divisible.

3. Again, *like is known by like.*[6] But the indivisible is more like the intellect than the divisible is, since *mind is simple.*[7] Therefore our intellect first knows the indivisible.

ON THE OTHER HAND, Aristotle says[8] that *indivisibles are realized in consciousness in the same manner as privations.* But since knowledge of privations comes later, so also, therefore, does the indivisible.

---

[7]ibid III, 4. 429a18; b23   [8]ibid III, 6. 430b21
[c]This response is an excellent brief description of St Thomas's understanding of individual differences and what is called the 'numerical distinction' of individuals.

RESPONSIO: Dicendum quod objectum intellectus nostri, secundum præsentem statum, est quidditas rei materialis, quam a phantasmatibus abstrahit, ut ex præmissis patet.[9] Et quia id quod est primo et per se cognitum a virtute cognoscitiva, est proprium ejus objectum, considerari potest quo ordine indivisibile intelligatur a nobis, ex ejus habitudine ad hujusmodi quidditatem.

Dicitur autem indivisibile tripliciter, ut dicitur.[10] Uno modo, sicut continuum est indivisibile, quia est indivisum in actu, licet sit divisibile in potentia. Et hujusmodi indivisibile prius est intellectum a nobis quam ejus divisio, quæ est in partes: quia cognitio confusa est prior quam distincta, ut dictum est.[11]

Alio modo dicitur indivisibile secundum speciem, sicut ratio hominis est quoddam indivisibile. Et hoc etiam modo indivisibile est prius intellectum quam divisio ejus in partes rationis, ut supra dictum est:[12] et iterum prius quam intellectus componat et dividat, affirmando vel negando. Et hujus ratio est, quia hujusmodi duplex indivisibile intellectus secundum se intelligit, sicut proprium objectum.

Tertio modo dicitur indivisibile quod est omnino indivisibile, ut punctus et unitas, quæ nec actu nec potentia dividuntur. Et hujusmodi indivisibile per posterius cognoscitur, per privationem divisibilis. Unde punctum privative definitur,[13] *punctum est cujus* pars non est:* et similiter ratio unius est quod sit *indivisibile,* ut dicitur.[14] Et hujus ratio est, quia tale indivisibile habet quandam oppositionem ad rem corporalem, cujus quidditatem primo et per se intellectus accipit.

Si autem intellectus noster intelligeret per participationem indivisibilium separatorum, ut Platonici posuerunt, sequeretur quod indivisibile hujusmodi esset primo intellectum: quia secundum Platonicos, priora† prius participantur a rebus.

1. Ad primum ergo dicendum quod in accipiendo scientiam, non semper principia et elementa sunt priora: quia quandoque ex effectibus sensibilibus devenimus in cognitionem principiorum et causarum intelligibilium. Sed in complemento scientiæ, semper scientia effectuum dependet ex cognitione principiorum et elementorum: quia, ut ibidem dicit Philosophus,[15] tunc opinamur nos scire, cum principia possumus in causas resolvere.

2. Ad secundum dicendum quod punctum non ponitur in definitione lineæ communiter sumptæ: manifestum est enim quod in linea infinita, et

---

*Piana: *cui* (meaning unchanged)
†Piana omits *priora*, the first things

[9]1a. 84, 7   [10]*De Anima* III, 6. 430b6
[11]art. 3   [12]ibid

REPLY: The object of our intellect, in its present state, is the whatness of material things which the intellect abstracts from sense images, as is clear from what has been said.[9] Now, since what is known first and essentially by a faculty is its proper object, whether the indivisible is known by us first or only later can be seen from its relationship to the whatness.

Now the term 'indivisible' has three senses, according to Aristotle.[10] First, the sense in which the continuous is indivisible, i.e., actually undivided but potentially divisible. The indivisible in this sense is understood by us before its division (into parts), since confused knowledge precedes distinct knowledge, as was mentioned.[11]

Second, the indivisible in specific nature is another sense, e.g., the meaning of 'man' is indivisible. In this sense also the indivisible is understood prior to a division into the elements in its definition (as mentioned before[12]), and also prior to the intellect's combining and separating in an affirmation or negation. The reason is that the intellect understands the indivisible, in this twofold sense, in itself just as it does its proper object.

Third, the indivisible can also mean what is entirely indivisible, for instance, the unit and points, which neither are nor can be divided. The indivisible in this sense is known later, as a privative aspect of the divisible. Thus the point is defined privatively:[13] *a point is that which has no parts;* and similarly the meaning of 'one' is 'to be indivisible', as Aristotle notes.[14] The reason is that the indivisible in this sense stands in opposition to corporeal reality, the whatness of which is primarily and essentially received by the intellect.

If, on the other hand, our intellect understood by participation in immaterial indivisibles, as the Platonists held, it would follow that such indivisibles would be understood first (for corporeal realities participate in the first things first, according to the Platonists).

Hence: 1. In the acquisition of demonstrative knowledge principles and elements do not always come first since, at times, we come to the knowledge of intelligible causes and principles from sensible effects. However, in the completion of a demonstration, demonstrative knowledge of effects always depends on a knowledge of principles and elements since, as Aristotle notes in the same place,[15] we do not think that we know a thing until we can justify principles in terms of causes.

2. Point is not included in the common definition of line, for it is evident that in an infinite or a circular line points exist only potentially. Euclid,

---

[13]Euclid, *Elements* I, definition 1   [14]*Metaphysics* IX, 1. 1052b16
[15]*Physics* I, lect. 1. 184a12: 'We do not think that we know a thing until we are acquainted with its primary conditions or first principles, and have carried our analysis as far as its simplest elements.'

etiam in circulari, non est punctum nisi in potentia. Sed Euclides definit lineam finitam rectam: et ideo posuit punctum in definitione lineæ, sicut terminum in definitione terminati.

Unitas vero est mensura numeri: et ideo ponitur in definitione numeri mensurati. Non autem ponitur in definitione divisibilis, sed magis e converso.

3. Ad tertium dicendum quod similitudo per quam intelligimus, est species cogniti in cognoscente. Et ideo non secundum similitudinem naturæ ad potentiam cognoscitivam est aliquid prius cognitum, sed per convenientiam ad objectum: alioquin magis visus cognosceret auditum quam colorem.

however, was defining a finite straight line, and he thus included points in the definition of a line as limits in the definition of something limited.

On the other hand, the unit is the measure of every number and is thus included in the definition of any measured number. It is not, however, included in the definition of the divisible, rather the opposite is true.

3. The likeness by which we understand is the species of the thing known in the knower. It is not, therefore, according to a likeness in nature with respect to the cognitive faculty, but by similarity with the object that a thing must be known first. Otherwise sight would know hearing rather than colour.

Quæstio 86. quid intellectus noster in rebus materialibus cognoscat

DEINDE CONSIDERANDUM EST quid intellectus noster in rebus materialibus cognoscat, et circa hoc quæruntur quatuor:

1. utrum cognoscat singularia;
2. utrum cognoscat infinita;
3. utrum cognoscat contingentia;
4. utrum cognoscat futura.

articulus 1. utrum intellectus noster cognoscat singularia

AD PRIMUM sic proceditur:[1] 1. Videtur quod intellectus noster cognoscat singularia. Quicumque enim cognoscit compositionem, cognoscit extrema compositionis. Sed intellectus noster cognoscit hanc compositionem, *Socrates est homo:* ejus enim est propositionem formare. Ergo intellectus noster cognoscit hoc singulare quod est Socrates.

2. Præterea, intellectus practicus dirigit ad agendum. Sed actus sunt circa singularia. Ergo cognoscit singularia.

3. Præterea, intellectus noster intelligit seipsum. Ipse autem est quoddam singulare: alioquin non haberet aliquem actum; actus enim singularium sunt. Ergo intellectus noster cognoscit singulare.

4. Præterea, quidquid potest virtus inferior, potest superior. Sed sensus cognoscit singulare. Ergo multo magis intellectus.

SED CONTRA est quod dicit Philosophus,[2] *universale secundum rationem est notum, singulare autem secundum sensum.*

RESPONSIO: Dicendum quod singulare in rebus materialibus intellectus noster directe et primo cognoscere non potest. Cujus ratio est, quia principium singularitatis in rebus materialibus est materia individualis: intellectus autem noster, sicut supra dictum est,[3] intelligit abstrahendo speciem intelligibilem ab hujusmodi materia. Quod autem a materia individuali abstrahitur est universale. Unde intellectus noster directe non est cognoscitivus nisi universalium.

Indirecte autem, et quasi per quandam reflexionem, potest cognoscere singulare: quia, sicut supra dictum est,[4] etiam postquam species intelligibiles abstraxit,* non potest secundum eas actu intelligere nisi

*Piana: *abstraxerit*
[1]cf IV *Sent.* 50, 1, 3. *De veritate* II, 5–6; X, 5. *In De anima* III, *lect.* 8. *Quodl.* XII, 8. *De principio individuationis*

Question 86. what our intellect knows with respect to material realities

WHAT OUR INTELLECT KNOWS with respect to material realities is next to be considered, and in this regard there are four points of inquiry:

1. whether it knows singulars;
2. whether it knows the infinite;
3. whether it knows contingent things;
4. whether it knows the future.

article 1. does our intellect know singulars?

THE FIRST POINT:[1] 1. It would seem that our intellect does know singulars. For whoever knows a combination knows the terms[a] in the combination. But our intellect knows the combination, *Socrates is a man*—it is, in fact, its function to formulate such a proposition. Therefore our intellect knows this singular, for instance Socrates.

2. Again, since it is directive of activities, and activities are concerned with singulars, the practical intellect must know singulars.

3. Again, our intellect understands itself. But it is something singular or else it could not act, since activities are of individuals. Therefore our intellect knows the singular.

4. Again, since a higher power can do whatever a lower one can, and the senses know singulars, therefore *a fortiori* the intellect must also.

ON THE OTHER HAND, Aristotle says[2] the *the universal is more knowable in the order of explanation, the particular in the order of sense.*

REPLY: Directly and immediately our intellect cannot know the singular in material realities. The reason is that the principle of singularity in material things is individual matter, and our intellect—as said before[3]—understands by abstracting species from this sort of matter. But what is abstracted from individual matter is universal. Therefore our intellect has direct knowledge only of universals.

Indirectly and by a quasi-reflection, on the other hand, the intellect can know the singular, because, as mentioned before,[4] even after it has abstracted species it cannot actually understand by means of them except

---

[2]*Physics* I, *lect.* 5. 189a5
[3]Ia. 85, 1
[4]Ia. 84, 7
[a]*extrema*, extremes: terms in a proposition. Singulars, i.e., individuals.

convertendo se ad phantasmata, in quibus species intelligibiles intelligit, ut dicitur.[5]

Sic igitur ipsum universale per speciem intelligibilem directe intelligit; indirecte autem singularia, quorum sunt phantasmata. Et hoc modo format hanc propositionem, *Socrates est homo.*

1. Unde patet solutio ad primum.

2. Ad secundum dicendum quod electio particularis operabilis est quasi conclusio syllogismi intellectus practici.[6] Ex universali autem propositione directe non potest concludi singularis, nisi mediante aliqua singulari propositione assumpta. Unde universalis ratio intellectus practici non movet nisi mediante particulari apprehensione sensitivæ partis.[7]

3. Ad tertium dicendum quod singulare non repugnat intelligibilitati* inquantum est singulare, sed inquantum est materiale, quia nihil intelligitur nisi immaterialiter. Et ideo si sit aliquod singulare† immateriale, sicut est intellectus, hoc non repugnat intelligibilitati.*

4. Ad quartum dicendum quod virtus superior potest illud quod potest‡ virtus inferior, sed eminentiori modo. Unde id quod cognoscit sensus materialiter et concrete, quod est cognoscere singulare directe, hoc cognoscit intellectus immaterialiter et abstracte, quod est cognoscere universale.

articulus 2. utrum intellectus noster possit cognoscere infinita

AD SECUNDUM sic proceditur:[1] 1. Videtur quod intellectus noster possit cognoscere infinita. Deus enim excedit omnia infinita. Sed intellectus noster potest cognoscere Deum, ut supra dictum est.[2] Ergo multo magis potest cognoscere omnia alia infinita.

2. Præterea, intellectus noster natus est cognoscere genera et species. Sed quorumdam generum sunt infinitæ species, sicut numeri, proportionis§ et figuræ. Ergo intellectus noster potest cognoscere infinita.

3. Præterea, si unum corpus non impediret aliud ab existendo in uno et eodem loco, nihil prohiberet infinita corpora in uno loco esse. Sed una species intelligibilis non prohibet aliam ab existendo simul in eodem intellectu: contingit enim multa scire in habitu. Ergo nihil prohibet intellectum nostrum infinitorum scientiam habere in habitu.

4. Præterea, intellectus, cum non sit virtus materiæ corporalis, ut supra dictum est,[3] videtur esse potentia infinita. Sed virtus infinita potest‖ super infinita. Ergo intellectus noster potest cognoscere infinita.

---

*Piana: *intelligenti*, to one who understands
†Piana adds *et*, and
§Piana: *proportiones*
[5]*De Anima* III, 7. 431b2

‡Piana omits *potest*
‖Piana adds *esse*, be
[6]*Nicomachean Ethics* VII, 3. 1147a28

by a return to sense images in which it understands the species, as Aristotle says.[5b]

Therefore, in this sense, it is the universal that the intellect understands directly by means of the species, and singulars (represented in sense images) only indirectly. And it is in this way that it formulates the proposition, 'Socrates is a man'.

Hence: 1. The first solution is evident.

2. The choice of a particular thing to be done is, as it were, the conclusion of a syllogism in the practical intellect.[6] But a singular proposition cannot be deduced from a universal proposition directly, but only on the assumption of a mediating singular proposition. Hence a universal argument in the practical intellect has no motivating force except by means of an apprehension of the particular in the sense part of man.[7]

3. The singular's repugnance to being intelligible is not because it is singular, but because it is material—since only the immaterial can be understood. Thus if there is such a thing as an immaterial singular—and the intellect is such—then it has no repugnance to being intelligible.

4. A higher power can do whatever a lower one can, but in a superior way. Thus what the senses know materially and concretely the intellect knows in an immaterial and abstract way, which is to know the universal.

article 2. can our intellect know the infinite?

THE FIRST POINT:[1] 1. It would seem that our intellect can know the infinite. For God exceeds all infinite things. But our intellect can know God, as said before.[2] Therefore it can, a fortiori, know all other infinite things.

2. Again, our intellect is by nature able to know classes and sub-classes. But some classes—for instance, number, proportion, and shape—have non-finite sub-classes. Therefore our intellect can know the infinite.

3. Again, if one body did not exclude another from existing in one and the same place, nothing would prevent an infinity of bodies from being in one place. But one species does not prevent another from existing at the same time in the same intellect, for we can know more than one thing—habitually. Therefore nothing prevents our intellect from having a knowledge of the infinite habitually.

4. Again, the intellect, since it is not a power of corporeal matter (as said before[3]), would seem to be an infinite power. But an infinite power extends to infinite things. Therefore our intellect can know the infinite.

---

[7]*De Anima* III, II. 434a16   [1]cf *De veritate* II, 9
[2]Ia. 12, I   [3]Ia. 76, I
[b]On his own terms, St Thomas should more properly say: '. . . understands the realities of which the species are images'; cf above, 85, 2.

SED CONTRA est quod dicitur,[4] *infinitum, inquantum est infinitum, est ignotum.*

RESPONSIO: Dicendum quod, cum potentia proportionetur suo objecto, oportet hoc modo se habere intellectum ad infinitum, sicut se habet ejus objectum, quod est quidditas rei materialis. In rebus autem materialibus non invenitur infinitum in actu, sed solum in potentia, secundum quod unum succedit alteri.[5] Et ideo in intellectu nostro invenitur infinitum in potentia, in accipiendo scilicet unum post aliud: quia nunquam intellectus noster tot intelligit, quin possit plura intelligere.

Actu autem vel habitu non potest cognoscere infinita intellectus noster. Actu quidem non, quia intellectus noster non potest simul actu cognoscere nisi quod per unam speciem cognoscit. Infinitum autem non habet unam speciem: alioquin haberet* rationem totius et perfecti. Et ideo non potest intelligi nisi accipiendo partem post partem, ut ex ejus definitione patet:[6] est enim infinitum *cujus quantitatem accipientibus semper est aliquid extra accipere.* Et sic infinitum cognosci non posset actu, nisi omnes partes ejus numerarentur: quod est impossibile.

Et eadem ratione non possumus intelligere infinita in habitu. In nobis enim habitualis cognitio causatur ex actuali consideratione: intelligendo enim efficimur scientes.[7] Unde non possemus habere habitum infinitorum secundum distinctam cognitionem, nisi consideravissemus omnia infinita, numerando ea secundum cognitionis successionem: quod est impossibile.

Et ita nec actu nec habitu intellectus noster potest cognoscere infinita, sed in potentia tantum, ut dictum est.

1. Ad primum ergo dicendum quod, sicut supra dictum est,[8] Deus dicitur infinitus sicut forma, quæ non est terminata per aliquam materiam: in rebus autem materialibus aliquid dicitur infinitum per privationem formalis terminationis. Et quia forma secundum se nota est, materia autem sine forma ignota, inde est quod infinitum materiale est secundum se ignotum. Infinitum autem formale, quod est Deus, est secundum se notum; ignotum autem quoad nos, propter defectum intellectus nostri, qui secundum statum præsentis vitæ habet naturalem aptitudinem ad materialia cognoscenda.

Et ideo in præsenti Deum cognoscere non possumus nisi per materiales effectus. In futuro autem tolletur defectus intellectus nostri per gloriam, et tunc ipsum Deum in sua essentia videre poterimus, tamen absque comprehensione.

---

*Piana adds *totam,* the whole
[4]*Physics* I, *lect.* 4. 187b7   [5]ibid III, *lect.* 6. 206a22
[6]ibid III, *lect.* 6. 207a7   [7]cf *Nicomachean Ethics* II, I. 1103a33   [8]Ia. 7, I

ON THE OTHER HAND, Aristotle says[4] that *the infinite qua infinite is unknowable.*

REPLY: Since faculties are proportioned to their object, the intellect must have the same relation to the infinite as does its object, which is the whatness of material things. But with respect to material realities there is no actual but only a potential infinity—in that one thing follows another to infinity.[5] Therefore in our intellect also there is a potential infinity—that, namely, of receiving one thing after another to infinity—in so far as our intellect can never understand so many things that it could not understand more.

Actually or habitually, however, our intellect cannot know the infinite. Not actually because our intellect, at one time, can only know what can be known in one species. But the infinite is not represented by one species—otherwise it would be total and complete—and thus cannot be understood except by receiving one part after another. (This is evident from its definition,[6] for the infinite is *a quantity such that we can always take a part outside what has been already taken.*) Therefore the infinite cannot be known actually unless all its parts are enumerated, which is impossible.

Nor, by the same reasoning, can we understand the infinite habitually. For our habitual knowledge is caused by our actual knowledge: we come to have science as a habit by acts of understanding.[7a] Hence we could only know the infinite habitually in a distinct way if we could consider everything that is infinite, successively enumerating all of them in our knowledge, which is impossible.

Therefore neither actually nor habitually can our intellect know the infinite, but only potentially, as mentioned.

Hence: 1. As said before,[8] God is spoken of as infinite as a form not limited by matter, whereas, in material reality, a thing is said to be infinite if it lacks a limit in the formal sense.

Now since forms are known in themselves, while matter without form remains unknown, it follows that the infinite in matter by itself remains unknown. On the other hand, the infinite in form—i.e., God—is in itself known but to us unknown, because of the deficiency of our intellect which in the present life is adapted by nature to know material things.

Therefore in the present life we can only know God through his material effects; in the future life, however, the deficiency of our intellect will be taken away by eternal glory and we will then be able to see God in his essence (though not 'comprehensively'[b]).

---

[a]The translation attempts to be fair to the sense rather than the words.
[b]Technical term: cf 1a. 12, 7. Also 1a2æ. 4, 3.

2. Ad secundum dicendum quod intellectus noster natus est cognoscere species per abstractionem a phantasmatibus. Et ideo illas species numerorum et figurarum quas quis non est imaginatus, non potest cognoscere nec actu nec habitu, nisi forte in genere et in principiis universalibus; quod est cognoscere in potentia et confuse.

3. Ad tertium dicendum quod, si duo corpora essent in uno loco, vel plura, non oporteret quod successive subintrarent locum, ut sic per ipsam subintrationis successionem numerarentur locata. Sed species intelligibiles ingrediunter intellectum nostrum successive: quia non multa simul actu intelliguntur. Et ideo oportet numeratas, et non infinitas species esse in intellectu nostro.

4. Ad quartum dicendum quod sicut intellectus noster est infinitus virtute, ita infinitum cognoscit. Est enim virtus ejus infinita, secundum quod non terminatur* per materiam corporalem. Et est cognoscitivus universalis, quod est abstractum a materia individuali, et per consequens non finitur ad aliquod individuum, sed, quantum est de se, ad infinita individua se extendit.

articulus 3. utrum intellectus sit cognoscitivus contingentium

AD TERTIUM sic proceditur:[1] 1. Videtur quod intellectus non sit cognoscitivus contingentium. Quia, ut dicitur,[2] intellectus et sapientia et scientia non sunt contingentium, sed necessariorum.

2. Præterea, sicut dicitur,[3] *ea quæ quandoque sunt et quandoque non sunt tempore mensurantur*. Intellectus autem a tempore abstrahit, sicut et ab aliis conditionibus materiæ. Cum igitur proprium contingentium sit quandoque esse et quandoque non esse, videtur quod contingentia non cognoscantur ab intellectu.

SED CONTRA, omnis scientia est in intellectu. Sed quædam scientiæ sunt de contingentibus; sicut scientiæ morales, quæ sunt de actibus humanis subjectis libero arbitrio; et etiam scientiæ naturales, quantum ad partem quæ tractat de generabilibus et corruptibilibus. Ergo intellectus est cognoscitivus contingentium.

RESPONSIO: Dicendum quod contingentia dupliciter possunt considerari. Uno modo, secundum quod contingentia sunt. Alio modo, secundum quod in eis aliquid necessitatis invenitur: nihil enim est adeo contingens quin

---

*Piana: *determinatur*
[1]cf *In Ethic.* VI, *lect.* I
[2]*Nicomachean Ethics* VI, 6. 1140b31

2. Our intellect by nature knows species[c] abstracted from sense images. Therefore a man can have neither actual nor habitual knowledge of those members of the classes of number and shape of which he has no images, except possibly in terms of the class itself or of general principles (and this would be knowing them vaguely and potentially).

3. If two or more bodies were in one place, they would not have to enter the place one after another (and thus be counted among the things located there by reason of successive entry). Species, on the other hand, enter our intellect one after another in so far as more than one thing cannot be understood at a time. Therefore there must be a limited number, and not an infinity, of species in our intellect.

4. In the sense in which our intellect is infinite in power, it does know the infinite. For its power is infinite in so far as it is not limited by corporeal matter. Furthermore, it has knowledge of the universal which is abstracted from individual matter and, as a consequence, is not limited to any individual object but, of itself, extends to an infinity of individuals.

article 3. does the intellect have knowledge of contingent things?

THE FIRST POINT:[1] It would seem that the intellect does not have knowledge of contingent things. For, as Aristotle says,[2] insight, wisdom, and demonstrative knowledge[a] are concerned, not with contingent things, but with necessary things.

2. Again, Aristotle also says:[3] *Those things which at one time exist, at another do not, are measured by time.* But the intellect abstracts from time as from other material conditions. Therefore since it is proper to contingent things that they at one time exist, at another do not, it would seem that contingent things cannot be known by the intellect.

ON THE OTHER HAND, all demonstrative knowledge is in the intellect. But some of the demonstrative sciences—for instance, the moral sciences (which are concerned with human acts governed by free will), and even the natural sciences (where they treat of realities subject to generation and corruption)—are concerned with contingent things. Therefore the intellect has knowledge of contingent things.

REPLY: Contingent things can be considered in two ways: precisely as contingent, and according as an element of necessity is found in them—for nothing is so contingent that it has nothing necessary in it. For instance,

---

[3]*Physics* IV, *lect.* 12. 221b29
[c]Rather: '. . . realities by way of species'; see art. 1, note *b*, and 85, 2 above.
[a]cf 1a2æ. 57, 2.

in se aliquid necessarium habeat. Sicut hoc ipsum quod est Socratem currere, in se quidem contingens est; sed habitudo cursus ad motum est necessaria: necessarium enim est Socratem moveri, si currit.

Est autem unumquodque contingens ex parte materiæ: quia contingens est quod potest esse et non esse; potentia autem pertinet ad materiam. Necessitas autem consequitur rationem formæ: quia ea quæ consequuntur ad formam ex necessitate insunt. Materia autem est individuationis principium: ratio autem universalis accipitur secundum abstractionem formæ a materia particulari. Dictum autem est supra quod per se et directe intellectus est universalium; sensus autem singularium, quorum etiam indirecte quodammodo est intellectus, ut supra dictum est.

Sic igitur contingentia, prout sunt contingentia, cognoscuntur directe quidem sensu, indirecte autem ab intellectu: rationes autem universales et necessariæ contingentium cognoscuntur per intellectum.

Unde si attendantur rationes universales scibilium,* omnes scientiæ sunt de necessariis. Si autem attendantur ipsæ res, sic quædam scientia est de necessariis, quædam vero de contingentibus.

Et per hoc patet solutio ad objecta.

articulus 4. utrum intellectus noster cognoscat futura

AD QUARTUM sic proceditur:[1] 1. Videtur quod intellectus noster cognoscat futura. Intellectus enim noster cognoscit per species intelligibiles, quæ abstrahunt† ab hic et nunc, et ita se habent indifferenter ad omne tempus. Sed potest cognoscere præsentia. Ergo potest cognoscere futura.

2. Præterea, homo quando alienatur a sensibus aliqua futura cognoscere potest; ut patet in dormientibus et phreneticis. Sed quando alienatur a sensibus magis viget‡ intellectu. Ergo intellectus, quantum est de se, est cognoscitivus futurorum.

3. Præterea, cognitio intellectiva hominis efficacior est quam cognitio quæcumque brutorum animalium. Sed quædam animalia sunt quæ cognoscunt quædam futura; sicut corniculæ frequenter crocitantes significant pluviam mox futuram. Ergo multo magis intellectus humanus potest futura cognoscere.

SED CONTRA est quod dicitur:[2] *Multa hominis afflictio, qui ignorat præterita,§ et futura nullo potest scire nuntio.*

---

*Piana: *sensibilium,* of sensible things   †Piana: *abstrahuntur* (passive)
‡Piana: *indiget,* needs   §Piana: *præsentia,* things present

[1]cf Ia. 57, 3. 2a2æ. 95, 1; 172, 1. II *Sent.* 7, 2, 2. *De veritate* VIII, 12. *CG* III, 154. *De malo* XVI, 7
[2]*Ecclesiastes* 8, 6–7 (Douay)

the fact that Socrates is running is of itself contingent, but the relationship between running and motion is necessary, for it is necessary that, if Socrates is running, he is also moving.

Now anything contingent is such by reason of matter, since the contingent is what has the potentiality to be or not be and potentiality pertains to matter. Necessity, on the other hand, is a natural consequence of form, since the requirements of form are necessary properties.[b] But matter is the principle of individuation, whereas the universal is such because it is received in the abstraction of a form from particular matter. Moreover, as said before, the direct and essential object of the intellect is universals; whereas singulars are the object of the senses, though also, as we have noticed, of the intellect indirectly.

Therefore contingent things, as contingent, are known by the senses directly, by the intellect indirectly; but universal and necessary aspects of contingent things are known by the intellect.

Thus if we look at the universal aspects of the objects of demonstrative knowledge, all the demonstrative sciences are concerned with necessary things. If, on the other hand, we look at things in themselves, some sciences are concerned with necessary things, others with contingent things.

This makes the solution of the difficulties clear.

article 4. does our intellect know the future?

THE FIRST POINT:[1] 1. It would seem that our intellect does know the future. For our intellect knows by means of species which abstract from the here and now and are thus in an undifferentiated state with respect to any particular time. But the intellect can know present things. Therefore it can also know things that are future.

2. Again, when a man is out of his senses, he can know certain things that are future, as is evident in those who are asleep or insane. But when someone is out of his senses, he is intellectually more active. Therefore the intellect, of itself, has knowledge of things that are future.

3. Again, the intellectual knowledge of man is capable of more than the knowledge of any of the brute animals. But some animals know certain things that are future—crows, for instance, when they caw repeatedly signify that there will soon be rain. Therefore, *a fortiori*, the human intellect can know the future.

ON THE OTHER HAND, Scripture says,[2] *There is great affliction for man, because he is ignorant of things past; and things to come he cannot know by any messenger.*

---

[b]The translation follows the sense rather than the words.

RESPONSIO: Dicendum quod de cognitione futurorum eodem modo distinguendum est, sicut de cognitione contingentium. Nam ipsa futura ut sub tempore cadunt, sunt singularia, quæ intellectus humanus non cognoscit nisi per reflexionem, ut supra dictum est. Rationes autem futurorum possunt esse universales, et intellectu perceptibiles; et de eis etiam possunt esse scientiæ.

Ut tamen communiter de cognitione futurorum loquamur, sciendum est quod futura dupliciter cognosci possunt: uno modo, in seipsis, alio modo, in suis causis.

In seipsis quidem futura cognosci non possunt nisi a Deo; cui etiam sunt præsentia dum in cursu rerum sunt futura, inquantum ejus æternus intuitus simul fertur supra totum temporis cursum, ut supra dictum est cum de Dei scientia ageretur.[3]

Sed prout sunt in suis causis, cognosci possunt etiam a nobis. Et si quidem in suis causis sint ut ex quibus ex necessitate proveniant, cognoscuntur per certitudinem scientiæ; sicut astrologus præcognoscit eclipsim futuram. Si autem sic sint in suis causis ut ab eis proveniant ut in pluribus, sic cognosci possunt per quandam conjecturam vel magis vel minus certam, secundum quod causæ sunt vel magis vel minus inclinatæ ad effectus.

1. Ad primum ergo dicendum quod ratio illa procedit de cognitione quæ fit per rationes universales causarum, ex quibus futura cognosci possunt secundum modum ordinis effectus ad causam.

2. Ad secundum dicendum quod, sicut Augustinus dicit,[4] anima habet quamdam vim sortis, ut ex sui natura possit futura cognoscere: et ideo quando retrahitur a corporeis sensibus, et quodammodo revertitur ad seipsam, fit particeps notitiæ futurorum. Et hæc quidem opinio rationabilis esset, si poneremus quod anima acciperet cognitionem rerum secundum participationem idearum, sicut Platonici posuerunt: quia sic anima ex sui natura cognosceret universales causas omnium effectuum, sed impeditur per corpus; unde quando a corporis sensibus abstrahitur, futura cognoscit.

Sed quia iste modus cognoscendi non est connaturalis intellectui nostro, sed magis ut cognitionem a sensibus accipiat; ideo* non est secundum naturam animæ quod futura cognoscat cum a sensibus alienatur; sed magis per impressionem aliquarum causarum superiorum spiritualium et corporalium.

Spiritualium quidem, sicut cum virtute divina ministerio angelorum intellectus humanus illuminatur, et phantasmata ordinantur ad futura

*Piana omits *ideo*, therefore

[3]1a. 14, 13   [4]*De Genesi ad litteram* XII, 13. PL 34, 464
ªA mistaken reference is given to *Confessions* XII; *Confessions* XI, 18-19 discusses

REPLY: With respect to knowing the future the same distinction has to be made as for knowing contingent things. For future things as being subject to time are singular, and the human intellect can only know them by reflection—as stated already. However, there can be, with respect to things that are future, universal aspects, perceptible to the intellect, and about these there can be demonstrative knowledge.

Nevertheless, in the ordinary way in which we speak of knowledge of the future, it should be noted that future things can be known in two ways; in themselves, and in their causes.

In themselves things that are future can be known only by God. To him they are present even while, in the course of events, they remain future, in so far as his eternal vision looks simultaneously on the whole course of time, as was shown in treating of God's knowledge.[3]

In their causes, however, they can be known even by us. In fact, if future things exist in causes from which they proceed necessarily, then they can be known with the certainty of demonstrative knowledge—as, for instance, an astronomer knows beforehand that an eclipse is to take place. If, however, they exist in causes from which they only proceed for the most part, then they can be known in terms of a more or less certain conjecture, according as the causes are more or less inclined to produce their effects.

Hence: 1. The argument assumes knowledge in terms of universal aspects of causes, and from these, things that are future can be known, according as there is an order of effect to cause.

2. Augustine says[4a] that the soul has a certain 'power of lots', allowing it to know the future by way of its own nature; thus when it is withdrawn from the corporeal senses and, in a sense, turned in upon itself, it becomes a sharer in the knowledge of the future. Now this opinion would be reasonable if we held that the soul receives knowledge of things by participation in Ideas (as the Platonists held)—for in this view the soul, by its very nature, knows the universal causes of all effects, though impeded by the body, so that when withdrawn from the corporeal senses, it knows the future.

However, since this mode of knowing is not connatural to our intellect, which, instead, receives its knowledge from the senses, it is not, therefore, according to the nature of the soul to know the future when withdrawn from the senses, but rather because of an impression received from superior spiritual or corporeal causes.

From spiritual causes for instance, when, by divine power, the human intellect is illumined by the ministry of angels, and sense images are so

knowledge of the future, but in terms closer to St Thomas's view here than to a 'power of lots' or the soul's knowing the future by its own nature.

aliqua cognoscenda; vel etiam cum per operationem dæmonum fit aliqua commotio in phantasia ad præsignandum aliqua futura quæ dæmones cognoscunt, ut supra dictum est.[5] Hujusmodi autem impressiones spiritualium causarum magis nata est anima humana suscipere cum a sensibus alienatur: quia per hoc propinquior fit substantiis spiritualibus, et magis libera ab exterioribus inquietudinibus.

Contingit autem et hoc per impressionem superiorum causarum corporalium.* Manifestum est enim quod corpora superiora imprimunt in corpora inferiora. Unde cum vires sensitivæ sint actus corporalium organorum, consequens est quod ex impressione cælestium corporum immutetur quodammodo phantasia. Unde cum cælestia corpora sint causa multorum futurorum, fiunt in imaginatione aliqua signa quorundam futurorum. Hæc autem signa magis percipiuntur in nocte et a dormientibus, quam de die et a vigilantibus: quia, ut dicitur,[6] *quæ deferuntur de die, dissolvuntur magis; plus est enim sine turbatione aër noctis, eo quod silentiores sunt noctes. Et in corpore faciunt sensum propter somnum: quia parvi motus interiores magis sentiuntur a dormientibus quam a vigilantibus. Hi vero motus faciunt phantasmata, ex quibus prævidentur futura.*

3. Ad tertium dicendum quod animalia bruta non habent aliquid supra phantasiam quod ordinet phantasmata, sicut habent homines rationem; et ideo phantasia brutorum animalium totaliter sequitur impressionem cælestem. Et ideo ex motibus hujusmodi animalium magis possunt cognosci quædam futura, ut pluvia et hujusmodi, quam ex motibus hominum, qui moventur per consilium rationis. Unde Philosophus dicit[7] quod *quidam imprudentissimi sunt maxime prævidentes: nam intelligentia horum non est curis affecta, sed tanquam deserta et vacua ab omnibus, et mota secundum movens ducitur.*

---

*Piana adds *materialium,* material

[5] Ia. 57, 3
[6] *De divinatione per somnum* 2. 464a12

arranged as to know certain future things; or else when, by the activity of demons, there is a stirring-up of the imagination to signify beforehand certain future things which the demons know, as mentioned earlier.[5] These impressions made by spiritual causes the human soul naturally receives better when withdrawn from the senses, because it is thereby brought nearer to spiritual substances and made freer of external disturbances.

By superior corporeal causes also can such an impression be made: for it is obvious that superior bodies make impressions on inferior bodies. Thus, since the sense faculties are forms of corporeal organs, it follows that certain changes can be effected in the imagination by celestial bodies and, since celestial bodies are the cause of many future events, signs of certain things in the future are produced in the imagination. But such signs are perceived at night and by those who are asleep better than during the day by those who are awake, because, as Aristotle says,[6] *when proceeding in the daytime they are more liable to dissolution (since at night the air is less disturbed, there being then less wind); they shall be perceived within the body owing to sleep, since persons are more sensitive even to slight sensory movements when asleep than when awake. It is these movements then that cause 'presentations', as a result of which sleepers foresee the future.*

3. Brute animals do not have anything higher than imagination to arrange sense images (as man has his reason), and therefore the imagination of brute animals is totally subject to celestial impressions. Thus certain kinds of future events—such as rain, etc.—can more easily be known from such changes in animals than from changes in men who are swayed also by the deliberations of reason. Hence Aristotle says[7] that *commonplace persons especially have foresight. For the mind of such persons is not given to thinking, but, as it were, derelict, or totally vacant, and, when once set moving, is borne passively on in the direction taken by that which moves it.*

---

[7]ibid 2. 464a18

Quæstio 87. quomodo anima intellectiva seipsam et ea quæ in ipsa sunt cognoscat

DEINDE CONSIDERANDUM EST quomodo anima intellectiva cognoscat seipsam et ea quæ in se sunt. Et circa hoc quæruntur quatuor:

1. utrum cognoscat seipsam per suam essentiam;
2. quomodo cognoscat habitus in se existentes;
3. quomodo intellectus cognoscat proprium actum;
4. quomodo cognoscat actum voluntatis.

articulus 1. utrum anima intellectiva seipsam cognoscat per suam essentiam

AD PRIMUM sic proceditur:[1] 1. Videtur quod anima intellectiva seipsam cognoscat per suam essentiam. Dicit enim Augustinus[2] quod *mens seipsam novit per seipsam, quoniam est incorporea.*

2. Præterea, angelus et anima humana conveniunt in genere intellectualis substantiæ. Sed angelus intelligit seipsum per essentiam suam. Ergo et anima humana.

3. Præterea, *in his quæ sunt sine materia, idem est intellectus et quod intelligitur,* ut dicitur.[3] Sed mens humana est sine materia: non enim est actus corporis alicujus, ut supra dictum est.[4] Ergo in mente humana est idem intellectus et quod intelligitur. Ergo intelligit se per essentiam suam.

SED CONTRA est quod dicitur:[5] *intellectus intelligit seipsum sicut et alia.* Sed alia non intelligit per essentias* eorum, sed per eorum similitudines. Ergo neque se intelligit per essentiam suam.

RESPONSIO: Dicendum quod unumquodque cognoscibile est secundum quod est in actu, et non secundum quod est in potentia:[6] sic enim aliquid est ens et verum, quod sub cognitione cadit, prout actu est. Et hoc quidem manifeste apparet in rebus sensibilibus: non enim visus percipit coloratum in potentia, sed solum coloratum in actu. Et similiter intellectus manifestum est quod, inquantum est cognoscitivus rerum materialium, non cognoscit nisi quod est actu: et inde est quod non cognoscit materiam

---

*Piana: *essentiam*
[1]cf *De veritate* x, 8. *CG* III, 46. *In De anima* III, *lect.* 9
[2]*De Trinitate* ix, 3. PL 42, 963
[3]*De Anima* III, 4. 430a3
[4]1a. 76, 1   [5]*De Anima* III, 4. 430a3
[6]Aristotle, *Metaphysics* VIII, 9. 1051a29
[a]For the place of this question in St Thomas's outline, see the prologue to question

Question 87. how the intellectual soul knows itself and the things in it

NEXT TO BE CONSIDERED is the way in which the intellectual soul knows itself and what are within it.[a] In this matter there are four issues for discussion:

1. whether the soul knows itself by its own essence;
2. how it knows the habitual dispositions[b] found in it;
3. how the intellect knows its own acts;
4. how it knows the acts of the will.

article 1. does the intellectual soul know itself by its own essence?

THE FIRST POINT:[1] 1. It would seem that the intellectual soul knows itself by its own essence. For Augustine says[2] that *the mind knows itself through itself because it is incorporeal.*

2. Again, angels and human souls belong to the same class of intellectual substance. But angels understand themselves by their own essence. So, therefore, does the human soul.

3. Again, *in the case of objects which involve no matter, what thinks and what is thought are identical,* as Aristotle says.[3] But the human mind has no matter since it is not the form of a body[a]—as mentioned before.[4] Therefore in the human mind the intellect is identical with what is understood, and thus it understands itself by its own essence.

ON THE OTHER HAND, Aristotle says[5] that *mind is itself thinkable in exactly the same way as its objects are.* But it understands other things, not by means of their essences, but by means of likenesses of them. Neither therefore does it understand itself by its own essence.

REPLY: Anything knowable is such in so far as it is actual and not as it is potential,[6] for a thing has being and truth, which is what falls under knowledge, in so far as it is actual. This is manifestly obvious with respect to sensible realities: sight does not perceive the potentially coloured, but only the actually coloured. Likewise it is clear that the intellect as having knowledge of material things knows only what is actual. This is the reason

---

84; after considering how man knows external things in the three preceding questions, he now turns to the knowledge of things within the soul.
[b]*habitus*, habits, but as St Thomas uses the term its connotations are much broader than the English 'habit'—'habitual disposition' (to know, to act virtuously, or even to exist in a certain way) seems better. Cf Vol. 22 of this series.
[a]i.e., of a bodily organ.

primam nisi secundum proportionem ad formam, ut dicitur.[7] Unde et in substantiis immaterialibus, secundum quod unaquæque earum se habet ad hoc quod sit in actu per essentiam suam, ita se habet ad hoc quod sit per suam essentiam intelligibilis.

Essentia igitur Dei, quæ est actus purus et perfectus, est simpliciter et perfecte secundum seipsam intelligibilis. Unde Deus per suam essentiam non solum seipsum, sed etiam omnia intelligit.

Angeli autem essentia est quidem in genere intelligibilium ut actus, non tamen ut actus purus neque completus. Unde ejus intelligere non completur per essentiam suam: etsi enim per essentiam suam se intelligat angelus, tamen non omnia potest per essentiam suam cognoscere, sed cognoscit alia a se per eorum similitudines.

Intellectus autem humanus se habet in genere rerum intelligibilium ut ens in potentia tantum, sicut et materia prima se habet in genere rerum sensibilium: unde *possibilis* nominatur.[8] Sic igitur in sua essentia consideratus, se habet ut potentia intelligens. Unde ex seipso habet virtutem ut intelligat, non autem ut intelligatur, nisi secundum id quod fit actu.

Sic enim etiam Platonici posuerunt ordinem entium intelligibilium supra ordinem intellectuum: quia intellectus non intelligit nisi per participationem intelligibilis*; participans autem est infra participatum, secundum eos.

Si igitur intellectus humanus fieret actu per participationem† formarum intelligibilium separatarum, ut Platonici posuerunt, per hujusmodi participationem rerum incorporearum intellectus humanus seipsum intelligeret. Sed quia connaturale est intellectui nostro, secundum statum præsentis vitæ, quod ad materialia et sensibilia respiciat, sicut supra dictum est;[9] consequens est ut sic seipsum intelligat intellectus noster, secundum quod fit actu per species a sensibilibus abstractas per lumen intellectus agentis, quod est actus ipsorum intelligibilium, et eis mediantibus‡ intellectus possibilis.

Non ergo per essentiam suam, sed per actum suum se cognoscit intellectus noster. Et hoc dupliciter. Uno quidem modo, particulariter, secundum quod Socrates vel Plato percipit se habere animam intellectivam, ex hoc quod percipit se intelligere. Alio modo, in universali, secundum quod naturam humanæ mentis ex actu intellectus consideramus.

Sed verum est quod judicium et efficacia hujus cognitionis per quam

---

*Piana: *intelligibilem*, intelligible (participation)
†Piana: *participationes*
‡Piana adds *intelligit*, understands
[7]*Physics* 1, lect. 7. 191a8
[8]Aristotle, *De Anima* III, 4. 429a22
[9]Ia. 84, 7

it only knows primary matter by analogy with form, as Aristotle says.[7] Hence also, among immaterial substances, as each stands with respect to being actual by its own essence, so will it stand with respect to being intelligible by its own essence.

Thus the essence of God, which is pure and complete act, is of itself simply and perfectly intelligible. Hence God understands, not only himself but all other things, by his own essence.

The essence of an angel, however, though its actuality is in the class of intelligible realities, is none the less not pure or complete act. Hence an angel's understanding does not have its completion by its own essence, for, although angels understand themselves by their own essence, they cannot know everything by their own essence, but know things other than themselves by likenesses of those things.

Now the human intellect only comes under the class of intelligible things as a potential being—in the way that primary matter is in the class of sensible things—hence its name, *possible intellect*.[8] Accordingly therefore, considered in its essence, it is potentially intelligent—thus it has, of itself, the power to understand but not to be understood except in so far as it is actualized.

(In this sense even the Platonists held that there is a superior order of 'intelligible beings' above the order of 'intellects', since an intellect understands, according to them, only by participation in the intelligible, and a participator is below what is participated in.)

Thus if the human intellect were actualized by participation in immaterial intelligible forms, as the Platonists held, the human intellect would also understand itself by participation in these incorporeal things. However, since it is connatural for our intellect in the present life to look to material, sensible things, as said before,[9] it follows that our intellect understands itself according as it is made actual by species abstracted from sensible realities by the light of the agent intellect, which is the actuality of intelligible objects and by means of them, also of the possible intellect.

Therefore our intellect knows itself, not by its own essence, but by means of its activity. And this in two senses. First, speaking particularly, as when Socrates or Plato perceives himself to have an intellectual soul from the fact that he perceives himself to be intellectually acting. Second, speaking universally, as when we consider the nature of the human mind from the nature of the intellect's activity.[b]

It is true, however, that the correctness[c] and effectiveness of this

---

[b]*particulariter* and *in universali*: here in the concrete and in the abstract, corresponding to self-awareness and scientific introspection.
[c]*judicium*, judgment: cf 84, 8 note *a*.

naturam animæ cognoscimus, competit nobis secundum derivationem luminis intellectus nostri a veritate divina, in qua rationes omnium rerum continentur, sicut supra dictum est.[10] Unde et* Augustinus dicit,[11] *Intuemur inviolabilem veritatem, ex qua perfecte, quantum possumus, definimus non qualis sit uniuscujusque hominis mens, sed qualis esse sempiternis rationibus debeat.*

Est autem differentia inter has duas cognitiones. Nam ad primam cognitionem de mente habendam, sufficit ipsa mentis præsentia, quæ est principium actus ex quo mens percipit seipsam. Et ideo dicitur se cognoscere per suam præsentiam. Sed ad secundam cognitionem de mente habendam, non sufficit ejus præsentia, sed requiritur diligens et subtilis inquisitio. Unde et multi naturam animæ ignorant, et multi etiam circa naturam animæ erraverunt. Propter quod Augustinus dicit,[12] de tali inquisitione mentis, *Non velut absentem se quærat mens cernere; sed præsentem quærat discernere,* idest cognoscere differentiam suam ab aliis rebus, quod est cognoscere quidditatem et naturam suam.

1. Ad primum ergo dicendum quod mens seipsam per seipsam† novit, quia tandem in sui ipsius cognitionem pervenit, licet per suum actum: ipsa enim est quæ cognoscitur, quia ipsa seipsam amat, ut ibidem subditur. Potest enim aliquid dici per se notum dupliciter: vel quia per nihil aliud in ejus notitiam devenitur, sicut dicuntur prima principia per se nota; vel quia non sunt cognoscibilia per accidens, sicut color est per se visibilis, substantia autem per accidens.

2. Ad secundum dicendum quod essentia angeli est sicut actus in genere intelligibilium, et ideo se habet et ut intellectus et ut intellectum. Unde angelus suam essentiam per seipsum apprehendit. Non autem intellectus humanus, qui vel est omnino in potentia respectu intelligibilium, sicut intellectus possibilis, vel est actus intelligibilium quæ abstrahuntur a phantasmatibus, sicut intellectus agens.

3. Ad tertium dicendum quod verbum illud Philosophi universaliter verum est in omni intellectu. Sicut enim sensus in actu est sensibile, propter similitudinem sensibilis, quæ est forma sensus in actu; ita intellectus in actu est intellectum in actu, propter similitudinem rei intellectæ, quæ est forma intellectus in actu. Et ideo intellectus humanus, qui fit in actu per speciem rei intellectæ, per eamdem speciem intelligitur, sicut per formam suam.

Idem autem est dicere quod *in his quæ sunt sine materia, idem est*

*Piana omits *et*
†Piana: *se* (meaning unchanged)

[10]Ia. 84, 5
[11]*De Trinitate* IX, 6. PL 42, 966
[12]*De Trinitate* X, 9. PL 42, 980

knowledge, whereby we know the nature of the soul, comes to us by the derivation of the light of our intellect from divine truth, in which, as said before,[10] the ideas of all things are contained. Hence Augustine says,[11] *We gaze upon indestructible truth, from which to define as fully as we can, not of what sort is the mind of any one particular man, but of what sort it ought to be by reason of the eternal plan.*

There is, moreover, a difference between these two kinds of knowledge. For, in order to have the first kind of knowledge of the mind the very presence of a mind is sufficient, since it is the principle of the act by means of which the mind perceives itself; thus it is said to know itself by being present to itself. To have the second kind of knowledge of the mind, however, mere presence is not sufficient, and a diligent, subtle inquiry is needed. Many, for this reason, are simply ignorant of the soul's nature and many are positively mistaken about it. Accordingly Augustine[12] speaks as follows about this mental inquiry, *Let the mind not strive merely to see itself as if it were absent, but strive to discern itself as present,* i.e., to know how it differs from other things, which is to know its whatness and nature.

Hence: 1. The mind knows itself by means of itself in that ultimately, though by means of its acts, it arrives at a knowledge of itself: it is what is known because it is what loves itself, as Augustine adds in the same place. For a thing can be spoken of as known of itself in two ways, either because knowledge of it is arrived at through nothing else (thus first principles are said to be known as self-evident), or because it is not known by another (thus colour is visible of itself, but substance only *per accidens*).[d]

2. The essence of an angel is something actual in the class of intelligible objects and thus stands as both understanding and what is understood; thus an angel, by means of itself, apprehends its own essence. But the human intellect does not, since it is either entirely potential with respect to intelligible objects (the possible intellect), or the actualization of intelligible objects abstracted from sense images (the agent intellect).

3. What Aristotle says there is true universally with respect to all intellects. For just as an actualized sense is identical with its sensible object by reason of a likeness of the object which is the form of the actualized sense, so actual understanding is identical with the actually understood by reason of a likeness of the thing understood which is the form of the actualized intellect. Consequently, the human intellect, which is actualized by a species of the thing understood, is itself understood through this same species as through its proper form.

Moreover, it means the same thing to say, 'with objects which involve

---

[d] *per accidens* here means *per aliud*; *per se* of itself. The distinction is drawn between the two meanings of *per se* evident, namely immediately evident and not indirectly evident.

intellectus et quod intelligitur, ac si diceretur quod *in his quæ sunt intellecta in actu, idem est intellectus et quod intelligitur:* per hoc enim aliquid est intellectum in actu, quod est sine materia. Sed in hoc est differentia, quia quorundam essentiæ sunt sine materia, sicut substantiæ separatæ quas angelos dicimus, quarum unaquæque et est intellecta et est intelligens: sed quædam res sunt quarum essentiæ non sunt sine materia, sed solum similitudines ab eis abstractæ. Unde et Commentator dicit,[13] quod propositio inducta non habet veritatem nisi in* substantiis separatis: verificatur enim quodammodo in eis quod non verificatur in aliis, ut dictum est.

articulus 2. utrum intellectus noster cognoscat habitus animæ per essentiam eorum

AD SECUNDUM sic proceditur:[1] 1. Videtur quod intellectus noster cognoscat habitus animæ per essentiam eorum. Dicit enim Augustinus,[2] *Non sic videtur fides in corde in quo est, sicut anima alterius hominis ex motibus corporis videtur; sed eam tenet certissima scientia, clamatque conscientia.* Et eadem ratio est de aliis habitibus animæ. Ergo habitus animæ non cognoscuntur per actus, sed per seipsos.

2. Præterea, res materiales, quæ sunt extra animam, cognoscuntur per hoc quod similitudines earum sunt præsentialiter in anima; et ideo dicuntur per suas similitudines cognosci. Sed habitus animæ præsentialiter per suam essentiam sunt in anima. Ergo per suam essentiam cognoscuntur.

3. Præterea, *propter quod unumquodque tale, et illud magis.*[3] Sed res aliæ cognoscuntur ab anima propter habitus et species intelligibiles. Ergo ista magis per seipsa ab anima cognoscuntur.

SED CONTRA, habitus sunt principia actuum, sicut et potentiæ. Sed, sicut dicitur,[4] *priores potentiis, secundum rationem, actus et operationes sunt.* Ergo eadem ratione sunt priores habitibus. Et ita habitus per actus cognoscuntur, sicut et potentiæ.

RESPONSIO: Dicendum quod habitus quodammodo est medium inter potentiam puram et purum actum. Jam autem dictum est quod nihil cognoscitur nisi secundum quod est actu. Sic ergo inquantum habitus deficit ab actu perfecto, deficit ab hoc, ut non sit per seipsum cognoscibilis, sed necesse est quod per actum suum cognoscatur: sive dum aliquis percipit se habere habitum, per hoc quod percipit se producere actum proprium habitus; sive dum aliquis inquirit naturam et rationem habitus, ex consideratione

---

*Piana omits *in*
[13]*Commentary on De anima* III, 15
[1]cf III *Sent.* 23, 1, 2. *De veritate* x, 9   [2]*De Trinitate* XIII, 1. PL 42, 1014

no matter, what thinks and what is thought are identical', as to say, 'with objects actually thought, what thinks and what is thought are identical', for a thing becomes actually understood in that it is without matter. But there is a difference here: the very essences of certain things are without matter (e.g., the immaterial substances that we call angels), and these are both understood and understanding; whereas other things have essences that are not without matter—only the likenesses abstracted from them are. For this reason Averroes says[13] that the statement in question is true only of immaterial substances—and, as we have just mentioned, it is in fact true of them in a way that it is not true of other things.

article 2. does our intellect know the habitual dispositions of the soul through their essences?

THE FIRST POINT.[1] 1: It would seem that our intellect does know the habitual dispositions of the soul through their own essences. For Augustine says,[2] *Faith is not seen in the heart in which it exists in the same way that the soul of another man is recognized by means of movements of the body; but we know it most certainly and conscience proclaims it aloud.* And the same argument applies to other habitual dispositions of the soul. Therefore they are known, not through their acts, but through themselves.

2. Again, material things outside the soul are known by means of the fact that their likenesses are in the soul as present to it; they are thus said to be known by means of their likenesses. But habitual dispositions of the soul are in the soul and present there by their very essence. Therefore they are known by means of their essences.

3. Again, *the cause of a quality itself has the quality to a higher degree.*[3] But other things are known by the soul because of species and habitual dispositions. Therefore the soul knows these both better and in themselves.

ON THE OTHER HAND, habitual dispositions—like faculties—are principles of activities. But, as Aristotle says,[4] *The question of what an agent does precedes the question of what enables it to do what it does,* and therefore also, by the same reasoning, precedes the question of habitual dispositions. Thus habitual dispositions are known by way of acts, just as faculties are.

REPLY: A habitual disposition is, in a sense, midway between pure potentiality and pure actuality. But it has already been mentioned that nothing is known except in so far as it is actual. Therefore to the extent that a habitual disposition has less than complete actuality, it will also be unknowable in itself and will have to be known by means of its actualization. As when, for

---

[3]*Posterior Analytics* I, 2. 72a29   [4]*De Anima* II, 4. 415a16

actus. Et prima quidem cognitio habitus fit per ipsam præsentiam habitus: quia ex hoc ipso quod est præsens actum causat, in quo statim percipitur. Secunda autem cognitio habitus fit per studiosam inquisitionem, sicut supra dictum est de mente.

1. Ad primum ergo dicendum quod, etsi fides non cognoscatur per exteriores corporis motus, percipitur tamen etiam ab eo in quo est, per interiorem actum cordis. Nullus enim fidem se habere scit, nisi per hoc quod se credere percipit.

2. Ad secundum dicendum quod habitus sunt præsentes in intellectu nostro, non sicut objecta intellectus (quia objectum intellectus nostri, secundum statum præsentis vitæ, est natura rei materialis, ut supra dictum est[5]); sed sunt præsentes in intellectu ut quibus intellectus intelligit.

3. Ad tertium dicendum quod, cum dicitur, *Propter quod unumquodque, illud magis*, veritatem habet, si intelligatur in his quæ sunt unius ordinis, puta in uno genere causæ: puta si dicatur quod sanitas est desiderabilis* propter vitam, sequitur quod vita sit magis desiderabilis. Si autem accipiantur ea quæ sunt diversorum ordinum, non habet veritatem: ut si dicatur quod sanitas est desiderabilis* propter medicinam, non ideo sequitur quod medicina sit magis desiderabilis, quia sanitas est in ordine finium, medicina autem in ordine causarum efficientium.

Sic igitur si accipiamus duo, quorum utrumque sit per se in ordine objectorum cognitionis; illud propter quod aliud cognoscitur, erit magis notum, sicut principia conclusionibus.

Sed habitus non est de ordine objectorum, inquantum est habitus; nec propter habitum aliqua cognoscuntur sicut propter objectum cognitum, sed sicut propter dispositionem vel formam qua cognoscens cognoscit: et ideo ratio non sequitur.

articulus 3. utrum intellectus cognoscat proprium actum

AD TERTIUM sic proceditur:[1] 1. Videtur quod intellectus non cognoscat proprium actum. Illud enim proprie cognoscitur, quod est objectum cognoscitivæ virtutis. Sed actus differt ab objecto. Ergo intellectus non cognoscit suum actum.

2. Præterea, quidquid cognoscitur, aliquo actu cognoscitur. Si igitur

---

*Leonine omits *desiderabilis*, desirable

[5]Ia. 84, 7   [1]cf III *Sent.* 23, 1, 2 ad 3. *De veritate* X, 9
[a]*mens*, see art. 1 above. The doctrine here of 'consciousness' without concepts, Augustinian in its inspiration, is a source for the studies of mystical theology on 'dwelling' in God's presence and friendship. See Vol. 1 of this series, Appendix 10.

instance, either someone perceives that he has a habitual disposition by perceiving that he produces the act proper to it, or else someone investigates the nature and definition of a habitual disposition by way of a consideration of its acts. The first kind of knowledge of a habitual disposition is produced by the very presence of the disposition—since by its very presence it causes an activity in which it is immediately perceived. The second kind, on the other hand, requires a diligent investigation, as we have mentioned with reference to the mind.[a]

Hence: 1. Although faith is not known by external movements of the body, it is perceived, even by the one in whom it dwells, through interior motions of the heart. For no one can know that he has faith except by perceiving his own acts of belief.

2. Habitual dispositions are not present in our intellect as objects of the intellect (since the object of our intellect in the present life is the nature of material things, as was said before[5]); they are present, rather, as *that by which* the intellect understands.

3. The dictum, *The cause of a quality itself has the quality to a higher degree*, is true if understood with respect to things of the same order, for instance to one class of explanatory principle,[b] e.g. if you were to say that health is desirable because of life, it follows that life is the more desirable of the two. If, however, we take things that belong to different orders it is not true, e.g., if you were to say that health is desirable on account of medicine, it does not therefore follow that medicine is the more desirable, since health belongs to the class of final causes, medicine to that of efficient causes.

Therefore if we take two things that are both essentially in the order of objects of knowledge, that on account of which something else is known will itself be better known, as premises are compared with conclusions.

However, a habitual disposition, as such, does not belong to the order of objects, nor are things known because a habitual disposition is an object known, but because this is a form or disposition by which a knower knows. The argument is thus a *non sequitur*.

article 3. does the intellect know its own acts?

THE FIRST POINT:[1] 1. It would seem that the intellect does not know its own acts. For that is known, properly speaking, which is the object of a cognitive faculty. But an activity is different from an object. Therefore the intellect does not know its acts.

2. Again, whatever one knows is known by means of an activity. Thus if

---

[b]*causæ*: cf 84, 1, note *k*.

intellectus cognoscit actum suum, aliquo actu cognoscit illum; et iterum illum actum* alio actu. Erit ergo procedere in infinitum: quod videtur impossibile.

3. Præterea, sicut se habet sensus ad actum suum, ita et intellectus. Sed sensus proprius non sentit actum suum, sed hoc pertinet ad sensum communem, ut dicitur.[2] Ergo neque intellectus intelligit actum suum.

SED CONTRA est quod Augustinus dicit,[3] *Intelligo me intelligere.*

RESPONSIO: Dicendum quod, sicut jam dictum est, unumquodque cognoscitur secundum quod est actu. Ultima autem perfectio intellectus est ejus operatio: non enim est sicut† actio tendens in alterum, quæ sit perfectio operati, sicut ædificatio ædificati; sed manet in operante ut perfectio et actus ejus.[4] Hoc igitur est primum quod de intellectu intelligitur, scilicet ipsum ejus intelligere.

Sed circa hoc diversi intellectus diversimode se habent.

Est enim aliquis intellectus, scilicet divinus, qui est ipsum suum intelligere. Et sic in Deo idem est quod intelligat se intelligere, et quod intelligat suam essentiam: quia sua essentia est suum intelligere.

Est autem‡ alius intellectus, scilicet angelicus, qui non est suum intelligere, sicut supra dictum est,[5] sed tamen primum objectum sui intelligere est ejus essentia. Unde etsi aliud sit in angelo, secundum rationem, quod intelligat se intelligere, et quod intelligat suam essentiam, tamen simul et uno actu utrumque intelligit: quia hoc quod est intelligere suam essentiam, est propria perfectio suæ essentiæ; simul autem et uno actu intelligitur res cum sua perfectione.

Est autem alius intellectus, scilicet humanus, qui nec est suum intelligere, nec sui§ intelligere est objectum primum ipsa ejus essentia, sed aliquid extrinsecum, scilicet natura materialis rei.

Et ideo id quod primo cognoscitur ab intellectu humano est hujusmodi objectum; et secundario cognoscitur ipse actus quo cognoscitur objectum; et per actum cognoscitur ipse intellectus, cujus est perfectio ipsum intelligere. Et ideo Philosophus dicit quod objecta præcognoscuntur actibus, et actus potentiis.[6]

1. Ad primum ergo dicendum, quod objectum intellectus est commune quoddam, scilicet ens et verum, sub quo comprehenditur etiam ipse actus intelligendi. Unde intellectus potest suum actum intelligere. Sed non primo: quia nec primum objectum intellectus nostri, secundum

---

*Piana omits *actum*, act   †Piana: *sic*, thus   ‡Piana: *etiam*, also   §Piana: *suum*
[2]*De Anima* III, 2. 425b12   [3]*De Trinitate* X, 11. PL 42, 984
[4]*Metaphysics* VIII, 8. 1050a36   [5]Ia. 54, 1–3. Vol. 9.   [6]*De Anima* II, 4. 415a16

the intellect knows its acts, it knows them by means of another act, and that by another, and so on to infinity. Which seems impossible.

3. Again, as the senses stand in relation to their acts, so does the intellect. But an external sense does not perceive its own acts—this belongs to the *sensus communis*, as Aristotle says.[2] Neither therefore does the intellect understand its own acts.

ON THE OTHER HAND, Augustine says,[3] *I understand that I understand.*

REPLY: As said before, a thing is known in so far as it is actual. But the ultimate perfection of the intellect is its own activity, for it is not the sort of activity that goes out to something else and to the completion of that, say the constructing of a building; it remains in the agent as its actuality and perfection.[4] Therefore what then is first understood about the intellect is its own act of understanding.

But different intellects have a different status with respect to this.

There is one intellect, namely the divine, that is identical with its act of understanding. Thus for God to understand his own understanding is the same thing as to understand his own essence, for his essence is his understanding.

There is also another kind of intellect, the angelic, which is not identical with its understanding, as we have said,[5] even though the primary object of its understanding is its own essence. Thus, although for an angel to understand its own understanding is not the same as understanding its own essence, the two are none the less understood at once and in one act—for the fact that it understands its own essence is the very perfection of its essence (and a thing and its perfection are understood at one time and in one act).

Finally there is a third kind of intellect, the human, which is not identical with its understanding nor is its own essence the primary object of its understanding, for this is something external, namely, the nature of material things.

Therefore what is first known by the human intellect is this object; then, in the second place, the act by which the object is known is itself known; and finally, by way of the act, the intellect, of which the act of understanding is the perfection, is itself known. This is why Aristotle says that objects are known before acts and acts before faculties.[6a]

Hence: 1. The object of the intellect is something general, namely, being real and being true, under which the act of understanding is also included. Thus the intellect can understand its own act—but not primarily.

---

[a]preceding article, *Sed contra.*

præsentem statum, est quodlibet ens et verum; sed ens et verum consideratum in rebus materialibus, ut dictum est;[7] ex quibus in cognitionem omnium aliorum devenit.

2. Ad secundum dicendum quod ipsum intelligere humanum non est actus et perfectio naturæ intellectæ materialis,* ut sic possit uno actu intelligi natura rei materialis et ipsum intelligere, sicut uno actu intelligitur res cum sua perfectione. Unde alius est actus quo intellectus intelligit lapidem, et alius est actus quo intelligit se intelligere lapidem, et sic inde.†
Nec est inconveniens in intellectu esse infinitum in potentia, ut supra dictum est.[8]

3. Ad tertium dicendum quod sensus proprius sentit secundum immutationem materialis organi a sensibili exteriori. Non est autem possibile quod aliquid materiale immutet seipsum; sed unum immutatur ab alio. Et ideo actus sensus proprii percipitur per sensum communem.

Sed intellectus‡ non intelligit per materialem immutationem organi: et ideo non est simile.

articulus 4. utrum intellectus intelligat actum voluntatis

AD QUARTUM sic proceditur:[1] 1. Videtur quod intellectus non intelligat actum voluntatis. Nihil enim cognoscitur ab intellectu nisi sit aliquo modo præsens in intellectu. Sed actus voluntatis non est præsens in intellectu: cum sint diversæ potentiæ. Ergo actus voluntatis non cognoscitur ab intellectu.

2. Præterea, actus habet speciem ab objecto. Sed objectum voluntatis differt ab objecto intellectus. Ergo et actus voluntatis speciem habet diversam ab objecto intellectus. Non ergo cognoscitur ab intellectu.

3. Præterea, Augustinus[2] attribuit affectionibus animæ quod cognoscuntur *neque per imagines, sicut corpora; neque per præsentiam, sicut artes;* *sed per quasdam notiones.* Non videtur autem quod possint esse aliæ notiones rerum in anima, nisi vel essentiæ rerum cognitarum vel earum similitudines. Ergo impossibile videtur§ quod intellectus cognoscat affectiones animæ, quæ sunt actus voluntatis.

SED CONTRA est quod Augustinus dicit,[3] *Intelligo me velle.*

RESPONSIO: Dicendum quod, sicut supra dictum est,[4] actus voluntatis nihil

---

*Piana omits *materialis*, material
‡Piana adds *noster*, our
[7]Ia. 84, 7
[1]Ia. 82, 4 ad 1. III *Sent.* 23, 1, 2 ad 3
[3]*De Trinitate* x, 11. PL 42, 983

†Piana: *deinde* (meaning unchanged)
§Piana: *est*, is
[8]Ia. 86, 2
[2]*Confessions* x, 17. PL 32, 790
[4]Ia. 59, 1

For the primary object of our intellect in its present state is not just any being or truth, but the being and truth found in material things, as mentioned,[7] and it comes to a knowledge of all else from these.

2. The human act of understanding is not the actuality and perfection of the material nature understood, as if the nature of the material thing and the act of understanding could be understood in one act, as by one act a thing and its perfection are understood. Hence the act whereby the intellect understands stone is different from the act whereby it understands that it understands stone, and so on. Nor is there any difficulty in the intellect being thus potentially infinite, as explained above.[8]

3. An external sense perceives according to a change effected in its material organ by an external sensible object. But it is impossible for anything material to bring about a change in itself; one is, rather, affected by another. For this reason the activity of an external sense is perceived by the *sensus communis*.

The intellect, on the other hand, does not understand by way of a change effected in an organ. Therefore the analogy does not hold.

article 4. *does the intellect understand acts of the will?*

THE FIRST POINT:[1] 1 It would seem that the intellect does not understand acts of the will. For nothing is known by the intellect unless it is in some sense present within the intellect. But an act of the will is not present within the intellect, since the two are distinct faculties. Therefore acts of the will are not known by the intellect.

2. Again, an activity is specified by[a] its objects. But the object of the will is different from the object of the intellect. Therefore acts of the will also have a specific nature distinct from the object of the intellect, so they cannot be known by the intellect.

3. Again, Augustine says,[2] of the affections of the soul, that they are not known *through images, as all bodies are,* nor *by the presence of the things themselves, as are the arts,* but *by some notion or observation.* But it would not seem that there could be, in the soul, notions of things other than either the essences of the things known or their likenesses. Therefore it seems impossible for the intellect to know those affections of the soul which are acts of the will.

ON THE OTHER HAND, there is what Augustine says,[3] *I understand that I will.*

REPLY: As said before,[4] an act of the will is nothing more than an inclination

---

[a]Activities get their specific character from and are what they are by reason of objects which engage them.

aliud est quam inclinatio quædam consequens formam intellectam, sicut appetitus naturalis est inclinatio consequens formam naturalem. Inclinatio autem cujuslibet rei est in ipsa re per modum ejus. Unde inclinatio naturalis est naturaliter in re naturali; et inclinatio* quæ est appetitus sensibilis, est sensibiliter in sentiente; et similiter inclinatio intelligibilis, quæ est actus voluntatis, est intelligibiliter in intelligente, sicut in principio et in proprio subjecto. Unde et Philosophus hoc modo loquendi utitur,[5] quod *voluntas in ratione est.*

Quod autem intelligibiliter est in aliquo intelligente, consequens est ut ab eo intelligatur. Unde actus voluntatis intelligitur ab intellectu, et inquantum aliquis percipit se velle, et inquantum aliquis cognoscit naturam hujus actus, et per consequens naturam ejus principii, quod est habitus vel potentia.

1. Ad primum ergo dicendum quod ratio illa procederet, si voluntas et intellectus, sicut sunt diversæ potentiæ, ita etiam subjecto differrent: sic enim quod est in voluntate esset absens ab intellectu. Nunc autem, cum utrumque radicetur in una substantia animæ, et unum sit quodammodo principium alterius, consequens est ut quod est in voluntate, sit etiam quodammodo in intellectu.

2. Ad secundum dicendum quod bonum et verum, quæ sunt objecta voluntatis et intellectus, differunt quidem† ratione, veruntamen unum eorum continetur sub alio, ut supra dictum est:[6] nam verum est quoddam bonum, et bonum est quoddam verum. Et ideo quæ sunt voluntatis cadunt sub intellectu; et quæ sunt intellectus possunt cadere sub voluntate.

3. Ad tertium dicendum quod affectus animæ non sunt in intellectu neque per similitudinem tantum, sicut corpora, neque per præsentiam ut in subjecto, sicut artes, sed sicut principiatum in principio, in quo habetur notio principiati. Et ideo Augustinus dicit affectus animæ esse in memoria per quasdam notiones.

---

*Piana adds *autem*
†Piana omits *quidem*, in fact
[5]*De Anima* III, 9. 432b5
[6]Ia. 16, 4 ad 1; 82, 4 ad 1
[b]This notion has sometimes been a bugaboo to Scholastics since the advent of modern science. While it is true that the concept of 'natural appetite', as applied (for instance) to the explanation of the gravitational motion of a heavy body, has an anthropomorphic ring, its meaning, certainly for St Thomas, is free from this.

consequent upon an understood form, just as a 'natural appetite'[b] is an inclination[c] consequent upon a natural form. But a thing's inclination is in it after the thing's own mode. Thus a natural inclination is in a natural thing in a natural mode; the inclination of sense appetite is in the sentient being in a sensible mode; and, similarly, an intellectual inclination—which is an act of the will—is in an intelligent being (as in its principle and its proper subject) in an intelligible mode. (Hence Aristotle, using this manner of speaking, says[5] that *will is found in reason*.)

But what exists in an intelligent being in an intelligible mode must, as a consequence, be understood by it. Therefore acts of the will are understood by the intellect, both inasmuch as a man perceives himself as willing things, and inasmuch as he perceives the nature of this act and, as a result, the nature of its principle, which is a habitual disposition or a faculty.

Hence: 1. The argument would follow if the will and the intellect were also distinct in terms of subject, just as they are distinct as faculties, for in this sense what is present in the will would be absent from the intellect. Now, however, since both are rooted in the same substance of the soul and one is a sort of principle for the other, it follows that what is in the will is, in a sense, also in the intellect.

2. Goodness and truth, which are the objects of the will and the intellect, do in fact differ in their definitions, but one is contained under the other (as said before[6]), for the true is a kind of good and the good a kind of true. Thus objects of will fall under intellect, and objects of intellect can fall under will.

3. The affective movements of the soul are in the intellect neither by likenesses only, like bodies, nor by presence as in a subject, like the arts, but as derivatives in their origin, which contains their notion. And so Augustine says the affective movements of the soul exist in the memory[d] by way of certain notions.

More often he seems to take *appetitus naturalis*, natural inclination (see the next note), as the more known reality in terms of which other 'appetites' (for instance a 'voluntary inclination' or act of choice) are to be explained.

[c]*inclinatio*: an excellent word to get the idea across, and one that transliterates very well into English, for English allows the same ambiguity; 'inclined' means either 'tending downward' or 'motivated to'.

[d]Not the internal sense of memory, but St Augustine's *memoria*, a pregnant and obscure notion. Cf 1a. 78, 4 & 79, 6, 7.

Quæstio 88. quomodo anima humana cognoscat ea quæ supra se sunt

DEINDE CONSIDERANDUM EST quomodo anima humana cognoscat ea quæ supra se sunt, scilicet immateriales substantias. Et circa hoc quæruntur tria:

1. utrum anima humana, secundum statum præsentis vitæ, possit intelligere substantias immateriales quas angelos dicimus, per seipsas;
2. utrum possit ad earum notitiam pervenire per cognitionem rerum materialium;
3. utrum Deus sit id quod primo a nobis cognoscitur.

articulus 1. utrum anima humana, secundum statum vitae præsentis, possit intelligere substantias immateriales per seipsas

AD PRIMUM sic proceditur:[1] 1. Videtur quod anima humana, secundum statum vitæ præsentis, possit intelligere substantias immateriales per seipsas. Dicit enim Augustinus,[2] *Mens ipsa, sicut corporearum rerum notitias per sensus corporis colligit, sic incorporearum rerum per semetipsam.* Hujusmodi autem sunt substantiæ immateriales. Ergo mens substantias immateriales intelligit.

2. Præterea, simile simili cognoscitur. Sed magis assimilatur mens humana rebus immaterialibus quam materialibus: cum ipsa* mens sit immaterialis, ut ex supradictis patet.[3] Cum ergo mens nostra intelligat res materiales, multo magis intelligit res immateriales.

3. Præterea, quod ea quæ sunt secundum se maxime sensibilia non maxime sentiantur a nobis, provenit ex hoc quod excellentiæ sensibilium corrumpunt sensum. Sed excellentiæ intelligibilium non corrumpunt intellectum, ut dicitur.[4] Ergo ea quæ sunt secundum se maxime intelligibilia sunt etiam maxime intelligibilia nobis. Sed cum res materiales non sint intelligibiles nisi quia facimus eas intelligibiles actu, abstrahendo a materia,

---

*Piana: *nostra,* our

[1]cf *De veritate* x, 11; xviii, 5 ad 8. *In De Trin.* VI, 3. *CG* III, 42–46. Disputations. *De anima* 16

[2]*De Trinitate* IX, 3. PL 42, 963   [3]1a. 76, 1   [4]*De Anima* III, 4. 429b2

[a]For the place of this question in St Thomas's outline, see the prologue to Question 84; after considering how man knows external things in the material world and things internal to the soul, he now turns to a consideration of the (natural) knowledge man can have of angels. He appends to the two articles on angels a special discussion of God as the first object of human knowledge.

Question 88. how the human soul knows things above it

NEXT TO BE CONSIDERED is the way in which the human soul knows the things that are above it, namely immaterial substances.[a] With respect to this there are three points of inquiry:

1. whether the human soul, in the present life, is able to understand the immaterial substances we call angels in themselves;
2. whether it can come to a knowledge of them by way of the knowledge of material things;
3. whether God is what we know first.

article 1. can the human soul, in the present life, understand immaterial substances in themselves?[b]

THE FIRST POINT:[1] 1. It would seem that the human soul, in the present life, can understand immaterial substances in themselves. For Augustine says:[2] *As the mind itself gathers the knowledge of corporeal things through the senses of the body, so of incorporeal things through itself.* But immaterial substances are of this kind. Therefore the mind understands immaterial substances.[c]

2. Again, like is known by like. But, since (as is evident from what was said before[3]) the human mind is itself immaterial, it has a greater similarity to immaterial than to material things. Therefore, since our minds understand material things, they will, *a fortiori*, understand immaterial things.

3. Again, the fact that things which are in themselves sensible to the highest degree are not best perceived by our senses happens by reason of the fact that sensible objects which exceed certain limits destroy the senses. But the most extremely intelligible objects do not destroy the intellect, as Aristotle notes;[4] the things in themselves most intelligible are also most intelligible to us. Now, since material things are actually intelligible only because we make them such by abstracting from matter, it is obvious that

---

[b]The present article may seem at first glance to be among the most archaic in the *Summa*. In fact, however, it is an excellent instance of St Thomas's struggle to transcend patterns of thinking among his contemporaries. As Appendix 6 will note, he carried on the struggle especially in defence of the rôle of genuinely natural knowledge—this comes through very clearly in the article (and the others of the question), and even more clearly when the present treatment is contrasted with that of Question 89.

[c]The response to this objection as much as notes that it is really not to the point.

manifestum est quod magis sint secundum se intelligibiles substantiæ quæ secundum suam naturam sunt immateriales. Ergo multo magis intelliguntur a nobis quam res materiales.

4. Præterea, Commentator dicit[5] quod si substantiæ abstractæ non possent intelligi a nobis, *tunc natura otiose egisset, quia fecit illud quod est naturaliter in se intellectum, non intellectum ab aliquo.* Sed nihil est otiosum sive frustra in natura. Ergo substantiæ immateriales possunt intelligi a nobis.

5. Præterea, sicut se habet sensus ad sensibilia, ita se habet intellectus ad intelligibilia. Sed visus noster potest videre omnia corpora, sive sint superiora et incorruptibilia, sive sint inferiora et corruptibilia. Ergo intellectus noster potest intelligere omnes substantias intelligibiles, et superiores et immateriales.

SED CONTRA est quod dicitur,[6] *Quæ in cælis sunt, quis investigabit?* In cælis autem dicuntur hujusmodi substantiæ esse; secundum illud,[7] *Angeli eorum in cælis* etc. Ergo non possunt substantiæ immateriales per investigationem humanam cognosci.

RESPONSIO: Dicendum quod secundum opinionem Platonis, substantiæ immateriales non solum a nobis intelliguntur, sed etiam sunt prima a nobis intellecta. Posuit enim Plato formas immateriales subsistentes, quas *ideas* vocabat, esse propria objecta nostri intellectus: et ita primo et per se intelliguntur a nobis. Applicatur tamen animæ cognitio rebus materialibus, secundum quod intellectui permiscetur phantasia et sensus. Unde quanto magis intellectus fuerit depuratus, tanto magis percipit immaterialium intelligibilem veritatem.

Sed secundum Aristotelis sententiam, quam magis experimur, intellectus noster, secundum statum præsentis vitæ, naturalem respectum habet ad naturas rerum materialium; unde nihil intelligit nisi convertendo se ad phantasmata, ut ex dictis patet.[8] Et sic manifestum est quod substantias immateriales, quæ sub sensu et imaginatione non cadunt, primo et per se, secundum modum cognitionis nobis expertum, intelligere non possumus.

Sed tamen Averroes ponit[9] quod in fine in hac vita homo pervenire potest ad hoc quod intelligat substantias separatas,* per continuationem vel unionem cujusdam substantiæ separatæ† nobis, quam vocat *intellectum agentem,* qui quidem, cum sit substantia separata, naturaliter substantias

---

*Piana: *substantiam separatam*
†Piana adds *a,* from
[5]*Commentary on Metaphysics* II, I [6]*Wisdom* 9, 16 [7]*Matthew* 18, 10
[8]Ia. 84, 7 [9]*Commentary on De anima* III, 36
ᵃThe heavenly bodies in Aristotle's outmoded cosmology; see Vol. 10 in this series.

substances which are by nature immaterial are in themselves more intelligible. They are thus also much better understood by us than material things.

4. Again, Averroes says[5] that if abstract substances could not be understood by us, *then nature would have operated in a futile way, for it made what is in itself naturally understood not understood by anything.* But nothing in nature is futile or in vain. Therefore immaterial substances can be understood by us.

5. Again, the intellect stands in the same relation to intelligible objects as the senses to sensible objects. But sight in us can see all bodies, whether incorruptible and of a higher order[d] or corruptible and inferior. Therefore our intellect can understand all intelligible substances, even those that are immaterial and of a higher order.

ON THE OTHER HAND, Scripture says,[6] *Who can discover what is in the heavens?* But, according to another passage,[7] these substances are said to be in heaven: *Their angels are in heaven.* Therefore immaterial substances cannot be known by way of human inquiry.

REPLY: According to Plato's opinion, immaterial substances are not only known by us, they are the primary things we understand. For Plato held that subsistent immaterial Forms, which he called Ideas, are the proper objects of our intellect, and thus are understood by us primarily and essentially. Nevertheless, the soul's knowledge gets bound up with material things according as imagination and the senses are mixed with understanding. Thus to the extent that the intellect becomes purified, it will that much better perceive the intelligible truth of immaterial things.

On the other hand, according to Aristotle's opinion, which is closer to our experience, in the present life our intellect has a natural relation to the natures of material things; thus it understands nothing except by turning to sense images (as is clear from what has been said[8]). In this sense it is obvious that we cannot, primarily and essentially, in the mode of knowing that we experience, understand immaterial substances since they are not subject to the senses and imagination.

However, Averroes, in still another opinion,[9] says that at the end of this life a man can arrive at an understanding of immaterial substances by means of a continuity or union with that immaterial substance which he calls the Agent Intellect.[e] The latter, since it is itself an immaterial substance,

---

[e]The best if not the only way to understand the long and difficult discussion that follows is to assume that St Thomas felt compelled to go into such detail, in language as close to the original as possible, because Averroism was one of the dominant schools of the day.

separatas intelligit. Unde cum fuerit nobis perfecte* unitus, sic ut per eum perfecte* intelligere possimus, intelligemus et nos substantias separatas; sicut nunc per intellectum possibilem nobis unitum intelligimus res materiales.

Ponit autem intellectum agentem sic nobis uniri. Cum enim nos† intelligamus per intellectum agentem et per intelligibilia speculata, ut patet cum conclusiones intelligimus per principia intellecta; necesse est quod intellectus agens comparetur ad intellecta speculata vel sicut agens principale ad instrumenta, vel sicut forma ad materiam. His enim duobus modis attribuitur actio aliqua duobus principiis: principali quidem agenti et instrumento, sicut sectio artifici et serræ; formæ autem et subjecto, sicut calefactio calori et igni. Sed utroque modo intellectus agens comparabitur ad intelligibilia speculata sicut perfectio ad perfectibile, et actus ad potentiam. Simul autem recipitur in aliquo perfectum et perfectio; sicut visibile in actu et lumen in pupilla. Simul igitur in intellectu possibili recipiuntur intellecta speculata et intellectus agens. Et quanto plura intellecta speculata recipimus, tanto magis appropinquamus ad hoc quod intellectus agens perfecte uniatur nobis. Ita quod cum omnia intellecta speculata cognoverimus, intellectus agens perfecte unietur nobis; et poterimus per eum omnia cognoscere materialia et immaterialia. Et in hoc ponit ultimam hominis felicitatem.

Nec refert, quantum ad propositum pertinet, utrum in illo statu felicitatis intellectus possibilis intelligat substantias separatas per intellectum agentem, ut ipse sentit: vel, ut ipse imponit Alexandro, intellectus possibilis nunquam intelligat substantias separatas (propter hoc quod ponit intellectum possibilem corruptibilem), sed homo intelligat‡ substantias separatas per intellectum agentem.

Sed prædicta stare non possunt. Primo quidem quia, si intellectus agens est substantia separata, impossibile est quod per ipsam formaliter intelligamus: quia id quo formaliter agens agit, est forma et actus agentis; cum omne agens agat inquantum est actu. Sicut etiam§ supra dictum est circa intellectum possibilem.[10]

Secundo quia, secundum modum prædictum, intellectus agens, si est

---

*Piana omits *perfecte*, completely   †Piana omits *nos*
‡Piana: *intelligit*   §Piana omits *etiam*, also
[10]Ia. 76, I

ᶠOn this capitalization see Ia. 84, 4, note g. It is carried on here because the *Summa* is attempting to present the view of Averroes as carefully and authentically as possible; in line with this purpose, the personified Agent Intellect is intended here rather than the agent intellect as a faculty.

ᵍ*Perfectio*, but abstract, static perfection is certainly not intended; this is one among many instances in which the medieval Scholastics would use an abstract and static

naturally understands immaterial substances. When, therefore, it is completely joined to us, so that we are able to understand completely through it, we shall also understand immaterial substances, just as now, in the view of Averroes, through the Possible Intellect as joined to us, we understand material realities.[f]

Averroes explains how the Agent Intellect is joined to us in this way. Since we humans understand by means of the Agent Intellect and intelligible objects we look at, as appears when we understand conclusions by way of principles previously understood, it must be that the Agent Intellect is related to known intelligible objects either as principal agent to instruments, or as form to matter. (For one activity is attributed to two principles in one of these two ways: to principal agent and instrument, for instance, as cutting to carpenter and saw; or to form and subject, as heating to heat and fire.) Now either way the Agent Intellect is related to known intelligible objects as perfecting[g] to perfectible and as actuality to potentiality. But perfecting and the perfected are received in a thing together, e.g., the actually visible, and light in the pupil of the eye. Therefore known intelligible objects and the Agent Intellect are received in the Possible Intellect together. And the more known intelligible objects we receive, the more we approach having the Agent Intellect perfectly joined to us. Thus, when we know all these intelligible objects, the Agent Intellect is perfectly united to us and we can, by means of it, understand all things, material and immaterial; it is in this that Averroes holds the ultimate happiness of man consists.

(Nor is it to the present point whether, in Averroes' own view, the Possible Intellect, in this state of happiness, understands immaterial substances by means of the Agent Intellect; or whether, in the view he ascribes to Alexander,[h] the Possible Intellect never understands immaterial substances—because, as he holds, the Possible Intellect is corruptible—but that a man understands immaterial substances by means of the Agent Intellect.)

These positions, however, cannot be upheld. First, because if the Agent Intellect is an immaterial substance, it would be impossible for us to understand by means of it, in the formal sense. For that by which an agent acts, in the formal sense, is a form and actuality of the agent, since every agent acts in accord with the actuality it has (as was also said already with respect to the possible intellect[10]).

Second, because if the Agent Intellect, in the above mode, is a subsistent

---

term when they intended to signify a concrete and dynamic reality—a practice that has led to many misunderstandings.
[h]Alexander of Aphrodisias (c. 200 A.D.); Greek commentator on Aristotle.

SUMMA THEOLOGIÆ, Ia, 88, I

substantia separata, non uniretur* nobis secundum suam substantiam; sed solum lumen ejus, secundum quod participatur in intellectis speculativis; et non quantum ad alias actiones intellectus agentis, ut possimus per hoc intelligere substantias immateriales. Sicut dum videmus colores illuminatos a sole, non unitur nobis substantia solis, ut possimus actiones solis agere; sed solum nobis unitur lumen solis ad visionem colorum.

Tertio quia, dato quod secundum modum prædictum uniretur nobis substantia intellectus agentis, tamen ipsi non ponunt quod intellectus agens totaliter uniatur nobis secundum unum intelligibile vel duo, sed secundum omnia intellecta speculata. Sed omnia intellecta speculata deficiunt a virtute intellectus agentis: quia multo plus est intelligere substantias separatas quam intelligere omnia materialia. Unde manifestum est quod etiam intellectis omnibus materialibus, non sic uniretur intellectus agens nobis, ut possemus intelligere per eum substantias separatas.

Quarto, quia intelligere omnia intellecta materialia vix contingit† alicui in hoc mundo; et sic nullus, vel pauci ad felicitatem pervenirent. Quod est contra Philosophum,[11] qui dicit quod felicitas est *quoddam bonum commune, quod potest pervenire omnibus non orbatis ad virtutem*. Est etiam contra rationem quod finem alicujus speciei ut in paucioribus consequantur ea quæ continentur sub specie.

Quinto, quia Philosophus dicit expresse[12] quod felicitas est *operatio secundum perfectam virtutem*. Et enumeratis multis virtutibus concludit[13] quod felicitas ultima, consistens in cognitione maximorum intelligibilium, est secundum virtutem sapientiæ, quam posuerat[14] esse caput scientiarum speculativarum. Unde patet quod Aristoteles posuit ultimam felicitatem hominis in cognitione substantiarum separatarum, qualis potest haberi per scientias speculativas: et non per continuationem intellectus agentis a quibusdam confictam.

Sexto, quia supra ostensum est[15] quod intellectus agens non est substantia separata, sed virtus quædam animæ, ad eadem active se extendens ad quæ se extendit intellectus possibilis receptive: quia, ut dicitur,[16] intellectus possibilis est *quo est omnia fieri*, intellectus agens *quo est omnia facere*. Uterque ergo intellectus se extendit, secundum statum præsentis vitæ, ad materialia sola; quæ intellectus agens facit intelligibilia actu, et recipiuntur in intellectu possibili.

---

*Piana: *unietur* †Piana: *competit*, belongs

[11]*Nicomachean Ethics* I, 9. 1099b18   [12]ibid I, 10. 1101a14   [13]ibid x, 8. 1178b24
[14]ibid VI, 7. 1141a20   [15]Ia. 79, 4   [16]*De Anima* III, 5. 430a14
iPossibly Averroist contemporaries of St Thomas, rather than Alexander or Averroes himself.
ji.e., all material objects.
k*Virtues,* taken broadly as including not only the moral virtues but also the 'intellec-

126

immaterial substance, not its substance, but only its light, would be joined to us—and even this as had by participation in speculative intellects; and not with respect to any other activities of the Agent Intellect which would allow us to understand immaterial substances by means of it. For example, when we see colours illuminated by the sun, the substance of the sun is not so joined to us as to allow us to do the things the sun can do; only the light of the sun is joined to us, for the seeing of colours.

Third, because, even granting that in the above mode the substance of the Agent Intellect would be joined to us, even so these authors[i] do not hold that the Agent Intellect is joined to us by reason of one or two intelligible objects, but when all intelligible objects are known. All intelligible objects[j] as known, however, still fall short of the scope of the Agent Intellect, since it is a much greater thing to understand immaterial substances than to understand all material things. Thus it is obvious that, even if all material things were understood, the Agent Intellect would not thereby be joined to us, allowing us to understand immaterial substances by means of it.

Fourth, because in this world understanding all material intelligible objects happens to hardly anyone. Thus no one, or very few, would achieve happiness—which is contrary to Aristotle,[11] who says that happiness is something *very generally shared; for all who are not maimed as regards virtue may win it.* It is also contrary to reason that the members of a class should only infrequently attain the goal of that class.

Fifth, because Aristotle says expressly[12] that happiness is *activity in accordance with complete virtue.* When he has enumerated all the virtues,[k] he concludes[13] that ultimate happiness—consisting in the knowledge of the highest intelligible objects—pertains to the virtue of wisdom, which he had set[14] as chief of the speculative sciences. Thus, obviously, Aristotle held that the ultimate happiness of man consists in the knowledge of immaterial substances as this can be had in the speculative sciences—not by way of the fictitious 'continuity of the Agent Intellect' supposed by certain authors.

Sixth, because as shown above,[15] the agent intellect is not a subsistent immaterial substance, but a faculty of the soul which extends in an active way to the same things as does the possible intellect in a receptive way, for, as Aristotle says,[16] the possible intellect *is what it is by virtue of becoming all things,* the agent intellect *by virtue of making all things.*[l] Thus the scope of both intellects, in the present life, extends only to material objects; these the agent intellect makes actually intelligible, and they are then received in the possible intellect.

---

tual virtues'—prudence, art, the sciences as habitual dispositions of the mind, etc. Cf 1a2æ. 55–67.   [l]i.e., making things intelligible.

Unde secundum statum præsentis vitæ, neque per intellectum possibilem neque per intellectum agentem, possumus intelligere substantias* immateriales secundum seipsas.

1. Ad primum ergo dicendum quod ex illa auctoritate Augustini haberi potest quod illud quod mens nostra de cognitione incorporalium rerum accipere potest, per seipsam cognoscere possit. Et hoc adeo verum est, ut etiam apud philosophos† dicatur quod scientia de anima est principium quoddam ad cognoscendum substantias separatas. Per hoc enim quod anima nostra cognoscit seipsam, pertingit ad cognitionem aliquam habendam de substantiis incorporeis, qualem eam contingit habere: non quod simpliciter et perfecte eas cognoscat, cognoscendo seipsam.

2. Ad secundum dicendum quod similitudo naturæ non est ratio sufficiens ad cognitionem: alioquin oporteret dicere quod Empedocles dixit, quod anima esset de natura omnium, ad hoc quod omnia cognosceret. Sed requiritur ad cognoscendum, ut sit similitudo rei cognitæ in cognoscente quasi quædam forma ipsius. Intellectus autem noster possibilis, secundum statum præsentis vitæ, est natus informari similitudinibus rerum materialium a phantasmatibus abstractis: et ideo cognoscit magis materialia quam substantias immateriales.

3. Ad tertium dicendum quod requiritur aliqua proportio objecti ad potentiam cognoscitivam, ut activi ad passivum, et perfectionis ad perfectibile. Unde quod excellentia sensibilia non capiantur a sensu, non sola ratio est quia corrumpunt organa sensibilia; sed etiam quia sunt improportionata potentiis sensitivis. Et hoc modo substantiæ immateriales sunt improportionatæ intellectui nostro, secundum præsentem statum, ut non possint ab eo intelligi.

4. Ad quartum dicendum quod illa ratio Commentatoris multipliciter deficit. Primo quidem, quia non sequitur quod, si substantiæ separatæ non intelliguntur a nobis, non intelligantur ab aliquo intellectu: intelliguntur enim a seipsis, et a se invicem. Secundo, quia non est finis substantiarum separatarum ut intelligantur a nobis. Illud autem otiose et frustra esse dicitur, quod non consequitur finem ad quem est. Et sic non sequitur substantias immateriales esse frustra, etiam si nullo modo intelligerentur a nobis.

5. Ad quintum dicendum quod eodem modo sensus cognoscit et superiora et inferiora corpora, scilicet per immutationem organi a sensibili. Non autem eodem modo intelliguntur a nobis substantiæ materiales, quæ intelliguntur per modum abstractionis; et substantiæ immateriales, quæ non possunt sic a nobis intelligi, quia non sunt earum aliqua phantasmata.

---

*Piana adds *separatas,* separate
†Piana: *Philosophum,* Aristotle

Therefore in the present life we cannot, by means of either the possible intellect or the agent intellect, understand immaterial substances in themselves.

Hence: 1. On Augustine's authority there it can be concluded that whatever knowledge of incorporeal realities our mind can receive, it can gain by itself. This is so true that, even among philosophers,[m] it is said that knowledge of the soul is a kind of principle for knowing immaterial substances. By the very fact that our soul knows itself, it comes to have a limited knowledge (the only kind it is able to have) of incorporeal substances; it does not, in knowing itself, know them simply and perfectly.

2. Likeness in nature is not a sufficient ground for knowledge, otherwise we would have to say with Empedocles, that the soul would have to be of the nature of all things in order to know all things. In order to know, however, what is required is a likeness of the thing known in the knower as its form. But our possible intellect, in the present life, is naturally adapted to being informed by likenesses of material things abstracted from sense images. Therefore what it knows is rather material things than immaterial substances.

3. A proportion is required between object and cognitive faculty, that, namely, of active to passive, and of perfecting[n] to perfectible. Thus that they destroy the sense organs is not the only reason that sensible objects exceeding certain limits are not received by the senses; it is also because they are disproportionate to the sense faculties. In the same way immaterial substances are disproportionate to our intellect in its present state, so that they cannot be understood by it.

4. This argument of Averroes is deficient for more than one reason. One is because it does not follow that, if immaterial substances are not understood by us, they would not be understood by any intellect; they are understood by themselves and by one another. Another is because it is not the purpose of immaterial substances to be understood by us. But only that is said to be futile and in vain which fails to achieve the purpose for which it exists. Thus it does not follow that immaterial substances would be in vain even if they were in no way understood by us.

5. The senses know bodies of a higher and lower order in the same way, namely through a change effected in the organ by the sensible object. But material substances, which are understood by way of abstraction, and immaterial substances, which cannot be understood by us in this way because there are no sense images of them, are not understood in the same way.

---

[m]Possibly philosophers in general, possibly the (largely Averroist) masters in the arts faculty at Paris, or possibly even Aristotle himself.
[n]See above, note *g*.

articulus 2. *utrum intellectus noster per cognitionem rerum materialium possit pervenire ad intelligendum substantias immateriales*

AD SECUNDUM sic proceditur:[1] 1. Videtur quod intellectus noster per cognitionem rerum materialium possit pervenire ad intelligendum substantias immateriales. Dicit enim Dionysius[2] quod *non est possibile humanæ menti ad immaterialem illam sursum excitari cælestium hierarchiarum contemplationem, nisi secundum se materiali manuductione utatur.* Relinquitur ergo quod per materialia manuduci possumus ad intelligendum substantias immateriales.

2. Præterea, scientia est in intellectu. Sed scientiæ et definitiones sunt de substantiis immaterialibus: definit enim Damascenus angelum;[3] et de angelis aliqua documenta traduntur tam in theologicis quam in philosophicis disciplinis. Ergo substantiæ immateriales intelligi possunt a nobis.

3. Præterea, anima humana est de genere substantiarum immaterialium. Sed ipsa intelligi potest a nobis per actum suum, quo intelligit materialia. Ergo et aliæ substantiæ immateriales intelligi possunt a nobis per suos effectus in rebus materialibus.

4. Præterea, illa sola causa per suos effectus comprehendi non potest, quæ in infinitum distat a suis effectibus. Hoc autem solius Dei est proprium. Ergo aliæ substantiæ immateriales creatæ intelligi possunt a nobis per res materiales.

SED CONTRA est quod Dionysius dicit,[4] *Sensibilibus intelligibilia, et compositis simplicia, et corporalibus incorporalia apprehendi non possunt.*

RESPONSIO: Dicendum quod, sicut Averroes narrat,[5] quidam Avempace nomine, posuit quod per intellectum substantiarum materialium pervenire possumus, secundum vera philosophiæ principia, ad intelligendum substantias immateriales. Cum enim intellectus noster natus sit abstrahere quidditatem rei materialis a materia, si iterum in illa quidditate sit aliquid materiæ, poterit iterato abstrahere: et cum hoc in infinitum non procedat, tandem pervenire poterit ad intelligendum* aliquam quidditatem quæ sit omnino sine materia. Et hoc est intelligere substantiam immaterialem.

Quod quidem efficaciter diceretur, si substantiæ immateriales essent formæ et species horum materialium, ut Platonici posuerunt. Hoc autem non posito, sed supposito quod substantiæ immateriales sint omnino

---

*Piana: *intelligibilium,* of intelligible objects
[1]cf IV *Sent.* 49, 2, 7 ad 12. *De veritate* XVIII, 5 ad 6. *CG* III, 41; *In De Trin.* VI, 4; Disputations *De anima* 16
[2]*De cælest. hierarchia* I, 3. PG 3, 124
[3]*De fide orthodoxa* II, 3. PG 94, 865

*article 2. can our intellect arrive at an understanding of immaterial substances by way
of the knowledge of material things?*

THE FIRST POINT:[1] 1. It would seem that our intellect can arrive at an
understanding of immaterial substances by way of the knowledge of
material things. For Dionysius says[2] that *it is not possible for the human
mind to be elevated to that immaterial contemplation of the celestial hierarchies
except in so far as it uses, according to its nature, material guidance.* We are
thus left with the conclusion that by way of material things we can be
guided to an understanding of immaterial substances.

2. Again, demonstrative knowledge is found in the intellect. But there
are both demonstrations and definitions with respect to immaterial substances, for Damascene gives a definition of an angel,[3] and treatises on the
angels are contained in both the theological and the philosophical disciplines.
Therefore immaterial substances can be understood by us.

3. Again, the human soul belongs to the class of immaterial substances.
But it can be understood by us, by means of the acts in which it understands
material things. Therefore other immaterial substances can also be understood by us, by means of their effects in material realities.

4. Again, only that cause cannot be fully comprehended through its
effects which is at an infinite distance from its effects. But this is proper to
God alone. Therefore the other immaterial substances can be understood
by us through material things.

ON THE OTHER HAND, Dionysius says[4] that *intelligible objects cannot be known
by sensible realities, nor simple objects by the composite, or the incorporeal by
the corporeal.*

REPLY: According to Averroes,[5] a philosopher named Avempace held that
we can, by way of an understanding of material substances, and according
to the true principles of philosophy, arrive at an understanding of immaterial substances. For, since our intellect is by nature capable of abstracting the whatness of material things from matter, if in that whatness there is
still something material it can abstract once again. And since this process
cannot go on to infinity, it will finally arrive at an understanding of a
whatness that is entirely without matter. But this is precisely to understand
an immaterial substance.

Now this would be spoken to good effect if immaterial substances were
the forms or specific natures of these material things, as the Platonists held.
But if this is not held, if on the other hand it is presupposed that immaterial

---

[4]*De divinis nominibus* I, lect. I. PG 3, 588
[5]*Commentary on De anima* III, 36. Ibn Badja (d. 1138)

alterius rationis a quidditatibus materialium rerum; quantumcumque intellectus noster abstrahat quidditatem rei materialis a materia, nunquam perveniet ad aliquid simile substantiæ immateriali.

Et ideo per substantias materiales non possumus perfecte substantias immateriales intelligere.

1. Ad primum ergo dicendum quod ex rebus materialibus ascendere possumus in aliqualem cognitionem immaterialium rerum, non tamen in perfectam: quia non est sufficiens comparatio rerum materialium ad immateriales, sed similitudines si quæ a materialibus accipiuntur ad immaterialia intelligenda, sunt multum dissimiles, ut Dionysius dicit.[6]

2. Ad secundum dicendum quod de superioribus rebus in scientiis maxime tractatur per viam remotionis: sic enim corpora cælestia notificat Aristoteles per negationem proprietatum inferiorum corporum. Unde multo magis immateriales substantiæ a nobis cognosci non possunt ut earum quidditates apprehendamus; sed de eis nobis in scientiis documenta traduntur per viam remotionis, et alicujus habitudinis ad res materiales.

3. Ad tertium dicendum quod anima humana intelligit seipsam per suum intelligere, quod est actus proprius ejus, perfecte demonstrans virtutem ejus et naturam. Sed neque per hoc neque per alia quæ in rebus materialibus inveniuntur, perfecte cognosci potest immaterialium substantiarum virtus et natura: quia hujusmodi non adæquant earum virtutes.

4. Ad quartum dicendum quod substantiæ immateriales creatæ in genere quidem naturali non conveniunt cum substantiis materialibus, quia non est in eis eadem ratio potentiæ et materiæ: conveniunt tamen cum eis in genere logico, quia etiam substantiæ immateriales sunt in prædicamento substantiæ, cum earum quidditas non sit earum esse. Sed Deus non convenit cum rebus materialibus neque secundum genus naturale, neque secundum genus logicum: quia Deus nullo modo est in genere, ut supra dictum est.[7]

Unde per similitudines rerum materialium aliquid affirmative potest cognosci de angelis secundum rationem communem, licet non secundum rationem speciei; de Deo autem nullo modo.

articulus 3. *utrum Deus sit primum quod a mente humana cognoscitur*

AD TERTIUM sic proceditur:[1] 1. Videtur quod Deus sit primum quod a mente humana cognoscitur. Illud enim in quo omnia alia cognoscuntur, et per quod de aliis judicamus, est primo cognitum a nobis; sicut lux ab

---

[6]*De cælest. hierarchia* II, 2. PG 3, 137
[7]1a. 3, 5

substances have a nature entirely different from the whatnesses of material things, then no matter how long our intellect goes on abstracting the whatness of a material thing from matter it will never arrive at anything like an immaterial substance.

Therefore, by way of material substances, we cannot understand immaterial substances perfectly.

Hence: 1. We can rise from material things to a limited knowledge of immaterial things, but not to a perfect knowledge because there is not a sufficient proportion between material and immaterial realities. Likenesses, if any are taken from material realities in order to understand the immaterial, are, rather, very much dissimilar, as Dionysius says.[6]

2. In the theological and philosophical sciences things of a higher order are treated for the most part in terms of what they do not have—thus the knowledge Aristotle offers with respect to the heavenly bodies is that of denying to them the properties of inferior bodies. Thus, *a fortiori*, immaterial substances can still less be known by us in the sense of apprehending their whatnesses. Rather, treatises on them are given to us in the theological and philosophical sciences in negative terms of what they are not, or by relationship to material things.

3. The human soul understands itself through its act of understanding, which is its own actuality and shows its power and nature perfectly. However, neither by means of this nor by means of anything else found among material realities can the power and nature of immaterial substances be known perfectly; these things are simply not proportionate to their powers.

4. Created immaterial substances, although they are in the same class, logically speaking, as material substances—for even immaterial substances are in the category of substance, since their whatness is not their existence —are nevertheless not in the same class of natural being since their potentiality and matter have not the same meaning. God, on the other hand, is not in the same class as material realities, either in the logical order or in the natural order—for God is not in any sense in a class, as said before.[7] Thus, by way of likenesses with material realities, something positive can be known about the angels, though in general, not specific, terms, but in no wise about God.

article 3. is God what is known first by the human intellect?

THE FIRST POINT:[1] 1. It would seem that God is what is first known by the human mind. For that in which all other things are known and in terms of which other things are judged by us is known first, e.g., light by the eye and

---

[1]cf *In De Trin.* 1, 3

oculo, et principia prima ab intellectu. Sed omnia in luce primæ veritatis cognoscimus, et per eam de omnibus judicamus; ut dicit Augustinus.² Ergo Deus est id quod primo cognoscitur a nobis.

2. Præterea, *propter quod unumquodque, et illud magis.*³ Sed Deus est causa omnis nostræ cognitionis: ipse enim est *lux vera, quæ illuminat omnem hominem venientem in hunc mundum.*⁴ Ergo Deus est id quod primo et maxime est cognitum nobis.

3. Præterea, id quod primo cognoscitur in imagine, est exemplar quo imago formatur. Sed in mente nostra est Dei imago, ut Augustinus dicit.⁵ Ergo id quod primo cognoscitur in mente nostra est Deus.

SED CONTRA est quod dicitur,⁶ *Deum nemo vidit unquam.*

RESPONSIO: Dicendum quod, cum intellectus humanus, secundum statum præsentis vitæ, non possit intelligere substantias immateriales creatas, ut dictum est; multo minus potest intelligere essentiam substantiæ increatæ. Unde simpliciter dicendum est quod Deus non est primum quod a nobis cognoscitur; sed magis per creaturas in Dei cognitionem pervenimus, secundum illud Apostoli,⁷ *Invisibilia Dei per ea quæ facta sunt, intellecta, conspiciuntur.* Primum autem quod intelligitur a nobis secundum statum præsentis vitæ, est quidditas rei materialis, quæ est nostri intellectus objectum, ut multoties supra dictum est.⁸

1. Ad primum ergo dicendum quod in luce primæ veritatis omnia intelligimus et judicamus, inquantum ipsum lumen intellectus nostri, sive naturale sive gratuitum, nihil aliud est quam quædam impressio veritatis primæ, ut supra dictum est.⁹ Unde cum ipsum lumen intellectus nostri non se habeat ad intellectum nostrum sicut quod intelligitur, sed sicut quo intelligitur; multo minus Deus est id quod primo a nostro intellectu intelligitur.

2. Ad secundum dicendum quod *propter quod unumquodque, illud magis,* intelligendum est in his quæ sunt unius ordinis, ut supra dictum est.¹⁰ Propter Deum autem alia cognoscuntur, non sicut propter primum cognitum, sed sicut propter primam cognoscitivæ virtutis causam.

3. Ad tertium dicendum quod, si in anima nostra esset perfecta imago Dei, sicut Filius est perfecta imago Patris, statim mens nostra intelligeret Deum. Est autem imago imperfecta. Unde ratio non sequitur.

²*De Trinitate* XII, 2. PL 42, 999. *De vera religione* 31. PL 34, 147
³*Posterior Analytics* I, 2. 72a29
⁴*John* I, 9
⁵*De Trinitate* XII, 4. PL 42, 1000
⁶*John* I, 18   ⁷*Romans* I, 20
⁸Ia. 84, 7 and *passim* throughout the treatise

first principles by the intellect. But we know everything by the light of the first truth, and by it we judge all things, as Augustine says.[2] Therefore God is what is first known by us.

2. Again, *the cause of a quality itself has the quality to a higher degree.*[3] But God is the cause of all our knowledge, for he is *the true light that enlightens every man who comes into the world.*[4] Therefore God is what is known first and most especially by us.

3. Again, what is known first in an image is the original after which the image is patterned. But, as Augustine says,[5] the image of God is in our minds. Therefore what is first known in our mind is God.

ON THE OTHER HAND Scripture says,[6] *No one has ever seen God.*

REPLY: Since, as was indicated, the human intellect in the present life cannot understand created immaterial substances, it can, *a fortiori*, still less understand the essence of an uncreated substance. Thus we must say simply that God is not the first thing known by us. Rather, we arrive at a knowledge of God by way of creatures, as St Paul says,[7] *The invisible things of God are there for the mind to see in the things he has made.* Instead, what is understood first by us in the present life is the whatness of material things, which is the object of our intellect, as said many times before.[8]

Hence: 1. We understand and judge all things in the light of the first truth because the light of our intellect, whether natural or the gift of grace,[a] is nothing more than an image[b] of the first truth, as said before.[9] Thus since the light of our intellect stands, in relation to our intellect, not as *that which* is understood, but as *that by which* we understand, therefore, *a fortiori*, God is even less that which is first understood by our intellect.

2. *The cause of a quality itself has the quality to a higher degree*, the dictum is to be understood as referring to things of one order (as said before[10]). But other things are known 'because of God', not in the sense, 'because of something known first', but 'by reason of the first cause of the cognitive faculty'.

3. If there were in our soul a perfect image of God (as the Son is the perfect image of the Father), our mind would understand God immediately. But the image is imperfect. Thus the argument is a *non sequitur*.

---

[9]Ia. 84, 5   [10]Ia. 87, 2 ad 3
[a]See Appendix 5 on faith and theological knowledge.
[b]*impressio*: the same word is used for the 'impressing' of a sensible object on the sense faculties—thus the choice of 'image' as a translation; the meaning is, however, actually closer to that of a wax impression made by a seal—but this can also be rendered as 'image'; cf Ia. 84, 5, where it is described as 'a participated likeness of the uncreated light'.

Quæstio 89. de cognitione animæ separatæ

DEINDE CONSIDERANDUM EST de cognitione animæ separatæ, et circa hoc quæruntur octo:

1. utrum anima separata a corpore possit intelligere;
2. utrum intelligat substantias separatas;
3. utrum intelligat omnia naturalia;
4. utrum cognoscat singularia;
5. utrum habitus scientiæ hic acquisitæ remaneat in anima separata;
6. utrum possit uti habitu scientiæ hic acquisitæ;
7. utrum distantia localis impediat cognitionem animæ separatæ;
8. utrum animæ separatæ a corporibus cognoscant ea quæ hic aguntur.

articulus 1. utrum anima separata aliquid intelligere possit

AD PRIMUM sic proceditur:[1] 1. Videtur quod anima separata nihil omnino intelligere possit. Dicit enim Philosophus[2] quod *intelligere corrumpitur, interius quodam corrupto.* Sed omnia interiora hominis corrumpuntur per mortem. Ergo et ipsum intelligere corrumpitur.

2. Præterea, anima humana impeditur ab intelligendo per ligamentum sensus, et perturbata imaginatione, sicut supra dictum est.[3] Sed morte totaliter sensus et imaginatio corrumpuntur, ut ex supra dictis patet.[4] Ergo anima post mortem nihil intelligit.

3. Præterea, si anima separata intelligit, oportet quod per aliquas species intelligat. Sed non intelligit per species innatas: quia a principio est *sicut tabula in qua nihil est scriptum.*[5] Neque per species quas abstrahat a rebus: quia non habet organa sensus et imaginationis, quibus mediantibus species

---

[1] cf III *Sent.* 31, 2, 4; IV *Sent.* 50, 1, 1. *De veritate* XIX, 1; Disputations *De anima* 15. *Quodl.* III, 9, 1
[2] *De Anima* I, 4. 408b24   [3] Ia. 84, 8
[4] Ia. 77, 8   [5] Aristotle, *De Anima* III, 4. 429b29

[a] On the face of it, this entire question, which is likely to appear to the modern reader a somewhat overstrained attempt to go far beyond the data of revelation into a mystery we cannot plumb, is obviously a product of St Thomas's time and not our own. Yet even here, his effort to do justice to natural knowledge (see Appendix 6) is everywhere in evidence, though the effort seems unsuccessful when contrasted with Question 88 (see art. 1 there, note *a*).

[b] For the place of the discussions in the scheme, see the prologue to Question 84; briefly, after man's knowledge in this life, the author now turns to the separated soul's natural knowledge.

Question 89. the knowledge of the soul separated from the body[a]

NEXT TO BE CONSIDERED is the knowledge of the separated soul,[b] and here there are eight points for discussion:

1. whether the soul, when separated from the body, is able to understand;
2. whether it understands immaterial[c] substances;
3. whether it understands all natural things;
4. whether it knows singular things;
5. whether knowledge acquired here in a habitual way remains in the separated soul;
6. whether it can make use of knowledge acquired in a habitual way here:
7. whether spatial[d] distance impedes the knowledge of the separated soul;
8. whether souls, when separated from their bodies, know what is going on here.

article 1. can the separated soul understand anything at all?

THE FIRST POINT:[1] 1. It would seem that the separated soul cannot understand anything at all. For Aristotle says[2] that *intellectual apprehension is destroyed through the decay of some inward part.* But all the inward parts of man are destroyed in death. Therefore understanding itself is also destroyed.

2. Again, the human soul is impeded from understanding when the senses are bound or the imagination disturbed, as said before.[3] But in death the senses and imagination are totally destroyed, as appears from what was said before.[4] Therefore the soul, after death, understands nothing.

3. Again, if the separated soul understands anything, it must do so by means of species. But it does not understand by means of innate species since it is, from the beginning, like *a writing-tablet on which as yet nothing is written.*[5] Nor yet by species it abstracts from things because it has no

---

[c]*separatæ*: the translation, as 'immaterial (substances)', here runs into a minor difficulty; much of the question will hang on the verbal similarity between 'separate substances' (spiritual substances which are complete things) and 'separated souls' (disembodied souls which are not complete things). However, it seems better to maintain uniformity in the translation (cf 84, 1, note *g*).
[d]On space rather than place, see 85, 3, note *d*.

intelligibiles abstrahuntur a rebus. Neque etiam per species prius abstractas, et in anima conservatas: quia sic anima pueri nihil intelligeret post mortem. Neque etiam per species intelligibiles divinitus influxas: hæc enim cognitio non esset naturalis, de qua nunc agitur, sed gratiæ. Ergo anima separata a corpore nihil intelligit.

SED CONTRA est quod Philosophus dicit,[6] *Si non est aliqua operationum animæ propria, non contingit ipsam separari.* Contingit autem ipsam separari. Ergo habet aliquam operationem propriam; et maxime eam quæ est intelligere. Intelligit ergo sine corpore existens.

RESPONSIO: Dicendum quod ista quæstio difficultatem habet ex hoc quod anima, quamdiu est corpori conjuncta, non potest aliquid intelligere nisi* convertendo se ad phantasmata, ut per experimentum patet. Si autem hoc non est ex natura animæ, sed per accidens hoc convenit ei ex eo quod corpori alligatur, sicut Platonici posuerunt, de facili quæstio solvi posset. Nam remoto impedimento corporis, rediret anima ad suam naturam, ut intelligeret intelligibilia simpliciter, non convertendo se ad phantasmata, sicut est de aliis substantiis separatis. Sed secundum hoc, non esset anima corpori unita propter melius animæ, si pejus intelligeret corpori unita quam separata; sed hoc esset solum propter melius corporis: quod est irrationabile, cum materia sit propter formam, et non e converso.

Si autem ponamus quod anima ex sua natura habeat ut intelligat convertendo se ad phantasmata, cum natura animæ per† mortem corporis non mutetur, videtur quod anima naturaliter nihil possit intelligere, cum non sint ei præsto phantasmata ad quæ convertatur.

Et ideo ad hanc difficultatem tollendam, considerandum est quod, cum nihil operetur nisi inquantum est actu, modus operandi uniuscujusque rei sequitur modum essendi ipsius. Habet autem anima alium modum essendi cum unitur corpori, et cum fuerit a corpore separata, manente tamen eadem animæ natura; non ita quod uniri corpori sit ei accidentale, sed per rationem suæ naturæ corpori unitur; sicut nec levis natura mutatur cum est in loco proprio, quod est ei naturale, et cum est extra proprium locum, quod‡ est ei præter naturam. Animæ igitur secundum illum modum essendi quo corpori est unita, competit modus intelligendi per conversionem ad phantasmata corporum, quæ in corporeis organis sunt: cum

---

*Piana: *non*, not
†Piana: *post*, after
‡Piana: *qui*, which (place)

organs of sense and imagination by means of which species are abstracted from things. Nor, again, by species previously abstracted and retained in the soul, for in this case the soul of a child would understand nothing after death. Nor, finally, by species which come from God, for this would not be the natural knowledge we are talking about, but a gift of grace. Therefore the soul, when separated from the body, understands nothing.

ON THE OTHER HAND, Aristotle says[6] that *if there is no way of acting proper to the soul, its separated existence is impossible.* But it does have a separated existence. Therefore it has a proper activity, above all that of understanding. Thus, when existing apart from the body, it still understands.

REPLY: This is a very difficult question by reason of the fact that the soul, while joined to the body, cannot understand anything except by turning to sense images, as appears from experience. If, on the other hand, this does not come from the nature of the soul, but happens only incidentally because it is tied down to a body (as the Platonists held), then the question could easily be resolved. For if the impediment of a body were removed, the soul would return to its true nature and understand intelligible objects simply, without turning to sense images, as other subsistent immaterial substances do. However, in this case the soul would not be joined to the body for the good of the soul, that is, if its understanding were worse when joined to the body than when separated, but only for the good of the body. Now this is unreasonable, since matter exists because of form and not the other way around.

But to come back to the problem, if we hold that the soul, by its very nature, has to understand by turning to sense images, then, since the nature of the soul is not changed by the death of the body, it would seem that the soul, naturally speaking, can understand nothing, for there are no sense images at hand for it to turn to.

So, to remove the difficulty, we should consider that, since nothing acts except according as it is actual, the mode of acting of each thing follows its mode of being. Now the soul has different modes of being when joined to the body and when separated from the body even while its nature remains the same. This does not imply that being joined to the body is something incidental to it, for that is by reason of its nature; we may draw a parallel. The nature of a light body does not change, whether it is in its proper place (which is natural to it) or whether it is outside its proper place (which is besides its nature). Thus to the soul according to its mode of being when united with the body belongs a mode of understanding which turns to the

---

[6]Aristotle, *De Anima* I, I. 403a11

autem fuerit a corpore separata, competit ei modus intelligendi per conversionem ad ea quæ sunt intelligibilia simpliciter, sicut et aliis substantiis separatis.

Unde modus intelligendi per conversionem ad phantasmata est animæ naturalis, sicut et corpori uniri: sed esse separatum* a corpore est præter rationem suæ naturæ, et similiter intelligere sine conversione ad phantasmata est ei præter naturam. Et ideo ad hoc unitur corpori, ut sit et operetur† secundum naturam suam.

Sed hoc rursus habet dubitationem. Cum enim natura‡ semper ordinetur ad id quod melius est; est autem melior modus intelligendi per conversionem ad intelligibilia simpliciter quam per conversionem ad phantasmata: debuit sic a Deo institui animæ natura, ut modus intelligendi nobilior ei esset naturalis, et non indigeret corpori propter hoc uniri.

Considerandum est igitur quod, etsi intelligere per conversionem ad superiora sit simpliciter nobilius quam intelligere per conversionem ad phantasmata, tamen ille modus intelligendi, prout erat possibilis animæ, erat imperfectior. Quod sic patet. In omnibus enim substantiis intellectualibus invenitur virtus intellectiva per influentiam divini luminis. Quod quidem in primo principio est unum et simplex; et quanto magis creaturæ intellectuales distant a primo principio tanto magis dividitur illud lumen et diversificatur, sicut accidit in lineis a centro egredientibus. Et inde est quod Deus per unam§ suam essentiam omnia intelligit; superiores autem intellectualium substantiarum, etsi per plures formas intelligant, tamen intelligunt per pauciores, et magis universales, et virtuosiores ad comprehensionem rerum, propter efficaciam virtutis intellectivæ quæ est in eis; in inferioribus autem sunt formæ plures, et minus universales, et minus efficaces ad comprehensionem rerum, inquantum deficiunt a virtute intellectiva superiorum.

Si ergo inferiores substantiæ haberent formas in illa universalitate in qua habent superiores, quia non sunt tantæ efficaciæ in intelligendo, non acciperent per eas perfectam cognitionem de rebus, sed in quadam communitate et confusione. Quod aliqualiter apparet in hominibus: nam qui sunt debilioris intellectus, per universales conceptiones magis intelligentium non accipiunt perfectam cognitionem, nisi eis singula in speciali explicentur.

Manifestum est autem inter substantias intellectuales, secundum naturæ ordinem, infimas esse animas humanas. Hoc‖ autem perfectio universi

---

*Piana: *separatam*
‡Piana: *res*, a thing
‖Piana: *Hæc*

†Piana: *ut sic operetur*, in order to act thus
§Piana omits *unam*, one

ⁿ*per conversionem ad*: this use of the same term for purely intelligible objects is

sense images of bodies found in corporeal organs, whereas when separated from the body its mode of understanding, as in other immaterial substances, is to turn[a] to things that are purely intelligible.

Hence to understand by turning to sense images is as natural to the soul as being joined to the body, whereas to be separated from the body is off-beat for its nature, and so likewise is understanding without turning to sense images.[b] The soul is joined to the body in order to be and act in accordance with its nature.

But here again a doubt comes up. For nature is always ordered to what is better, and since understanding by turning to purely intelligible objects is a better mode than turning to sense images, the nature of the soul ought to have been constituted by God in such a way that the higher mode would be natural to it, and for this it would not need to be joined to the body.

We must therefore consider that, although understanding by turning to superior beings is better, simply speaking than by turning to sense images, nevertheless, as a possible mode of understanding for the soul it would not be so well. The following makes this clear. In all intellectual substances the power of intelligence comes from the influence of divine light. Now this at its source, is one and simple, and the further intellectual creatures are from this origin, the more the light will be divided and diversified, as with lines radiating from a centre. Thus God, by his one essence, understands all things. The higher intellectual substances, although they understand through more than one form, nevertheless do so by forms that are relatively few and more universal, as well as more powerful with respect to comprehending things, because of the strength of their minds. Among lower substances the forms are more numerous and less universal, and also less powerful in comprehending things, because their intellectual faculties fall short of those of higher substances.

Thus if lower substances had forms with the universality that higher ones have, then they would not—because they do not have the same efficacy in understanding—receive through them a complete knowledge of things, but a general and confused knowledge. Some sort of parallel to this appears among human minds: men of weaker intelligence do not reach through general conceptions the full knowledge of those more intelligent without having individual applications explained to them in detail.

Now evidently among intellectual substances, in the order of nature, human souls are the lowest. (And the perfection of the universe demanded this, so as to have a scale of beings.[c] Therefore were human souls so

helpful in understanding the contrasted 'turning to sense images'—cf 84, 7, note *a*.
[b]*præter naturam*, outside its nature, even unnatural.
[c]cf 1a. 47, 1 & 2. Vol. 8 of this series.

exigebat, ut diversi gradus in rebus essent. Si igitur animæ humanæ sic essent institutæ a Deo ut intelligerent per modum qui competit substantiis separatis, non haberent cognitionem perfectam, sed confusam in communi. Ad hoc ergo quod perfectam et propriam cognitionem de rebus habere possent, sic naturaliter sunt institutæ ut corporibus uniantur, et sic ab ipsis rebus sensibilibus propriam de eis cognitionem accipiant;* sicut homines rudes ad scientiam induci non possunt nisi per sensibilia exempla.

Sic ergo patet quod propter melius animæ est ut corpori uniatur, et intelligat per conversionem ad phantasmata; et tamen esse potest separata, et alium modum intelligendi habere.

1. Ad primum ergo dicendum quod, si diligenter verba Philosophi discutiantur, Philosophus hoc dixit ex quadam suppositione prius facta, scilicet quod intelligere sit quidam motus conjuncti, sicut et sentire: nondum enim differentiam ostenderat inter intellectum et sensum.

Vel potest dici quod loquitur de illo modo intelligendi qui est per conversionem ad phantasmata. De quo etiam procedit secunda ratio.

3. Ad tertium dicendum quod anima separata non intelligit per species innatas, nec per species quas tunc abstrahit, nec solum per species conservatas, ut objectio probat; sed per species ex influentia divini luminis participatas, quarum anima fit particeps sicut et aliæ substantiæ separatæ, quamvis inferiori modo. Unde tam cito cessante conversione ad corpus, ad superiora convertitur. Nec tamen propter hoc cognitio† non est naturalis: quia Deus est auctor non solum influentiæ gratuiti luminis, sed etiam naturalis.

articulus 2. utrum anima separata intelligat substantias separatas

AD SECUNDUM sic proceditur:[1] 1. Videtur quod anima separata non intelligat substantias separatas. Perfectior enim est anima corpori conjuncta, quam a corpore separata: cum anima sit naturaliter pars humanæ naturæ; quælibet autem pars perfectior est in suo toto. Sed anima conjuncta corpori non intelligit substantias separatas, ut supra habitum est.[2] Ergo multo minus cum fuerit a corpore separata.

2. Præterea, omne quod cognoscitur, vel cognoscitur per sui præsentiam vel per suam speciem. Sed substantiæ separatæ non possunt cognosci ab anima per suam præsentiam: quia nihil illabitur animæ nisi solus Deus. Neque etiam per aliquas species quas anima ab angelo abstrahere possit:

---

*Piana: *accipiunt*
†Piana adds *vel potentia*, or the power
[1]cf Disputations *De anima* 17. *Quodl.* III, 9, 1

constituted by God that they understood in the mode proper to immaterial substances, they would not have perfect, but confused and general knowledge. And so in order that they might have perfect and proper knowledge of things, they were so constituted as to be joined to bodies and to receive proper knowledge of sensible things from these things themselves; thus unlearned men are led to demonstrative knowledge only by way of sensible examples.

Manifestly, then, it is for the good of the soul to be joined to the body and to understand by turning to sense images; yet all the same it can be separated from the body and enjoy another mode of understanding.

Hence: 1. If these words of Aristotle are analysed carefully, it will be clear that he made the statement on the basis of an earlier supposition, namely that understanding, like sensation, is a sort of change in the composite. For he had not yet shown the difference between the intellect and the senses.

Or else it can be said that he is talking about the mode of understanding by way of turning to sense images—which is also the assumption in the second argument.

3. The separated soul does not understand by means of innate species, nor by species it abstracts then, nor by retained species alone—as the objection alleges—but by species participated in by the influence of the divine light. The soul is made a sharer in these just like other immaterial substances, though in an inferior mode. Thus as soon as it ceases to turn to the body it turns to higher beings. It does not follow on this account that the knowledge is not natural, for God is the author of the inflowing of light, not only of grace, but also of nature.

article 2. does the separated soul understand immaterial substances?

THE FIRST POINT:[1] 1. It would seem that the separated soul does not understand immaterial substances. For the soul when joined to the body is in a more perfect state than when separated from the body, since the soul is naturally a part of human nature, and a part is more perfect when in its whole. But the soul joined to the body does not understand immaterial substances, as we have already agreed.[2] Much less, therefore, does it when separated from the body.

2. Again, everything known is known either by being present itself or by a species of itself. But immaterial substances cannot be known by the soul by way of their being present, because nothing enters within the soul except God alone. Nor again by way of species which the soul can abstract

_____
[2] Ia. 88, 1

SUMMA THEOLOGIÆ, Ia. 89, 2

quia angelus simplicior est quam anima. Ergo nullo modo anima separata potest cognoscere substantias separatas.

3. Præterea, quidam philosophi posuerunt in cognitione separatarum substantiarum consistere ultimam hominis felicitatem. Si ergo anima separata potest intelligere substantias separatas, ex sola sua separatione consequitur felicitatem. Quod est inconveniens.

SED CONTRA est quod animæ separatæ cognoscunt alias animas separatas; sicut dives in inferno positus vidit Lazarum et Abraham.³ Ergo* vident etiam et dæmones et angelos animæ separatæ.

RESPONSIO: Dicendum quod, sicut Augustinus dicit,⁴ *Mens nostra cognitionem rerum incorporearum per seipsam accipit,* idest cognoscendo seipsam, sicut supra dictum est.⁵ Per hoc ergo quod anima separata cognoscit seipsam, accipere possumus qualiter cognoscit alias substantias† separatas. Dictum est autem quod quamdiu anima corpori est unita, intelligit convertendo se ad phantasmata. Et ideo nec seipsam potest intelligere nisi inquantum fit actu intelligens per speciem a phantasmatibus abstractam: sic enim per actum suum intelligit seipsam, ut supra dictum est.⁶ Sed cum fuerit a corpore separata, intelliget non convertendo se ad phantasmata, sed ad ea quæ sunt secundum se intelligibilia: unde seipsam per seipsam intelliget.

Est autem commune omni substantiæ separatæ quod *intelligat id quod est supra se, et id quod est infra se, per modum suæ substantiæ:*⁷ sic enim intelligitur aliquid secundum quod est in intelligente; est autem aliquid in altero per modum ejus in quo est. Modus autem substantiæ animæ separatæ est infra modum substantiæ angelicæ, sed est conformis modo aliarum animarum separatarum. Et ideo de aliis animabus separatis perfectam cognitionem habet; de angelis autem imperfectam et deficientem, loquendo de cognitione naturali animæ separatæ. De cognitione autem gloriæ est alia ratio.

1. Ad primum ergo dicendum quod anima separata est quidem imperfectior, si consideretur natura qua communicat cum natura‡ corporis: sed tamen quodammodo est liberior ad intelligendum, inquantum per gravedinem et occupationem corporis a puritate intelligentiæ impeditur.

2. Ad secundum dicendum quod anima separata intelligit angelos per

---

*Piana omits *Ergo,* Therefore
†Piana: *res,* things
‡Piana omits *qua communicat cum natura,* (that) it shares with the nature

³*Luke* 16, 23   ⁴*De Trinitate* IX, 3. PL 42, 963
⁵Ia. 88, 1 ad 1   ⁶Ia. 87, 1
⁷*Liber de causis,* prop. 8

from angels since an angel is simpler than the soul.[a] Therefore in no sense can the separated soul know immaterial substances.

3. Again, certain philosophers have held that the ultimate happiness of man consists in the knowledge of immaterial substances. Therefore if the separated soul can understand immaterial substances, it will achieve happiness by the fact of separation alone, which is an embarrassing conclusion.

ON THE OTHER HAND, separated souls know other separated souls, for instance, the rich man sent to hell saw Lazarus and Abraham.[3] Therefore separated souls also see angels and demons.

REPLY: As Augustine says,[4] *The mind gathers the knowledge of incorporeal things through itself*, i.e., by knowing itself, as said before.[5] Thus from the fact that the separated soul knows itself we can learn how it knows other immaterial substances. Now it has already been mentioned that while the soul is joined to the body it understands by turning to sense images; it cannot even understand itself except in that it comes to be actually understanding through a species abstracted from sense images; and it is thus that it understands itself by way of its acts, as said before.[6] On the other hand, when separated from the body, it understands not by turning[b] to sense images, but to things that arc intelligible in themselves; and so it understands itself through itself.

Now it is common to all immaterial substances for each to understand *what is above it and what is beneath it according to the mode proper to its substance*,[7] for a thing is understood in this way, namely, as existing in the one who understands, and a thing exists in another in the mode proper to that other. But the mode proper to the substance of a separated soul is beneath the mode proper to the substance of an angel, though in conformity with the mode of other separated souls. Therefore the separated soul has perfect knowledge of other separated souls, but only an imperfect, deficient knowledge of the angels, to speak in terms of the knowledge which is natural to it. (The explanation is different when it comes to the knowledge of eternal glory.)

Hence: 1. The separated soul is indeed in an imperfect state looked at in the nature it shares with the body. However in a way it is freer to understand, in that the heaviness and preoccupations of the body keep it from pure intelligence.

2. The separated soul understands angels through likenesses shed on it

---

[a]and it is from complexity that the mind abstracts.
[b]see above, art. 1, note *a*.

similitudines divinitus impressas. Quæ tamen deficiunt a perfecta repræsentatione eorum, propter hoc quod animæ natura est inferior quam angeli.

3. Ad tertium dicendum quod in cognitione substantiarum separatarum non quarumcumque,* consistit ultima hominis felicitas, sed solius Dei, qui non potest videri nisi per gratiam. In cognitione vero aliarum substantiarum separatarum est magna felicitas, etsi non ultima, si tamen perfecte intelligantur. Sed anima separata naturali cognitione non perfecte eas intelligit, ut dictum est.

articulus 3. utrum anima separata omnia naturalia cognoscat

AD TERTIUM sic proceditur:[1] 1. Videtur quod anima separata omnia naturalia cognoscat. In substantiis enim separatis sunt rationes omnium rerum naturalium. Sed animæ separatæ cognoscunt substantias separatas. Ergo cognoscunt omnia naturalia.

2. Præterea, qui intelligit magis intelligibile multo magis potest intelligere minus intelligibile. Sed anima separata intelligit substantias separatas, quæ sunt maxima intelligibilium. Ergo multo magis potest intelligere omnia naturalia, quæ sunt minus intelligibilia.†

3. Sed contra, in dæmonibus magis viget naturalis cognitio quam in anima separata. Sed dæmones non omnia naturalia cognoscunt; sed multa addiscunt per longi temporis experientiam, ut Isidorus dicit.[2] Ergo neque animæ separatæ omnia naturalia cognoscunt.

4. Præterea, si anima statim cum est separata omnia naturalia cognosceret, frustra homines studerent ad rerum scientiam capessendam. Hoc autem est inconveniens. Non ergo anima separata omnia naturalia cognoscit.

RESPONSIO: Dicendum quod, sicut supra dictum est, anima separata intelligit per species‡ quas recipit ex influentia divini luminis, sicut et angeli: sed tamen, quia natura animæ est infra naturam angeli, cui iste modus cognoscendi est connaturalis,§ anima separata per hujusmodi species non accipit perfectam rerum cognitionem, sed quasi in communi et confusam. Sicut igitur se habent angeli ad perfectam cognitionem rerum naturalium per hujusmodi species, ita animæ separatæ ad imperfectam et confusam. Angeli autem per hujusmodi species cognoscunt cognitione perfecta omnia

---

*Piana: *quarumcumque non* †Piana: *intelligibilia minus*
‡Piana adds *separatas*, separate §Piana: *naturalis*

[1]cf Disputations *De anima* 18
[2]*Sententiarum libri tres* I, 10. PL 83, 556
cPerfectly or completely: see 84, 8, note *b*. For human happiness in knowledge by grace and nature see 1a2æ. 3, 5–8. Vol. 16 of this series.

by God. These, however, fall short of a perfect representation, because the soul's nature is inferior to an angel's.

3. The ultimate happiness of man consists in the knowledge, not of just any immaterial substances, but of God alone, and he cannot be seen except by grace. There is, however, great, though not the ultimate, happiness in knowing other immaterial substances—if, that is, they are understood perfectly.[c] And, as we have mentioned, the separated soul, by its connatural knowledge, does not understand them perfectly.

article 3. does the separated soul know all natural things?

THE FIRST POINT:[1] 1. It would seem that the separated soul does know all natural things. For immaterial substances possess the ideas of all natural things. But separated souls know immaterial substances. Therefore they know all natural things.

2. Again, anyone who understands the more intelligible can, *a fortiori*, understand the less intelligible. But the separated soul understands immaterial substances, and these are the highest of intelligible objects. Therefore, *a fortiori*, it can understand still better all natural things since these are less intelligible.

3. On the other hand, the natural knowledge of demons has greater power than that of the separated soul. But demons do not know all natural things—rather, they learn many things by experience over a long period of time, as Isidore says.[2] Neither, therefore, do separated souls know all natural things.

4. Besides, if as soon as separated the soul were to know all natural things, it would be useless for men to study in order to acquire demonstrative knowledge of things. Awkward this. Therefore the separated soul does not know all natural things.[a]

REPLY: As said before, the separated soul understands through species received under the influence of divine light, as the angels do. However, even so, since the nature of the soul is beneath the nature of an angel (to which this mode of knowing is connatural), the separated soul through these species does not receive a perfect, but a sort of general and confused, knowledge of things; these species set separated souls to imperfect and confused knowledge of natural things as they set the angels to perfect knowledge. But the angels, by means of these species, know all natural

---

[a]Note the double *sed contra*. The *corpus* will take a middle position between the two sets of arguments; all four are replied to.

SUMMA THEOLOGIÆ, Ia. 89, 4

naturalia: quia omnia quæ Deus fecit in propriis naturis fecit in intelligentia angelica, ut dicit Augustinus.[3] Unde et animæ separatæ de omnibus naturalibus cognitionem habent, non certam et propriam, sed communem et confusam.

1. Ad primum ergo dicendum quod nec ipse angelus per suam substantiam cognoscit omnia naturalia, sed per species quasdam, ut supra dictum est.[4] Et ideo non propter hoc sequitur quod anima cognoscat omnia naturalia quia cognoscit quoquo modo* substantiam separatam.

2. Ad secundum dicendum quod, sicut anima separata non perfecte intelligit substantias separatas, ita nec omnia naturalia perfecte cognoscit, sed sub quadam confusione, ut dictum est.

3. Ad tertium dicendum quod Isidorus loquitur de cognitione futurorum; quæ† nec angeli nec dæmones nec animæ separatæ cognoscunt, nisi vel in suis causis, vel per revelationem divinam. Nos autem loquimur de cognitione naturalium.‡

4. Ad quartum dicendum quod cognitio quæ acquiritur hic per studium, est propria et perfecta; illa autem est confusa. Unde non sequitur quod studium addiscendi sit frustra.

articulus 4. utrum anima separata cognoscat singularia

AD QUARTUM sic proceditur:[1] 1. Videtur quod anima separata non cognoscat singularia. Nulla enim potentia cognoscitiva remanet in anima separata nisi intellectus, ut ex supra dictis patet.[2] Sed intellectus non est cognoscitivus singularium, ut supra habitum est.[3] Ergo anima separata singularia non cognoscit.

2. Præterea, magis est determinata cognitio qua cognoscitur aliquid in singulari, quam illa qua cognoscitur aliquid in universali. Sed anima separata non habet§ determinatam cognitionem de speciebus rerum naturalium. Multo igitur minus cognoscit singularia.

3. Præterea si cognoscit singularia, et non per sensum, pari ratione omnia singularia cognosceret.‖ Sed non cognoscit omnia singularia. Ergo nulla cognoscit.

SED CONTRA est quod dives in inferno positus dixit, *Habeo quinque fratres.*[4]

RESPONSIO: Dicendum quod animæ separatæ aliqua singularia cognoscunt, sed non omnia, etiam quæ sunt præsentia. Ad cujus evidentiam,

---

*Piana omits *quoquo modo*, somehow
†Piana: *qua* ‡Piana: *naturali*, natural (knowledge)
§Piana adds *aliquam*, any ‖Piana: *cognoscit*, knows

148

things with a perfect knowledge, for, as Augustine says,[3] all the things God made with a proper nature he also produced in the understanding of the angels. Therefore separated souls also have a knowledge of all natural things, but one that is general and confused, not certain and proper.

Hence: 1. Not even the angels know all natural things in their own substance, but by means of species, as said before.[4] And so, from the fact that it somehow knows immaterial substances, it does not follow that the soul knows all natural things.

2. As the separated soul does not perfectly understand immaterial substances, so also it does not know all natural things perfectly, but as we have mentioned, in a confused fashion.

3. Isidore is talking about knowledge of future things, and these neither angels nor demons nor separated souls know except either in their causes or by divine revelation. But here we are talking about the knowledge of natural things.

4. The knowledge acquired here by study is perfect and proper, whereas that knowledge is confused. Thus it does not follow that studying in order to learn is useless.

article 4. does the separated soul know singulars?

THE FIRST POINT:[1] 1. It would seem that the separated soul does not know singulars. For the only cognitive faculty that remains in the separated soul is the intellect, as is obvious from what was said before.[2] But the intellect does not know singulars, as was held before.[3] Therefore the separated soul does not know singulars.

2. Again, the knowledge in which something is known in a singular way is more determinate than that in which it is known in a universal way. But the separated soul does not have determinate knowledge of even the specific natures of natural things. Much less, then, can it know singulars.

3. Again, if it knows singulars—and not by way of the senses—by the same reasoning it should know all singulars. But this it does not. Therefore it knows none of them.

ON THE OTHER HAND, the rich man sent to hell said,[4] *I have four brothers.*

REPLY: Separated souls know some singulars but not all (even of those that are temporally present). For evidence on this we should consider that there

---

[3]*De Genesi ad litteram* II, 8. PL 34, 269   [4]Ia. 55, 1; 87, 1
[1]cf IV *Sent.* 50, 1, 3. *De veritate* XIX, 2; Disputations *De anima* 20
[2]Ia. 77, 8   [3]Ia. 86, 1   [4]*Luke* 16, 28

considerandum est quod duplex est modus intelligendi. Unus per abstractionem a phantasmatibus: et secundum istum modum singularia per intellectum cognosci non possunt directe, sed indirecte, sicut supra dictum est.[5] Alius modus intelligendi est per influentiam specierum a Deo: et per istum modum intellectus potest singularia cognoscere. Sicut enim ipse Deus per suam essentiam, inquantum est causa universalium et individuallium principiorum, cognoscit omnia et universalia et singularia, ut supra dictum est;[6] ita substantiæ separatæ per species, quæ sunt quædam participatæ similitudines illius divinæ essentiæ, possunt singularia cognoscere.

In hoc tamen est differentia inter angelos et animas separatas, quia angeli per hujusmodi species habent perfectam et propriam cognitionem de rebus, animæ vero separatæ confusam. Unde angeli, propter efficaciam sui intellectus, per hujusmodi species non solum naturas rerum in speciali cognoscere possunt, sed etiam singularia sub speciebus contenta. Animæ vero separatæ non possunt cognoscere per hujusmodi species nisi solum singularia illa ad quæ quodammodo determinantur, vel per præcedentem cognitionem, vel per aliquam affectionem, vel per naturalem habitudinem, vel per divinam ordinationem: quia omne quod recipitur in aliquo, determinatur in eo secundum* modum recipientis.

1. Ad primum ergo dicendum quod intellectus per viam abstractionis non est cognoscitivus singularium. Sic autem anima separata non intelligit, sed sicut dictum est.

2. Ad secundum dicendum quod ad illarum rerum species vel individua cognitio animæ separatæ determinatur, ad quæ anima separata habet aliquam determinatam habitudinem, sicut dictum est.

3. Ad tertium dicendum quod anima separata non se habet æqualiter ad omnia singularia, sed ad quædam habet aliquam habitudinem quam non habet ad alia. Et ideo non est æqualis ratio ut omnia singularia cognoscat.

---

articulus 5. utrum habitus scientiæ hic acquisitæ remaneat in anima separata

AD QUINTUM sic proceditur:[1] 1. Videtur quod habitus scientiæ hic acquisitæ non remaneat in anima separata. Dicit enim Apostolus,[2] *Scientia destruetur.*

2. Præterea, quidam minus boni in hoc mundo scientia pollent, aliis magis bonis carentibus scientia. Si ergo habitus scientiæ permaneret etiam

---

*Piana: *recipitur in eo per*, received in it in

[5]1a. 86, 1   [6]1a. 14, 11
[1]cf 1a2æ. 67, 2. IV *Sent.* 50, 1, 2. *In* I *Cor.* XIII, *lect.* 3   [2]I *Corinthians* 13, 8
[a]This article and the next carry on very similar discussions, first with respect to habitual, then actual knowledge. The point of the discussion is stated succinctly

are two modes of understanding. One is by abstraction from sense images, and in this manner singulars cannot be known by the intellect directly, but indirectly, as said before.[5] The other manner of understanding is by the infusion of species by God, and according to this manner the intellect can know singulars. For, just as God, by his own essence (since it is the cause of both universal and individual principles), knows all things, whether universal or singular, as said before,[6] so also immaterial substances can know singulars by way of species which are participated likenesses of the divine essence.

There is, however, a difference between angels and separated souls, for angels, by means of these species, have proper and perfect knowledge, but separated souls only a confused knowledge. Thus angels, because of the efficaciousness of their understanding, can by way of these species know not only the natures of things in terms of their proper class, but also the singulars contained in each class. Separated souls, on the other hand, by means of these species can know only those singulars to which they have some determinate order, by earlier knowledge, by affection, by natural relationships, or by divine dispensation. For a thing, when received in something else, becomes determinate in the receiver according to the mode proper to the receiver.

Hence: 1. The intellect does not know singulars by way of abstraction. Neither, then, does a separated soul understand thus, but in the way mentioned.

2. The knowledge of the separated soul is confined to the specific or individual natures of those things to which it has a determinate relationship, as mentioned above.

3. The separated soul is not set on all singulars, but has a relationship to some that it does not have to others. There is, thus, not an equal reason for its knowing them all.

article 5. does knowledge acquired here in a habitual way remain in the separated soul?[a]

THE FIRST POINT:[1] 1. It would seem that knowledge acquired here in a habitual way does not remain in the separated soul. For St Paul says,[2] *Knowledge will fail.*

2. Again, some men in this world who are less good have a power in knowledge lacking in others who are better. Were habitual knowledge to

in the second objection of article 6: 'In no sense can the separated soul understand by means of species acquired here.' Thus, though the term *scientia*—translated throughout as 'demonstrative knowledge'—is used, the point is not to emphasize demonstration, but *any* knowledge acquired in the present life. Thus the term 'demonstrative' has been dropped in the two articles wherever feasible.

post mortem in anima, sequeretur quod aliqui minus boni etiam in futuro statu essent potiores aliquibus magis bonis. Quod videtur inconveniens.

3. Præterea, animæ separatæ habebunt scientiam per influentiam divini luminis. Si igitur scientia hic acquisita in anima separata remaneat, sequetur quod duæ erunt formæ unius speciei in eodem subjecto. Quod est impossibile.

4. Præterea, Philosophus dicit[3] quod *habitus est qualitas difficile mobilis; sed ab ægritudine, vel ab aliquo hujusmodi, quandoque corrumpitur scientia.* Sed nulla est ita fortis immutatio in hac vita sicut immutatio quæ est per mortem. Ergo videtur quod habitus scientiæ per mortem corrumpatur.

SED CONTRA est quod Hieronymus dicit,[4] *Discamus in terris, quorum scientia nobis perseveret in cælo.*

RESPONSIO: Dicendum quod quidam posuerunt habitum scientiæ non esse in ipso intellectu, sed in viribus sensitivis, scilicet imaginativa, cogitativa et memorativa; et quod species intelligibiles non conservantur in intellectu possibili. Et si hæc opinio vera esset, sequeretur quod, destructo corpore, totaliter habitus scientiæ hic acquisitæ destrueretur.

Sed quia scientia est in intellectu, qui est *locus specierum,* ut dicitur,[5] oportet quod habitus scientiæ hic acquisitæ partim sit in prædictis viribus sensitivis, et partim in ipso intellectu. Et hoc potest considerari ex ipsis actibus ex quibus habitus scientiæ acquiritur: nam *habitus sunt similes actibus ex quibus acquiruntur,* ut dicitur.[6] Actus autem intellectus ex quibus in præsenti vita scientia acquiritur, sunt per conversionem intellectus ad phantasmata, quæ sunt in prædictis viribus sensitivis. Unde per tales actus et ipsi intellectui possibili acquiritur facultas quædam ad considerandum per species susceptas; et in prædictis inferioribus viribus acquiritur quædam habilitas ut facilius per conversionem ad ipsas intellectus possit intelligibilia speculari.

Sed sicut actus intellectus principaliter quidem et formaliter est in ipso intellectu, materialiter autem et dispositive in inferioribus viribus, idem etiam dicendum est de habitu. Quantum ergo ad id quod aliquis præsentis scientiæ habet in inferioribus viribus non remanebit in anima separata: sed quantum ad id quod habet in ipso intellectu, necesse est ut remaneat.

---

[3]*Categories* 6. 8b28
[4]*Epist. 53, ad Paulinum.* PL 22, 549
[5]*De Anima* III, 4. 429a27
[6]*Nicomachean Ethics* II, 1. 1103b21

remain in the soul even after death, it would follow that some men who are less good would in the future state still have an advantage over others who are better. This does not seem credible.

3. Again, the separated souls will get their knowledge under the influence of divine light. Thus if knowledge acquired here remains in the separated soul, it follows that there will be two forms of the same species in the same subject. But this is impossible.

4. Again, Aristotle says[3] that a *habitual disposition is a quality difficult to displace, though knowledge can sometimes be destroyed by disease or something similar*. But no change in this life is as thorough as that brought about in death. Therefore it would seem that habitual knowledge is destroyed in death.

ON THE OTHER HAND, Jerome says,[4] *Let us learn on earth those things whose knowledge will remain with us in heaven.*

REPLY: Some have held that knowledge as a habitual disposition exists, not in the intellect, but in the sense faculties (that is, imagination, the cogitative faculty, and sense memory[b]), and that species are not retained in the possible intellect. Now were this opinion true, it would follow that when the body is destroyed so also would be, and totally, the habitual knowledge we have here acquired.

Since, however, knowledge is in the intellect (which is, as Aristotle says,[5] *the place of forms*), it must be that knowledge acquired here in a habitual way is partly in the sense faculties mentioned and partly in the intellect. And this can be seen in terms of the acts by which this habitual knowledge is acquired, for, as Aristotle says,[6] *habitual dispositions arise out of like activities*. Now the acts by which, in the present life, knowledge is acquired include a turning of the intellect to sense images found in the sense faculties we have mentioned. Thus through these acts, there is on one hand, in the possible intellect, a certain ability acquired for considering things received through the species and, on the other hand, in the lower faculties alluded to, a certain aptitude acquired for seconding the intellect, so that it can see intelligible objects more easily by turning to them.

But just as acts of the intellect are principally and formally seated in the intellect itself, but materially and in the manner of a disposition in the lower faculties, so also must the same be said of habitual dispositions. Therefore as to man's present knowledge, the part that is in the lower faculties will not remain in the separated soul, but what is in the intellect will necessarily remain.

---

[b]cf 84, prol. note *g*.

SUMMA THEOLOGIÆ, 1a. 89, 6

Quia, ut dicitur,[7] dupliciter corrumpitur aliqua forma: uno modo per se, quando corrumpitur a suo contrario, ut calidum a frigido; alio modo per accidens, scilicet per corruptionem subjecti. Manifestum est autem quod per corruptionem subjecti, scientia quæ est in intellectu humano, corrumpi non potest: cum intellectus sit incorruptibilis, ut supra ostensum est.[8] Similiter etiam nec per contrarium corrumpi possunt species intelligibiles quæ sunt in intellectu possibili: quia intentioni intelligibili nihil est contrarium; et præcipue quantum ad simplicem intelligentiam, qua intelligitur *quod quid est.*

Sed quantum ad operationem qua* intellectus componit et dividit, vel etiam ratiocinatur, sic invenitur contrarietas in intellectu, secundum quod falsum in propositione vel in argumentatione est contrarium vero. Et hoc modo interdum scientia corrumpitur per contrarium, dum scilicet aliquis per falsam argumentationem abducitur a scientia veritatis. Et ideo Philosophus[9] ponit duos modos quibus scientia per se corrumpitur: scilicet *oblivionem,* ex parte memorativæ, et *deceptionem,* ex parte argumentationis falsæ.

Sed hoc non habet locum in anima separata. Unde dicendum est quod habitus scientiæ, secundum quod est in intellectu, manet in anima separata.

1. Ad primum ergo dicendum quod Apostolus non loquitur ibi de scientia quantum ad habitum, sed quantum ad cognitionis actum. Unde ad hujus probationem inducit, *Nunc cognosco ex parte.*

2. Ad secundum dicendum quod, sicut secundum staturam corporis aliquis minus bonus erit major aliquo magis bono; ita nihil prohibet aliquem minus bonum habere aliquem scientiæ habitum in futuro, quem non habet aliquis magis bonus. Sed tamen hoc quasi nullius momenti est in comparatione ad alias prærogativas quas meliores habebunt.

3. Ad tertium dicendum quod utraque scientia non est unius rationis. Unde nullum inconveniens sequitur.

4. Ad quartum dicendum quod ratio illa procedit de corruptione scientiæ quantum ad id quod habet† ex parte sensitivarum virium.

articulus 6. *utrum actus scientiæ hic acquisitæ maneat in anima separata*

AD SEXTUM sic proceditur:[1] 1. Videtur quod actus scientiæ hic acquisitæ non maneat in anima separata. Dicit enim Philosophus[2] quod corrupto

---

*Piana: *quia*   †Piana: *est,* is

[7]*De longitudine et brevitate vitæ* 2. 465a19
[8]1a. 75, 6
[9]*De longitudine et brevitate vitæ* 2. 465a23
[1]cf III *Sent.* 31, 2, 4; IV *Sent.* 50, 1, 2
[2]*De Anima* I, 4. 408b27

For, as Aristotle says,[7] a form can be destroyed in two ways, first, in itself, when it is destroyed by its contrary,[c] e.g., heat by cold; second, incidentally,[d] that is, by the destruction of its subject. Now it is obvious that demonstrative knowledge in the human intellect cannot be destroyed by the destruction of its subject, because, as shown before,[8] the intellect is immortal. Nor, similarly, can species in the possible intellect be destroyed by their contrary, since nothing is contrary to an intellectual intention, especially in a matter of the simple understanding in which the *whata-thing-is*[e] is understood.

On the other hand, with respect to the activity in which the intellect combines and separates, or reasons, contrariety is found in the intellect in the sense that falsity in a proposition or argument is contrary to truth. And thus also demonstrative knowledge is sometimes destroyed by its contrary, namely, when a person is led away from the truth by a false argument. Thus Aristotle holds[9] that there are two ways in which demonstrative knowledge is destroyed in itself, i.e., by forgetting, on the part of memory, and deception, in terms of a false argument.

But this has no place in the separated soul. Therefore we must say that this habitual knowledge, as it is found in the intellect, remains in the separated soul.

Hence: 1. St Paul is not speaking there of habitual, but of actual, knowledge. And to prove his point he adds, *The knowledge that I have now is imperfect.*

2. Just as a person who is less good may be bigger in terms of bodily stature than someone better, so nothing prevents someone less good from having a habitual knowledge in the future life which a better person does not have. Nevertheless, this will be of practically no importance in comparison with the other prerogatives that those who are better will have.

3. The two kinds of knowledge do not have the same nature. So no awkward consequence is implied.

4. The argument assumes that destruction of demonstrative knowledge which happens by reason of the sense faculties.

article 6. does the use of knowledge acquired here remain in the separated soul?

THE FIRST POINT:[1] 1. It would seem that knowledge acquired here does not remain in an actual state in the separated soul. For Aristotle says[2] that,

---

[c] i.e., its logical contrary—an opposite quality within the same class; by definition such qualities must be mutually exclusive.

[d] *per accidens, per aliud*: that is, destroyed by the removal of a condition for its existence.

[e] Same as *quidditas*; see Appendix 2.

corpore, anima *neque reminiscitur neque amat.* Sed considerare ea quæ prius aliquis* novit, est reminisci. Ergo anima separata non potest habere actum scientiæ quam hic acquisivit.

2. Præterea, species intelligibiles non erunt potentiores in anima separata quam sint in anima corpori unita. Sed per species intelligibiles non possumus modo intelligere, nisi convertendo nos super phantasmata, sicut supra habitum est.[3] Ergo nec anima separata hoc poterit. Et ita nullo modo per species intelligibiles hic acquisitas anima separata intelligere poterit.

3. Præterea, Philosophus dicit[4] quod habitus similes actus reddunt actibus per quos acquiruntur.† Sed habitus scientiæ hic acquiritur per actus intellectus convertentis se supra phantasmata. Ergo non potest alios actus reddere. Sed tales actus non competunt animæ separatæ. Ergo anima separata non habebit aliquem actum scientiæ hic acquisitæ.

SED CONTRA est quod dicitur[5] ad divitem in inferno positum, *Recordare quia recepisti bona in vita tua.*

RESPONSIO: Dicendum quod in actu est duo considerare, scilicet speciem actus et modum ipsius. Et species quidem actus consideratur ex objecto in quod actus cognoscitivæ virtutis dirigitur per speciem; quæ est objecti similitudo: sed modus actus pensatur ex virtute agentis. Sicut quod aliquis videat lapidem, contingit ex specie lapidis quæ est in oculo: sed quod acute videat, contingit ex virtute visiva oculi.

Cum igitur species intelligibiles maneant in anima separata, sicut dictum est, status autem animæ separatæ non sit idem sicut modo est, sequitur quod secundum species intelligibiles hic acquisitas, anima separata intelligere possit quæ prius intellexit; non tamen eodem modo, scilicet per conversionem ad phantasmata, sed per modum convenientem animæ separatæ.

Et ita manet quidem in anima separata actus scientiæ hic acquisitæ, sed non secundum eundem modum.

1. Ad primum ergo dicendum quod Philosophus loquitur de reminiscentia, secundum quod memoria pertinet ad partem sensitivam: non autem secundum quod memoria est quodammodo in intellectu, ut dictum est.[6]

2. Ad secundum dicendum quod diversus modus intelligendi non provenit ex diversa virtute‡ specierum, sed ex diverso statu animæ intelligentis.

3. Ad tertium dicendum quod actus per quos acquiritur habitus, sunt

---

*Piana omits *aliquis,* a person

†Leonine gives *habitus similes actus reddunt actibus per quos acquiruntur* (habitual dispositions produce acts similar to those acts by which they are acquired) as a direct quote

when the body is destroyed, *memory and love cease in the soul*. But for a person to consider things he has known previously is to remember. Therefore the separated soul cannot have an act of knowledge acquired here.

2. Again, species in the separated soul will not be more powerful than they would be in the soul joined to the body. But we cannot understand now through species except by turning to sense images, as we have stated.[3] Neither, therefore, will the separated soul be able to do this. Thus in no sense can the separated soul understand by means of species acquired here.

3. Again, Aristotle says[4] that habitual dispositions produce acts similar to the acts by which they are acquired. Now demonstrative knowledge is acquired here in a habitual way by acts of the intellect turning to sense images. Accordingly it cannot produce acts of any other kind. But such acts are not found in the separated soul. Therefore the separated soul will not, in an actual way, retain the demonstrative knowledge acquired here.

ON THE OTHER HAND, there is what is said[5] to the rich man sent to hell, *Remember that during your life good things came your way*.

REPLY: There are two things to consider in acts, namely the kind of act and its mode. Now the kind of act is considered in terms of the object toward which the act of a cognitive faculty is directed by means of a species (which is a likeness of the object), whereas the mode of an act is thought of in terms of the power of an agent. For example, the fact that someone sees a stone happens because the stone's image is found in the eye, but that he sees it with keenness happens because of good eyesight.

Thus since species remain in the separated soul (as mentioned) and the condition of the separated soul is not the same as now, it follows that, by means of species acquired here, the separated soul can understand the things it understood before, though not in the same way (by turning to sense images), but in the mode that belongs to the separated soul.

Therefore knowledge acquired here remains in the separated soul in an actual way, but not according to the same mode.

Hence: 1. Aristotle is speaking of remembering as of the memory which belongs to the sense part of man, and not as of the sort of memory which, as we have mentioned, is in the intellect.[6]

2. A distinct mode of understanding does not come from the power of the species, but from the different condition of the soul that understands.

3. The acts by which an habitual disposition is acquired are similar to

---

‡Piana: *ex diversitate*, from the diversity

[3]1a. 84, 7　　　　　　　　　　[4]*Nicomachean Ethics* II, I. 1103b21
[5]*Luke* 16, 25　　　　　　　　　[6]1a. 79, 6

similes actibus quos habitus causant, quantum ad speciem actus: non autem quantum ad modum agendi. Nam operari justa, sed non juste, idest delectabiliter, causat habitum justitiæ politicæ, per quem delectabiliter operamur.

articulus 7. utrum localis distantia impediat cognitionem animæ separatæ

AD SEPTIMUM sic proceditur:[1] 1. Videtur quod distantia localis impediat cognitionem animæ separatæ. Dicit enim Augustinus[2] quod *animæ mortuorum ibi sunt, ubi ea quæ hic fiunt scire non possunt.* Sciunt autem ea quæ apud eos aguntur. Ergo distantia localis impedit cognitionem animæ separatæ.

2. Præterea, Augustinus dicit[3] quod *dæmones, propter celeritatem motus, aliqua nobis ignota denuntiant.* Sed agilitas motus ad hoc nihil faceret, si distantia localis cognitionem dæmonis non impediret. Multo igitur magis distantia localis impedit cognitionem animæ separatæ, quæ est inferior secundum naturam quam dæmon.

3. Præterea, sicut distat aliquis secundum locum, ita secundum tempus. Sed distantia temporis impedit cognitionem animæ separatæ: non enim cognoscunt futura. Ergo videtur quod etiam distantia secundum locum animæ separatæ cognitionem impediat.

SED CONTRA est quod dicitur[4] quod dives, *cum esset in tormentis, elevans oculos suos, vidit Abraham a longe.* Ergo distantia localis non impedit animæ separatæ cognitionem.

RESPONSIO: Dicendum quod quidam posuerunt quod anima separata cognosceret singularia abstrahendo a sensibilibus. Quod si esset verum, posset dici quod distantia localis impediret animæ separatæ cognitionem: requireretur enim quod vel sensibilia agerent in animam separatam, vel anima separata in sensibilia; et quantum ad utrumque, requireretur distantia determinata.

Sed prædicta positio est impossibilis: quia abstractio specierum a sensibilibus fit mediantibus sensibus et aliis potentiis sensitivis, quæ in anima separata actu non manent. Intelligit autem anima separata singularia per influxum specierum ex divino lumine, quod quidem lumen æqualiter se habet ad propinquum et distans. Unde distantia localis nullo modo impedit animæ separatæ cognitionem.

[1]cf IV *Sent.* 50, 1, 4
[2]*De cura pro mortuis agenda* 13. PL 40, 605
[3]*De divinatione dæmonum* 3. PL 40, 584
[4]*Luke* 16, 23

the acts which habitual dispositions cause in one respect, the kind of act, but not with respect to the mode of acting. For instance, performing just deeds, though not justly, that is, with ease, sets up the habitual disposition of being a good citizen, and from that we can act pleasurably.[a]

article 7. does spatial[b] distance impede the knowledge of the separated soul?

THE FIRST POINT:[1] 1. It would seem that spatial distance does impede the knowledge of the separated soul. For Augustine says[2] that *the souls of the dead are there where they cannot know what is done here.* But they know what is happening among themselves. Therefore spatial distance impedes the knowledge of the separated soul.

2. Again, Augustine says[3] that *the demons, because of the rapidity of their movements, announce certain things that are unknown to us.* But agility of movement would contribute nothing if spatial distance did not impede the knowledge of a demon. Therefore, *a fortiori*, spatial distance impedes the knowledge of the separated soul, since it is by nature inferior to a demon.

3. Again, as a man can be distant in space, so also in time. But temporal distance impedes the knowledge of the separated soul—for they do not know the future. Therefore it would seem distance in space would also impede the knowledge of the separated soul.

ON THE OTHER HAND, Scripture says[4] that the rich man, *in his torment in hell, looked up and saw Abraham a long way off.* Thus spatial distance does not impede the knowledge of the separated soul.

REPLY: Some have held that the separated soul knows singulars by abstraction from sensible objects. Now if this were true, it could be said that spatial distance would impede the knowledge of the separated soul. For it would be required either that the sensible objects would act on the separated soul, or the separated soul on the sensible objects, and in either case a determinate distance would be required.

However, this position is impossible. For the abstraction of species from sensible objects is done by means of the external senses and other sense faculties, and none of these retain their actuality in the separated soul. Instead, the separated soul understands singulars by the infusion of species from the divine light, which is indifferent to what is far or near. Thus spatial distance in no sense impedes the knowledge of the separated soul.

---

[a] an echo from Aristotle on 'habits' as second-nature, dispositions to act congenially, that is pleasurably: cf 1a2æ. 49–54. Vol. 22.
[b] See above 89, 1, note *d*, & 85, 3, note *d*.

1. Ad primum ergo dicendum quod Augustinus non dicit quod propter hoc quod ibi sunt animæ mortuorum, ea quæ hic sunt videre non possunt, ut localis distantia hujus ignorantiæ causa esse credatur: sed hoc potest propter aliquid aliud contingere, ut infra dicetur.

2. Ad secundum dicendum quod Augustinus ibi loquitur secundum opinionem illam qua aliqui posuerunt quod dæmones habent corpora naturaliter sibi unita: secundum quam positionem, etiam potentias sensitivas habere possunt, ad quarum cognitionem requiritur determinata distantia. Et hanc opinionem etiam in eodem libro[5] Augustinus expresse tangit: licet eam magis recitando quam asserendo tangere videatur, ut patet per ea quæ dicit.[6]

3. Ad tertium dicendum quod futura, quæ distant secundum tempus, non sunt entia in actu. Unde in seipsis non sunt cognoscibilia: quia sicut deficit aliquid ab entitate, ita deficit a cognoscibilitate. Sed ea quæ sunt distantia secundum locum, sunt entia in actu, et secundum se cognoscibilia. Unde non est eadem ratio de distantia locali et de distantia temporis.

articulus 8. *utrum animæ separatæ cognoscant ea quæ hic aguntur*

AD OCTAVUM sic proceditur:[1] 1. Videtur quod animæ separatæ cognoscant ea quæ hic aguntur. Nisi enim ea cognoscerent, de eis curam non haberent. Sed habent curam de his quæ hic aguntur; secundum illud,[2] *Habeo quinque fratres, ut testificetur illis, ne et ipsi veniant in hunc locum tormentorum.* Ergo animæ separatæ cognoscunt ea quæ hic aguntur.

2. Præterea, frequenter mortui vivis apparent, vel dormientibus vel vigilantibus, et eos admonent de iis quæ hic aguntur; sicut Samuel apparuit Sauli.[3] Sed hoc non esset, si ea quæ hic sunt non cognoscerent. Ergo ea quæ hic aguntur cognoscunt.

3. Præterea, animæ separatæ cognoscunt ea quæ apud eas aguntur. Si ergo quæ apud nos aguntur non cognoscerent, impediretur earum cognitio per localem distantiam. Quod supra negatum est.

SED CONTRA est quod dicitur,[4] *Sive fuerint filii ejus nobiles, sive ignobiles, non intelliget.*

RESPONSIO: Dicendum quod, secundum naturalem cognitionem, de qua nunc hic agitur, animæ mortuorum nesciunt quæ hic aguntur. Et hujus ratio ex dictis accipi potest.[5] Quia anima separata cognoscit singularia per hoc quod quodammodo determinata est ad illa, vel per vestigium alicujus

---

[5]*De divinatione dæmonum* 3. PL 40, 584   [6]*De civitate Dei* XXI, 10. PL 41, 724
[1]cf 2a2æ. 83, 4 ad 2. IV *Sent.* 45, 3, 1 ad 1 & 2   [2]*Luke* 16, 28

Hence: 1. Augustine says that the souls of the departed cannot see what is done here, not because they are *there*. He does not leave us to believe that spatial distance is the reason for the ignorance. There is another, as we shall explain in the next article.

2. Augustine is speaking there according to the opinion of certain authors who held that demons by nature are united to bodies, and so can even have sense faculties, whose knowledge requires a determinate distance. Again in the same book[5] Augustine touches on this opinion expressly, though, it seems from statements elsewhere, more in the sense of reporting it than of asserting it.[6]

3. Future things, distant in time, are not actual beings. And so they are not knowable in themselves, since a thing lacks knowability to the degree that it lacks being. Things that are distant in space, on the other hand, are actual beings, knowable in themselves. Thus the reasoning is not the same with respect to spatial and temporal distance.

article 8. do separated souls know what is happening here?

THE FIRST POINT:[1] 1. It would seem that separated souls do know what is happening here. For if they did not know them they would not be concerned about them. But they are concerned about things that happen here, for instance, the man who pleaded,[2] *I have five brothers, to give them warning so that they do not come to this place of torment too.* Therefore separated souls know what is happening here.

2. Again, the dead frequently appear to the living, whether asleep or awake, to advise them about things that are happening here: Samuel, for instance, appeared to Saul.[3] But this would not be so if they did not know things that exist here. Therefore they know things that happen here.

3. Again, separated souls know the things that are done among themselves. If, therefore, they did not know the things that happen among us, it would be spatial distance that impeded their knowledge. But this has been denied.[a]

ON THE OTHER HAND: Scripture says,[4] *Let his sons achieve honour, he does not know of it, humiliation, he gives it not a thought.*

REPLY: In terms of natural knowledge, which is our concern here, the souls of the dead do not know what happens here, and the reason for this can be learned from what has been said.[5] For the separated soul knows singulars by being made somehow determinate with respect to them, whether

---

[3]1 *Samuel* 28, 11   [4]*Job* 14, 21   [5]art. 4 above
[a]In the previous article.

præcedentis cognitionis seu affectionis, vel per ordinationem divinam. Animæ autem mortuorum, secundum ordinationem divinam, et secundum modum essendi, segregatæ sunt a conversatione viventium, et conjunctæ conversationi spiritualium substantiarum quæ sunt a corpore separatæ. Unde ea quæ apud nos aguntur ignorant.

Et hanc rationem assignat Gregorius,[6] dicens, *Mortui vita in carne viventium post eos, qualiter disponatur, nesciunt: quia vita spiritus longe est a vita carnis; et sicut corporea atque incorporea diversa sunt genere, ita sunt distincta cognitione.* Et hoc etiam Augustinus videtur tangere,[7] dicens quod *animæ mortuorum rebus viventium non intersunt.*

Sed quantum ad animas beatorum, videtur esse differentia inter Gregorium et Augustinum. Nam Gregorius ibidem subdit, *Quod tamen de animabus sanctis sentiendum non est: quia quæ intus omnipotentis Dei claritatem vident, nullo modo credendum est quod sit foris aliquid quod ignorent.* Augustinus vero[8] expresse dicit quod *nesciunt mortui, etiam sancti, quid agant vivi et eorum filii,* ut habetur in glossa[9] super illud, *Abraham nescivit nos.*[10] Quod quidem confirmat per hoc quod a matre sua non visitabatur, nec in tristitiis consolabatur, sicut quando vivebat; nec est probabile ut sit facta vita feliciore crudelior. Et per hoc quod Dominus promisit Josiæ regi quod prius moreretur, ne videret mala quæ erant populo superventura.[11] Sed Augustinus hoc dubitando dicit: unde præmittit, *ut volet, accipiat quisque quod dicam.* Gregorius autem assertive: quod patet per hoc quod dicit, *nullo modo credendum est.*

Magis tamen videtur, secundum sententiam Gregorii, quod animæ sanctorum Deum videntes, omnia præsentia quæ hic aguntur cognoscant. Sunt enim angelis æquales: de quibus etiam Augustinus asserit[12] quod ea quæ apud vivos aguntur non ignorant. Sed quia sanctorum animæ sunt perfectissime justitiæ divinæ conjunctæ, nec tristantur, nec rebus viventium se ingerunt, nisi secundum quod justitiæ divinæ dispositio exigit.

1. Ad primum ergo dicendum quod animæ mortuorum possunt habere curam de rebus viventium, etiam si ignorent eorum statum; sicut nos curam* habemus de mortuis, eis suffragia impendendo, quamvis eorum statum ignoremus.

Possunt etiam facta viventium non per seipsos cognoscere, sed vel per

---

*Piana omits *curam*, concern

[6]*Moralia* XII, 21. PL 75, 999
[7]*De cura pro mortuis agenda* 13. PL 40, 604; 16. PL 40, 607
[8]*De cura pro mortuis agenda* 13. PL 40, 604
[9]*Glossa interlin.* IV, 102
[10]*Isaiah* 63, 16
[11]II *Kings* 22, 20

by a vestige of previous knowledge or affection, or by divine dispensation. But the souls of the dead, according to divine dispensation and their mode of existence, are set apart from intercourse with the living and enter into intercourse with spiritual and bodiless substances. Therefore they are ignorant of what goes on among us.

This is the reason Gregory gives,[6] *The dead do not know how things are with those left behind living the life of the flesh, for the life of the spirit is far from the life of the flesh. Again, as corporeal and incorporeal realities are different in kind, so also are they different in knowledge.* Augustine also would seem to touch on the same argument when he says[7] that *the souls of the dead do not associate with the affairs of the living.*

However, with respect to the souls of the blessed, there seems to be a difference between Gregory and Augustine. For Gregory, in the same place, continues, *Nevertheless, this should not be thought to be the case with the souls of the saints, for in no sense can it be believed that there is anything outside unknown to those who see the brilliance of almighty God from within.* Whereas Augustine says expressly[8] that *the dead, even the saints, do not know what the living, even their own children, are doing* (at least as the statement is reported in a gloss[9] on the statement:[10] *Abraham does not acknowledge us*). And he says in confirmation that he was not visited by his mother or consoled by her in his sorrows as he had been when she was alive, and how unlikely it is that by the greater happiness of life she had become more cruel. And again that the Lord promised to Josiah that he would die before he saw the evils that were going to befall his people.[11]

Augustine leaves all this, however, as a matter of doubt. Thus he prefaces his remarks, *Let each one accept what I say as he will.* Gregory, on the other hand, is speaking assertively, as appears from the fact that he says *it can in no sense be believed.*

All this aside, it seems, following the opinion of Gregory, more likely that the souls of the saints, seeing God, know all that at present passes here. For they are like the angels, with respect to which even Augustine asserts[12] that they are not ignorant of things that happen among the living on earth. But since the hearts of the saints most perfectly cleave to divine justice, neither are they saddened nor do they involve themselves in the affairs of the living, except as the dispositions of divine justice demand.

Hence: 1. The souls of the dead can be concerned about the affairs of the living even if they are ignorant of how they are going, just as we care for the dead by offering suffrages for them, even though we do not know what their condition is.

The deeds of the living they can also know, not in themselves, but

---

[12]*De cura pro mortuis agenda* 15. PL 40, 605

animas eorum qui hinc ad eos accedunt; vel per angelos seu dæmones; vel etiam *Spiritu Dei revelante*, sicut Augustinus dicit.[13]

2. Ad secundum dicendum quod hoc quod mortui viventibus apparent qualitercumque, vel contingit per specialem Dei dispensationem, ut animæ mortuorum rebus viventium intersint: et est inter divina miracula computandum. Vel hujusmodi apparitiones fiunt per operationes angelorum bonorum vel malorum, etiam ignorantibus mortuis: sicut etiam vivi ignorantes aliis viventibus apparent in somnis, ut Augustinus dicit.[14]

Unde et de Samuele dici potest quod ipse apparuit per revelationem divinam; secundum hoc quod dicitur:[15] *dormivit, et notum fecit regi finem vitæ suæ*. Vel illa apparitio fuit procurata per dæmones: si tamen *Ecclesiastici* auctoritas non recipiatur, propter hoc quod inter canonicas scripturas apud Hebræos non habetur.

3. Ad tertium dicendum quod ignorantia hujusmodi non contingit ex locali distantia, sed propter causam prædictam.

---

[13]*De cura pro mortuis agenda* 15. PL 40, 606
[14]ibid 12. PL 40, 600

through the souls of those arriving there from here, or through angels or demons, or even *by a revelation from the Spirit of God*, as Augustine says.[13]

2. The fact that the dead appear, in whatever way it may be, to the living happens either because by special dispensation of God the souls of the dead interfere in the affairs of the living, which should be counted a divine miracle. Or else such apparitions happen through the activity of good or bad angels, even without the knowledge of the dead themselves (as also living people, unknown to themselves, appear in dreams to other living persons, as Augustine observes).[14]

Thus with respect to Samuel it can be said that he appeared through divine revelation, according to the saying,[15] that *after he fell asleep he prophesied again, warning the king of his death.* Or else—if the authority of *Ecclesiasticus* is not accepted because it was not included among the canonical Scriptures by the Hebrews—that the apparition was brought about by demons.

3. This kind of ignorance does not happen by reason of spatial distance, but for the reason mentioned.

---

[15]*Ecclesiasticus* 46, 23

Appendix 1

IDEAS, SPECIES, IMAGES

A COMPACT account of the main technical terms relating to the problem of human knowledge in the present treatise can best be provided, it seems to me, by taking two passages from St Thomas, the first from the *Contra Gentes*, the second from the *Summa Theologiæ*.

'Species intelligibilis' and 'intentio intellecta' (*CG* 1, 53)

The intellect, given form (*formatus*[1]) by the species of a thing, in understanding formulates (*format*[2]) in itself an intention (*intentio*[3]) of the thing understood which is the aspect (*ratio*) of the thing signified by a definition.

Now this understood intention (*intentio intellecta*), since it is in one way the term of the intellectual act, is distinct from the species (*species intelligibilis*) which puts the intellect in a state of actuality, and which, therefore, must be looked at as the principle of the intellectual act, though both are a likeness (*similitudo*[4]) of the thing understood. For since the species which is the form of the intellect and the principle of the act of understanding is a likeness of the thing outside, it follows that the intention formulated by the intellect must also be similar to the thing, for the effects a thing produces are according to the mode of its being. And from the fact that the understood intention is similar to a thing, it follows that the intellect in formulating such an intention understands that thing.

In addition to those already explained in the footnotes, other key terms here are *intentio intellecta* and *ratio*. It should be noted that St Thomas employs a number of synonyms for *intentio intellecta: conceptio* (*De potentia* VIII, 1) and *conceptus* (*CG* IV, 11), both roughly equivalent to 'concept'; *verbum mentis* and *verbum interius* (*CG* IV, 11), 'mental word' and 'interior

---

[1]Form as actualizing potentiality, here cognitive. Elsewhere St Thomas says *informatus*, emphasizing the 'informational' rôle, and speaks of the process as a *passio* of the intellect similar to that of the senses receiving impressions from their objects; e.g., 1a. 85, 2 ad 3

[2]The etymological sense is 'forms', 'shapes', 'gives form to', but the important point here is what is formed, namely an *intentio* or *ratio*

[3]Simple transliteration suffices because 'intentionality' has become standard in English to express the relatedness of knower to known. For translation of *ratio* as 'aspect', see below

[4]Likeness in form, but 'form' has many senses—shape, tonal quality, etc., with reference to the external senses; the recomposed *species sensibilis* and its expression, the 'sense image' or *phantasma*, with reference to the internal senses; the 'separated forms'; etc. In human intellectual knowledge, both the *species intelligibilis* and *intentio* or *conceptio* are more properly likenesses in *formula* than form as shape, etc.

word'; and, seemingly, even *ratio*, *definitio*, and *enuntiatio*.[5] Perhaps in recognition of Platonic usage, he reserves *idea* for a form *outside* things—the 'idea' or pattern in the mind of an artist or maker;[6] the English term 'idea' could be used in many contexts where St Thomas uses either *species intelligibilis* or *intentio-conceptio*, but the decision was made in the text to use 'species' uniformly throughout the translation.

Now for the terms to be explained. First, *intentio intellecta*. Very likely this is shorthand for *intentio rei intellectæ*. In any case the meaning is not 'intention' or 'concept', as taken reflexively; although there is an *intentio universalitatis* consequent upon the intention as universal which is known reflexively (Ia. 85, 2 ad 2). St Thomas is clearly speaking here of direct knowledge, as appears from the final words in the quotation. Second, *ratio*. This is perhaps *the* key word, most difficult to interpret and therefore to translate, and used with many meanings. In the present context the simplest explanation is that *ratio* is a synonym of the *immobilis habitudo* in Ia. 84, I ad 3. This is an unchanging aspect (*respectus*) or relationship in a changing reality. *In the thing* it is individual, singular, actually intelligible only to God in terms of a divine exemplar idea (Ia. 14, 11). To us it is only potentially intelligible, universalizable rather than universal. Such also seems to be the meaning of *ratio* in many passages. In the present case *ratio* would mean 'that which presents itself (as "lighted up" by the agent intellect) to reason', i.e., the *rationabile* with respect to *ratio* taken as reason or intelligence.

As understood, then, the *ratio* or *immobilis habitudo* of the thing is no longer singular but universal. It is in this sense that St Thomas here identifies *ratio* with *intentio* (the concept or *species expressa*—see below). Both of these are then signified by a definition—a *ratio* or combination or balance of universals (in the conceptual order) or words (in imagination, speech or writing).

In summary, what St Thomas is saying thus far is that in intellectual knowledge there must be what the scholastics have come to call a *species impressa* (*qua*, the *id quo*) and a *species expressa* (*in qua*, that *in quo*, the term). However important the distinction, the present treatise makes explicit reference to it only in one place, Ia. 85, 2 ad 3. We may thus presume that *species intelligibilis*, the term used regularly throughout, is often meant to include *both* aspects—such is certainly the case in the treatment of 'innate species' and probably also wherever illuminationist theories are in question.

Intellectual Knowledge in relation to Sense Knowledge (Ia. 85, 2 ad 3)

In the sense-part of man there are two kinds of activity. One by way of a change (*immutatio*) effected from outside; thus the activity of the senses is fully carried out through a change effected by sensible objects. The other

---

[5] See Ia. 85, 2 ad 3
[6] cf Ia. 15, I ad 2; *De veritate* III, I

activity is the 'formation' by which the faculty of imagination forms for itself a model of something absent or even of something never seen.

Now both of these activities are joined in the intellect. For there is indeed an effect (*passio*) produced in the possible intellect in so far as it is informed by a species; further, when it is thus informed, it formulates either a definition or else an affirmative or negative proposition, which is then signified by words.

Here the important terms are *immutatio* with respect to the external senses, *formatio* with respect to imagination, and the clear distinction between the two. In all the senses, external and internal, there is a passive aspect, *immutatio* or *passio*, by way of an impressed image, *species sensibilis*. However, only in the external senses is this sufficient for knowledge. In the internal senses, imagination, sense memory, and cogitative faculty, a further, active rôle is required, a *formatio* producing what I have translated throughout as a 'sense image', *phantasma*; this is the *species expressa* of the internal senses.

Note that St Thomas attributes to the imagination a further productive power, going beyond the mere representing of what has been impressed in the *species impressa*. Thus he admits a collating or rearranging of sense images, especially for the purpose of getting at the intelligibility of the material world (2a2æ. 173, 2); and also a *ratio particularis*, a sort of reasoning process of which the internal senses are capable (1a. 78, 4).

Appendix 2

THE SIMPLE UNDERSTANDING OF *QUIDDITAS*

JARRING TO the modern ear is the repeated assertion that, with respect to the 'whatness' (*quidditas*) of a thing, speaking essentially or *per se*, the intellect is infallible (1a. 85, 6 and *passim*). Even a friendly critic can read this as, 'What our understanding grasps primarily and most readily is the specific nature (*quod quid est*) of material substances',[1] 'specific nature' being taken to mean the specific essence or proper nature of the object. There is a misapprehension here, occasioned perhaps by the frequent equation of *quidditas* and *essentia*. In fact 'whatness' does mean 'what a thing is', but not necessarily nor even usually the *specific* or *proper* nature, or the substantial essence of a thing. This can be shown, first, by St Thomas's clear statements that truly proper knowledge of the substantial form of material things is infrequent, and second, by recalling and drawing the implications of a basic text in the present treatise (1a. 85, 3). So, then, we address ourselves to what is really meant by the statement, *per se loquendo cognitio quidditatis est infallibilis*.

Knowledge of Specific Natures

Numerous texts bear witness to our limitations in the ordinary run of knowledge. For instance:—'The essential principles of things are unknown to us' (*In De anima* I, *lect.* 1); 'Essential differences are unknown to us' (*De veritate* IV, 1 ad 8; cf X, 1, & ad 6); 'Substantial forms are *per se* unknown to us' (*De spiritualibus creaturis* 11 ad 3); 'We are ignorant of many of the properties of sensible things, and in many cases we are unable to discover the proper nature even of those properties that we perceive by the senses' (*CG* I, 3); 'We do not know even the essence of a fly' (*In Symbolo apostolorum* I); and finally: 'Substantial differences, because they are unknown, are manifested by accidental differences' (*In De generatione* I, *lect* 1.).

However, the inadequacy should not be overstated, for 'Sometimes the properties and incidental characteristics (*accidentia*) of a thing disclosed by the senses adequately manifest its nature' (*In De Trinitate* VI, 2). All the same the normal condition is suggested in the final quotation of the preceding paragraph. Thus also: 'Sometimes necessity compels us to use incidental differences in place of essential differences in so far as incidental differences are signs of essential differences unknown to us' (*In Meta.* VII, *lect.* 12); and, 'But even in the case of sensible things, essential differences

---

[1]Peter Geach. *Mental Acts: Their Content and Their Objects.* New York. 1957, pp. 130–1

170

are unknown to us; thus we have to signify them by incidental differences, which have their origin in what is essential, as when we designate a cause in terms of its effect' (*De ente et essentia* 5).

Thus the ordinary way we know and define material realities, which are the proper object of our intellect, is in terms of incidental characteristics (*accidentia*). Does this mean that St Thomas is merely holding up an ideal seldom attained when he speaks of infallible knowledge of the 'whatness' or essence ? Decidedly not, as the analysis to follow will show; rather, what he is saying is that the intellect attains a *quid*, a 'whatness', or essence every time it functions, but that this can be more or less generic, and indeed can be either substantial or accidental.

Knowledge of the More Universal Comes First (1a. 85, 3)

The text concludes: 'In us the knowledge of singulars precedes the knowledge of universals in so far as sense knowledge precedes intellectual knowledge. But both in the senses and in the intellect more general precedes less general knowledge.' The reason is given: because both senses and intellect go from potentiality to actuality.

Left as a bald statement, not much seems to be said. However, the passage from potentiality to actuality here involves more than appears at first sight, as becomes clear when the article is examined in the carefully worked-out context of the whole Question, on the 'mode and order' according to which human knowledge unfolds, in which all the conclusions flow from the premise of the *abstractive mode* of human knowledge.

For example, to take as the key the second act of the mind, in which truth and falsity are found. The intellect has to combine and separate because its first apprehension is imperfect or incomplete. The incompleteness of abstractive knowledge is explained in article 1 and clarified in article 2 (which rejects representationalism). Next, article 3, the implication is drawn that the abstractions must begin with the most general, each successive one adding detail to ones that have gone before. Then, turning to the composition that puts together again what abstraction has separated, the teaching is confirmed in article 4, set out formally in article 5, and related to the problem of truth in article 6.

The picture emerges of original broad vistas being progressively narrowed down and filled in with more and more details, and this on the sense level as well as that of the intellect. Once awakened in its original act, the intellect will ordinarily perceive in its fashion nearly every object perceived by the senses, internal or external, but the perception will always be limited by the degree of elaboration in the sense image.

Infallible Knowledge?

What then is left of the claim to infallibility in knowing essences ? We have noted how limited this is; it is not claimed that men usually or normally or easily attain the specific natures even of the most common realities in their environment. Next, the knowledge of any particular material being is progressive from most general 'whatnesses' to more and more specific notes as experience uncovers new facets, though, as St Thomas explicitly recognizes, a genuinely proper and specific knowledge is almost never yielded. All the same each *quidditas*, when made intelligible by the agent intellect, is either seen as such or not at all; no mistake, no partial apprehension, is possible. For every *quidditas* is a *ratio*, a balance of composing elements, which if varied or 'partially seen' is simply not seen. If anything at all is seen, it is something else, some other *ratio* or balance of intelligibilities.

Appendix 3

COMPLEX KNOWLEDGE, THE SECOND ACT OF THE MIND

ST THOMAS takes up matter, treated in the manuals under the heading, 'Judgment', in terms of a question: Does our intellect understand by way of combining and separating (*componendo et dividendo*)? Before taking up the content of the question, we should first note the care and delicacy with which the question is presented.

The Structure of 1a. 85, 4–5

The two articles are carefully linked. Article 4 concludes: 'Therefore it is impossible for the same intellect to be perfected by different species which allow it to understand actually different things at one time.' Article 5 begins: 'It would seem that our intellect does not understand by combining and separating. For the intellect cannot understand more than one thing at a time.' Then giving his explanation of the combinative act of mind, St Thomas turns to its mode in the reply to objection 1. 'The intellect's combinations and separations come about by way of a comparison or contrast. The intellect thus knows several objects by combining and separating in the same way that it compares or contrasts things', that is, as explained in article 4, reply to objection 4, by knowing 'two things compared or contrasted under the aspect of the very comparison or contrast.'

This unity in composition finds no exact parallel elsewhere in his writings, though there may be a shift from the earliest to the latest works in emphasis and precision of argument.[1]

The Act of Composition

As indicated, the key to the treatment of the second act of the mind is to be found in the solution of the difficulty: Combining and separating can only take place with respect to more than one thing; but the intellect cannot understand more than one thing at a time; therefore it cannot understand by combining and separating. The reply is to show that composition and division involve a unity-in-composition, a reduction to simplicity of the multiple data of abstraction.

Composition is the operative term, and a sketch of the various compositions leading up to or involved in judgment (as the ultimate product of the second act of the mind) will be helpful. Most fundamental of all is the composite

---

[1] cf II *Sent.* 3, 3, 4. *De veritate* VIII, 14. *CG* I, 55. 1a. 12, 10; 58, 2; *Quodl.* VII, 1, 2

mode of being which is, properly speaking, the object of judgment. Secondly, there is the composite image (*phantasma*) which represents the composition of the object to the mind. On the intellectual level there are two further compositions, the so-called 'enunciable' and enunciation, and that which 'compares' the enunciation with or applies it to reality. This final composition has been interpreted in two ways: as the essence of the judgmental act;[2] or as a property of judgment, in which case the essence of judgment would lie in the enunciation, joining two concepts, and the application would be a reflex judgment on the truth value of the enunciation.[3]

This is not the place to go into this controversy,[4] but some points may be made. As mentioned, the ultimate product of the second act of the mind is a judgment in which the mind affirms (or denies) a composition as true, or as adequate to represent reality. This affirmation is not based on prior, reflexive knowledge of the adequacy of the composition to represent the reality.[5] Nor does it consist in a comparison, in the proper sense, of a composition in the mind with the reality outside. To state what it does involve would require a full phenomenological and analytical outline of the psychological stages leading up to it; here it will suffice to return to some of the compositions we have mentioned.

The composition in the sense image is non-judgmental, even when it is a verbal representation of the affirmation ultimately to be made. In simple apprehension there is no composition as such, but a verb-concept does imply and lead to composition. Within the second act of the mind, which is better thought of as complex, the central composition is that of the enunciation or joining of concepts—although as *species expressa* (see Appendix 1) it is preceded by the quasi *species impressa* of the 'enunciable' composition. The enunciation itself can be considered in two ways: first, as combination of concepts in the single *ratio* of which St Thomas speaks—and thus it is the enunciative composition properly-so-called; secondly, as image or representation of reality, and thus it is the matter for the affirmational composition, the affirmation itself.[6]

Thus there are within the second act of the mind two distinct operations, a synthesis of concepts (in an entitatively simple reduction-to-unity) and an

---

[2]Peter Hoenen. *Reality and Judgment according to St Thomas*. Chicago. 1952, p. 137
[3]L. M. Regis: *Epistemology*. New York. 1959, p. 323
[4]For a full discussion, and an attempt at a solution, see my article: 'Unity and Composition in Judgment', *The Thomist*, XXXI (1967), Washington. pp. 83–120
[5]cf John of St Thomas: *Cursus theologicus* (Solesmes edition), II, 625, no. 18
[6]The best textual arguments for this dual composition within the second act of the mind are to be found in passages which balance 'composition and division' with affirmation and denial: *componit et dividit, affirmando et negando* (*De veritate* XIV, 1. 1a. 85, 8). See also the clear expository passage, *In Periherm.* 1, *lect.* 3

affirmation.[7] In my opinion the term 'judgment' is more appropriate as applied to the second of these operations, since it is a (non-reflexive 'judging' of the objective validity of the enunciation according to the proper measure[8] which fits the composite mode of being real.

---

[7] cf John of St Thomas. *Cursus theologicus*, II, 622, no. 11. It seems to me that this is an important point as an opening to recent theories in cognitive psychology (see references to Jerome Bruner in Appendix 7), namely the 'projection' of tentative, possible meanings on to the chaos of experience as preparation for any decisions (affirmations) that have to be made

[8] *De veritate* X, 9

Appendix 4

REASONING: DEMONSTRATIVE AND DIALECTICAL

THE ALMOST total absence, throughout the six questions in the treatise, of any references to less-than-certain knowledge is striking. *Opinio*, in the sense of a probable assertion (even allowing for such a synonym as *conjectura*) appears no more than four or five times,[1] and *fides*, in the sense of knowledge on the authority of another (human or divine), even fewer times. Intellectual knowledge is virtually equated with *scientia*, usually to be translated as 'demonstrative knowledge.'

The Nature of 'Scientia'

So much has been written by so many about Aristotle's ideal of science, *epistéme* or *scientia*, that little more than a reminder of familiar points is needed here. *Posterior Analytics* I. 2 begins with the definition: 'We suppose ourselves to possess unqualified scientific knowledge of a thing, as opposed to knowing it in the accidental way in which the sophist knows, when we think that we know the cause on which the fact depends, as the cause of that fact and of no other, and, further, that the fact could not be other than it is' (71b8–12). This is clearly the ideal of demonstrative knowledge, as found in classical plane geometry, and Aristotle in fact goes on to describe demonstration as that type of syllogistic reasoning which produces knowledge of this kind, and then adds, 'The premises of demonstrated knowledge must be true, primary [underived], immediate [self-evident], better known than and prior to the conclusion, which is related to them as effect to cause' (71b20–22).

One side of demonstrative knowledge that plays an important part in St Thomas's thinking is that of *habitus scientiæ*—the habitual disposition acquired by way of learning in the man who becomes immersed in a particular demonstrative discipline. Contemporary ideals of science pay little attention to this, but it is implicit when we recognize, say, a mathematician as having a 'feel' for his subject.

Science can also be considered as an ordered system, to be outlined in a course or textbook. There is some misunderstanding here, when Aristotelianism is described as a closed system or even a closed deductive system. St Thomas is very clear that scientific method differs from discipline to discipline, and that only mathematics is demonstrative in the sense that we would describe as a 'deductive science' (*In De Trin.* VI, 1). As for a closed system, Aristotle explicitly affirms that 'a science expands, not by the interposition of fresh middle terms, but by the apposition of fresh extreme terms'

---

[1] Aside from references to 'the opinion of Plato', etc

176

(78a13–14), i.e., new notes that enter into demonstrations about the subject of the science. St Thomas teaches also that a *habitus scientiæ* can grow both intensively and extensively (1a2æ. 52, 2).

This gives a certain flexibility and openness to the demonstrative method. *Scientia* also makes an opening for non-demonstrative reasoning or 'dialectical arguments'. As is well known, such arguments are often employed by Aristotle throughout his philosophical works. Their rôle is commonly interpreted by Thomists as ancillary—one author sums up the matter by saying that dialectical proofs are intended: first, to persuade popular audiences; second, to supply a substitute argument where no proper proofs are available; and third, to confirm demonstrations already given.[2] This may well not be the whole story on Aristotle's attitude toward dialectics,[3] but at least it does give an Aristotelean place, a subordinate one, for non-certain reasoning.

Dialectical Reasoning (*'Opinio'*)

Is this small allowance all that St Thomas gives to less-than-certain knowledge? No. If not here in the *Summa*, then at least in other places St Thomas has a fairly detailed theory of dialectical reasoning, which can be summarized as follows. 1. He takes the general nature of dialectics to be the art of applying 'common, logical principles', not to logical considerations, but to knowledge of the real (*In Poster.* 1, lect. 20. *In Meta.* IV, lect. 4). 2. These principles include, in addition to such logical entities as class and sub-class, the formal definitions of things, i.e., definitions of material things without their material element (*In De anima* I, lect. 2. *In Physic.* III, lect. 8. *In Meta.* VII, lect. 2). 3. Dialectics as a 'scientific' discipline is distinct from the philosophical disciplines in which it is used (1a2æ. 57, 6 ad 3), but it is a necessary part—the discovery or tentative part (*pars inventiva vel tentativa: In Poster.* proëm.; *In Meta.* IV, lect. 4) of *scientia* as a discipline. 4. The appropriate middle term, correspondingly 'tentative', in such usages is the 'universal *ut nunc*' (*In Poster.* 1, lect. 9).[4] 5. Both 'doctrinal demonstrative logic' and 'doctrinal dialectical logic' (*logica docens*) are 'scientific', but (*a*) the use of demonstrative logic is not logic, but a demonstration in some particular

---

[2]B. M. Ashley. *Aristotle's Sluggish Earth: The Problematics of the 'De Cælo'.* River Forest, Ill. 1958, pp. 37–9
[3]According to another account, the basic pattern of argument for Aristotle was set in his earliest logical work, the *Topics*, and then formalized definitively in the *Prior Analytics.* The pattern is that of convincing an opponent in discussion. If a conclusion can be shown to follow necessarily from agreed-upon principles, the discussion is closed with 'scientific knowledge'; otherwise the argument remains dialectical. Cf Ernst Kapp. *Greek Foundations of Traditional Logic.* New York. 1942, pp. 15–18
[4]cf John Oesterle. 'The Significance of the Universal *ut nunc*', in *The Dignity of Science*, ed. J. A. Weisheipl. Washington. 1961, pp. 27–38. Cf *The Thomist*, XXIV (1961), 163–74

philosophical discipline, whereas (*b*) dialectical logic is the *logica utens* of all the sciences (*In Meta.* IV, *lect.* 4).

If all this is so, according to St Thomas, why is a doctrine so important missing from the treatise on human knowledge? One response is that it is not. Josef Pieper maintains that he was the master dialectician of an age recognized as outstanding in dialectics.[5] This mastery is displayed in the *disputatio* method. On this view, dialectics is never absent even from the most rigorous proofs in the *Summa*; it is usually to be found in the preliminary formulations of the *Quæstiones Disputatæ* which prepare the way for the *Summa*.

I believe that this contention is, in the main, true. But it does not explain the absence of references to non-certain knowledge in the present treatise in the *Summa*, and this must be counted a lack.

---

[5]Josef Pieper. *Guide to Thomas Aquinas*, New York. 1962, chap. 7. Mortimer Adler. *The Conditions of Philosophy*. New York. 1965, p. 255

Appendix 5

FAITH AND THEOLOGICAL KNOWLEDGE

IN RECENT decades one of the most persistent criticisms of St Thomas has been that so much of his supposedly theological synthesis is in fact little more than a development along the lines of Aristotelean philosophy. And one of the chief targets for such a criticism could be this treatise on human knowledge, where references to Scripture and other theological sources are scant. He himself would have found these objections strange, coming, as they do, from a different cultural background and different ideal models of knowledge (see Appendix 6). For the starting-point to be properly theological, by the appeal to the living tradition of the Word, it was sufficient for him if the development followed a theological rather than a philosophical order (*CG* II, 4), and nothing in the speculations ran counter to Sacred Scripture or the authority of the Church.

This is not the contemporary approach; all the same the intent is theological throughout the *Summa*, though this includes protecting the natures of things. He begins the present treatise by ruling out certain matters, saying they 'do not directly concern the theologian', but there is more to it than that. It is intrinsically theological, first, by its place within the grand design of the *Summa*, and secondly, because it lays the groundwork for the study of faith.

Place of Treatise in the Grand Design

As an integral part of St Thomas's synthesis of theology, it is suffused throughout with his understanding of the science of faith. By etymology and definition, theology is about God; other topics enter only to the extent that they are somehow related to God who has revealed himself. This *sacra doctrina* is a *doctrina sacræ paginæ*, founded on the Scriptures and therefore centred on God's interventions in history.[1]

This determines the general plan of the *Summa*, which treats of God and creatures as coming forth from God, man's return to God, and Christ as image of the Father and 'the way' of return to God (1a. 2, prol.). Moreover, although its exegetical method may appear archaic to modern scholars, the Scriptures are not merely integrated into but are the main inspiration of its discourse.[2]

The present treatise falls into its place within the ampler treatise on man as a creature coming forth from God the creator, which is focused on the

---

[1] cf Vol. I of this series. Appendices 5, 7, & 11
[2] It has been remarked how St Thomas strikes his superb form as a theologian in his commentaries on Scripture.

Scriptural teaching on the creation of man.[3] Yet man's nature and powers are part of the scene, and it is to do justice to them, in the light of the philosophy and science of the day, much of which is by no means obsolete, that the present treatise on natural knowledge is introduced (see Appendix 6).

It is a necessary preparation for the subsequent discussions, manifestly theological, of man made to God's image. Hence critics may well pause, for even though they may reject its Aristotelean presuppositions, they will have others of their own, which they should spell out, as St Thomas does, before stating a 'pure' theology.

Groundwork for Study of Faith

Does this then mean that the treatise is still, after all, philosophical, merely an explicit affirmation of a non-theological conceptual framework to be used in the interpretation of Scripture? It is certainly that, but it is also much more. Despite its mannerisms, the *Summa* is profoundly non-repetitious, in the sense that teaching given formally in one treatise is not repeated, but only alluded to in other treatises. There, however, it is firmly implicit. When this is recognized further evidence for the theological intent of the present treatise can be gathered from the retrospective made to it in the treatise on faith (2a2æ. 1–16).

These references run throughout to the philosophy of knowledge. Mostly they are implicit, but one, in particular, is quite explicit, and it is very important. A theme, quite properly close to the hearts of contemporary theologians, is that the act of faith goes out, not to a set of propositions, but directly to God himself and to the person of Christ. Based on findings of the present question, the distinction is drawn between him in whom we believe and the enunciation of our belief (2a2æ. 1, 2). 'The mode proper to the human intellect is knowing a truth by way of combining and separating, as was said in the *Prima Pars*. Thus the human intellect knows in a complex way things that are simple in themselves. And so the object of faith can be considered in two ways; first, on the part of the thing believed—in this sense the object of faith is something non-complex, namely the reality concerning which we have faith; secondly, on the part of the believer, and in this respect the object of faith is something complex in that it is stated in a proposition.'

To end with a qualification. The present treatise is an integral part of a theology, which even in the treatise on faith is cast in an Aristotelean mode. There it draws the conclusion that our beliefs must be expressed in propositions, not that these must be framed in terms of the Aristotelean philosophy, which form an idiom less close than phenomenological modes of speaking to Scriptural language. In this matter it may be that the pendulum has swung back and that we are witnessing a revival of the Augustinianism against which St Thomas rebelled in defending the rights of natural knowledge.

[3]Ia. 44–49. Vol. 8 of this series. Also Ia. 90–102. Vol. 13. For a development of this line of thought see Vol. 13 of this series, Introduction by Edmund Hill.

Appendix 6

ST THOMAS AND THE HISTORY OF THEORIES OF KNOWLEDGE

THAT HUMAN knowledge is that aspect of people's behaviour by which they take their environment into account, moreover somehow dependent on the senses, and a legitimate object of investigations by empirical psychology, is an assumption generally made today. But it is one that will be challenged by men from other backgrounds than ours.

One indication of this difference is the difficulty encountered in attempting to disseminate Western science among 'underdeveloped' peoples. For though its advantages seem obvious to the Western mind—technology, the offspring of science, will without doubt improve living conditions, bolster developing economies, lower death rates, and so forth—many cultures in fact will not buy the package. Nor is the reason, as anthropology shows, a lack of intellectual adultness on the part of the intended beneficiaries. Just the opposite: their cultural evaluation of knowledge, just because it is so mature, simply does not accord the high place we do to scientific empiricism, if they recognize it at all.

There is, then, a socio-cultural context of knowledge, which shapes and moulds the thinking of the characteristic knowers of a particular region and period. Yet exaggeration is to be avoided here, just as it is in viewing knowledge in total isolation from history, for the treatment of knowledge culturally is attended by the temptation to cast various epochs in simplistic terms. Each does have its ideals and priorities, but that does not mean the privileged ideal completely dominates the culture to the exclusion of all others. Our age is pragmatic and experimental, true, but there still exist in Western nations groups devoted to mysticism, to non-scientific humanisms of one sort or another, to astrology, etc. The very existence of this edition of the *Summa* is witness to the lasting value accorded to a kind of theology that antedates modern science by hundreds of years.

What is suggested is that in every highly developed culture various ideals of knowledge may exist. The intellectual sub-culture with the highest prestige will necessarily influence the others, but except under the extremes of authoritarianism it will not eliminate them. It is against such a background that St Thomas's place in the history of theories of knowledge can best be seen. Outlining stages in cultural evolution is notoriously hazardous, but the following grand stages should be generally acceptable even where the reasons for distinguishing them may vary.

The Rise of the Philosophical Ideal

It is generally agreed that theories of knowledge began with the Greek philosophers. This need not be questioned if we mean that it was they who first gave explicit accounts of the nature of human knowledge. These, however, arose in a context of implicit views of knowledge, each with its own order of priorities and prestige. What the Greeks of the Golden Age managed to do was to give birth to a new sub-culture with a new ideal of knowledge. Mythical or dramatic views of man's nature were not supplanted but henceforth there would always be in Western culture a legitimate place for a philosophical interpretation.

It is as hard to mark the steps in this process as to distinguish myth from rational explanation in the Pre-Socratics. But certainly by the time of Plato and Aristotle, coinciding roughly with the breakdown of classical Greek culture and the rise of Hellenism, it became possible for schools of men, within the larger culture, to devote themselves to the purely rational, non-mythological elaboration of theories of knowledge. To what extent the new ideal supplanted the old, each must judge for himself, but the theorizing of a Plato or an Aristotle cannot be understood apart from this struggle to vindicate the rights of the disinterestedly scientific approach.

The Renaissance of the Thirteenth Century

Christianity brought with it profound cultural changes, which were heightened by the breakdown of social order in Europe under the barbarian invasions. Out of the gradual collapse of pagan cultural ideals rose a hegemony, a single knowledge-ideal of supernatural theologizing in opposition to all that was pagan, myth, religion, literature, and philosophy. If any cultural ideal can be said to have prevailed, at least in the West, it would be the grand synthesis of St Augustine of Hippo. His prestige in the early Middle Ages was enormous, and even when Arabian Aristoteleanism invaded the West it was Neo-Platonic enough in parts to coalesce with Augustinianism.

What was chiefly lacking in the Augustinian ideal was the due recognition of the place of natural knowledge in a radically other-worldly theology. The history of the latter part of the thirteenth century in the West can be interpreted as a struggle for the rights of natural knowledge within a supernatural system. It has a political parallel, in the growing power of Nation States and the supporting efforts of contemporary political theorists. The periodic condemnations of Aristotle, the struggles of the divines with the secular masters in the arts faculty of the University of Paris, the very condemnation of St Thomas and the Averroists in 1277 are all indications of the birth pangs of a new cultural ideal, in which philosophy was recognized as a legitimate preparation for theology.

In this struggle, according to the judgment of history, no thinker was more successful in vindicating the rights of a natural view of knowledge within a supernatural economy than St Thomas Aquinas. And it is in the light of this struggle that his theory of knowledge must be viewed.

The Renaissance and the Birth of the New Science

The next two stages in this panoramic view of theories of knowledge, because they come after St Thomas, can be treated more briefly. Yet it is necessary to see something of these developments, both to see him and his influence on later thinkers in better perspective.

The thirteenth and fourteenth centuries witnessed a justification of the rights of natural knowledge, but it remained for the later Renaissance to emancipate reason from faith, and to devote itself to natural knowledge independently and in conscious contrast with the supernatural. Not all practitioners of the 'new science' were anti-religious, of course, but it is often the hallmark of a new society of knowers that they see themselves in opposition to the old ways. And certainly they were aware of themselves as a special society forming a sub-culture distinctively organized to promote the new knowledge. Only in a cultural context of this sort can the birth of epistemology in the modern sense, and the work of Descartes and the British empiricists and Kant, be properly appreciated. Their aim was to ground and justify the new scientific approach and safeguard it from what they saw as the defects of the old approaches to science. Yet it should always be remembered that a revival of Thomism was still alive contemporaneously with Descartes, that theology flourished in these centuries (in terms of numbers of theologians if not of new ideas), and that a humanist literature was rapidly growing up in opposition to science and technology. Epistemology had come to birth along with the new science, but both had to find a place for themselves in the larger society of knowledge.

Non-Philosophical Theory of Knowledge

After Kant epistemology became so theoretically specialized that it lost interest for the practising scientist; the problem of knowledge fell more and more to the lot of the pure philosophers. Then in the late nineteenth and early twentieth centuries two movements developed and gradually merged into the contemporary view of how we should approach knowledge: these were the spread of experimental psychology and the emancipation of science from the philosophical ideal of certitude with which it had been burdened since Descartes. As science began to be seen as hypothetico-deductive, rather than inductive in a Baconian sense, it became possible for the first time to study human knowledge in terms of experimentally verifiable hypotheses rather than of philosophical systems. The results of this approach, and its relation to the analyses of St Thomas, will be considered in Appendix 7.

In this schematic survey[1] the work of St Thomas fits into stage 2, the

---

[1]Useful sources for a study of the complex history of theories of knowledge include the following. On philosophical problems as seen against a historical background: Bertrand Russell. *A History of Western Philosophy*. New York. 1945. For an enlightening historical survey of epistemology (though one unfriendly to Aristotle): Marjorie Grene. *The Knower and the Known*. New York. 1966. A good survey of

defence of the rights of natural knowledge within a supernatural world-view. There his work parallels that of the Parisian Averroists (even when it is in opposition to them), and of Roger Bacon; it is in line with that of Albertus Magnus and John of Paris; it also is a foil to the work of William of Ockham. See him in this setting, and it becomes singularly inappropriate to judge him by the concerns of later ages. Unlike Descartes, he was not attempting to establish an independent ground for natural science and thereby inaugurate a new philosophy. Unlike behaviorists, he was not attempting to establish hypotheses on the basis of experimentation.

---

recent Thomistic thinking on problems of epistemology: Georges Van Riet. *Thomistic Epistemology*, trans. G. Franks, Vol. I. St Louis. 1963. A good survey of current empiricist concerns: Roderick M. Chisholm. *Theory of Knowledge*. Englewood Cliffs, N.J. 1966. Mortimer Adler offers a realist critique of these and other contemporary philosophical positions in *The Conditions of Philosophy*. New York. 1965. Robert K. Merton. *Social Theory and Social Structure*. Glencoe, Ill. 1957. Parts III and IV provide an excellent introduction to the socio-cultural conditioning of knowledge.

Appendix 7

NAIVE REALISM

IF NEWTONIAN science was marked by naive realism, then it goes without saying that so was medieval science. Taking it for granted that Scholastic realism was naive, many authors do not bother to apply the term to St Thomas, but, for instance, to Thomas Reid and the Scottish philosophers of commonsense, and consider that Aristotle and St Thomas are 'out of the main stream of epistemological thinkers'.[1] This verdict, if it is well-founded, deserves consideration, which will involve looking at the psychological data that make it plausible, and evaluating the present treatise on human knowledge in their light.

Human Knowledge in Experimental Psychology

The findings of experimental psychology are readily available,[2] and only the briefest summary will be offered here. It is important to keep in mind the fundamental distinction drawn between sensation, perception, and thinking. Sensation is most often[3] presented in terms of simple sensory stimuli; perception is then defined as that complex process in which men select, organize, and interpret sensory stimulations, forming them into a meaningful and coherent picture of the world; finally, thinking is defined, not in terms of direct experience, but of the manipulation of symbolic experience, of the use of symbols.

The major findings on sensation have to do with stimulus thresholds, the levels of stimulation below which a sensory stimulus is not received, and the quantitative correlations between them, such as Weber's law with respect to the least detectable change in intensity as a function of the initial intensity of a stimulus. One item in this field is 'unconscious sensation' in the presence of near-threshold stimuli, where some receptors are triggered, but not enough for conscious sensation.

An experimental finding on perception—one that is reasonably well established scientifically—is that sensory stimuli alone are not sufficient to explain the coherent picture of the world that men have. The natures of stimuli (as unexpected, particularly intense, etc.) are received selectively in accordance with prior experience, and as dictated by needs and other motivations. From the beginnings of simplest experience, stimuli are organized and objects are perceived as integrated wholes. Especially when a relatively complete picture

---

[1] cf *Realism and the Background of Phenomenology*. Edited by Roderick M. Chisholm. Glencoe, Ill. 1960. Index, *s.v.* 'Realism'.
[2] cf Bernard Berelson and Gary Steiner. *Human Behavior: An Inventory of Scientific Findings*. New York. 1964, chapters 4–5
[3] But not always; cf James Gibson. *The Senses Considered as Perceptual Systems*. Boston. 1966

of the world emerges, objects sensed only partially are 'filled in' in accord with the need for homogeneity and other expectations; ambiguous stimuli are interpreted, especially in line with the familiar, and people tend to 'see' things as they want to or need to.

How much of this organization and interpretation is the result of thinking and not mere perception? This is a difficult question, not yet answered by experimentation. But a great deal of work—we may cite that of Jean Piaget—has gone into the development and nature of the thinking process which does unquestionably accompany the elaboration of a perceptual world-picture. One of the most studied but least conclusive areas of concern is the mutual interaction between verbal learning and conceptual growth.

In the field of thinking proper we cite the work of Jerome Bruner.[4] His model of the thinking process can be outlined as follows: conceptual growth takes place, not by passive learned habit formation in accord with reinforcement, but by active search, by the projection of 'hypotheses' which are then tested according to a relatively fixed strategy. These strategies can be 'wholist' or 'partist' (according to the generality of a hypothesis in relation to the problematic stimuli); so far the wholist strategies seem to be the more creative or productive.

Though there is excellent experimental support for these assertions, the theoretical models invoked are not unchallenged.[5] Nevertheless, a clear picture of developing human knowledge that is empirically verifiable in greater or less degree does begin to emerge. It is a highly complex one in which sensation, perception, and thinking largely merge into a unified whole, of 'developing consciousness'. Here the tentative, hypothesis-testing, 'projective' conception of the nature of thinking engages those who follow St Thomas's thought.[6] However, more pressing than any detail of the scheme, is the question of how his straightforward account of human knowledge squares with this highly complex process.

St Thomas and Realism

As mentioned in Appendix 6, his treatment of human knowledge must be seen in the light of the concerns of his day, not our own. He was, quite

[4]cf J. S. Bruner, J. J. Goodnow, and G. A. Austin. *A Study of Thinking*. New York. 1956. *Studies in Cognitive Growth*. New York. 1966. An interesting complement to Bruner's work, covering the same material in an entirely different perspective, is: *Pattern Recognition: Theory, Experiment, Computer Simulations, and Dynamic Models of Form Perception and Discovery*. Edited by Leonard Uhr. New York. 1966
[5]cf E. E. Harris. *The Foundations of Metaphysics in Science*. New York. 1965, chapters 20–21
[6]I have suggested earlier (Appendix 3) that the first operation within the second act of the mind, the formation of 'enunciations', especially when done tentatively as in the actual thinking process of a science, i.e., in probable reasoning (see Appendix 4) offers a sort of opening for Bruner's approach

obviously, not offering a theoretical framework for the kind of experimentation just indicated. What he did offer was a defence of natural knowledge, of the way in which man understands as this can be known through reason. Within these limits the actual working out of the theory is not experimental, certainly, not even empirical in the narrow modern sense, but an analytical development of the requirements of knowledge, *granting that it exists.* If man has genuinely intellectual knowledge, then it follows that such knowledge must exist in an intellectual mode, as universal and necessary. If man's knowledge is not derived from superior beings but comes through the senses, then the mode of human intellectual knowing must be abstractive; and if abstractive, then the partial data of abstraction must be put together in propositions and arguments. If the cognitive faculties go from potentiality to actuality, then they require a form (the *species sensibilis* or *species intelligibilis*) to do so. If an object of a faculty is not directly present, then an image is required to make it present (a *species expressa,* the *phantasma* or *conceptio*); but if knowledge is to be of the reality and not the image, then this image must be, not an object *quod,* but that in which, *in quo,* the external object is known directly. And so on.

Now no one needs to accept these as valid analytical statements to recognize that at least the process is valid. Even the most rigid adherent of behaviourism must begin his investigations by laying down a series of assumptions, about the meanings of terms, the limits of the investigation, the existence of the problems to be solved, etc. Every psychological system, no matter what claims it might make to the contrary, must have some analytical apparatus in order to begin. That St Thomas never went beyond this analysis, probably owing to an assumption that analysis is sufficient if it accounts for the data of experience (as he felt Plato's theory did not), may be regarded as a lack. That his analytical apparatus may also not be amenable to experimental verification may also be entertained as possible, though the point would have to be proved. But neither consideration invalidates his analytical apparatus. This could be done only by a contrary analysis which either demonstrated its falsity or else showed it to be implausible in accounting for experimental data.

Finally, it should be noted what St Thomas's treatise is not. First and most obviously, as stated in the terms of a psychology, it is not an answer to the epistemological problem, though later Thomists have thought they found in it the seeds of one. Second, his treatise on human knowledge is not an empirical investigation into developing human consciousness.

Glossary

absoluta consideratio, see *simple understanding*.

abstract substances, forms, ideas, see *ideas*.

abstraction (*abstractio, abstrahere*), mode of understanding proper to the human intellect by reason of the fact that its activity requires a material or bodily contribution; St Thomas's straightforward explanation of the process, in 1a. 85, 1, avoids many of the difficulties associated with the use of the term in later authors.

action, activity (*actio*): (1) *tendens in alterum, transiens in rem exteriorem*, so-called 'transient (or transitive) activity', affects something outside the agent or efficient cause; (2) *manens in agente*, so-called 'immanent activity', remains in the agent as its perfection—knowledge is an instance of the latter type of activity.

active and passive power (*potentia activa, passiva*), whereas a passive power only receives, an active power is productive; the example used by St Thomas is imagination, which not only represents sense objects which are no longer present but can also combine images in novel ways; see *formation*.

actus organi corporalis, the form of a corporeal organ—St Thomas's description of the sense faculties, internal and external; though the soul is the form of the human body, its intellectual faculty is not the form of a bodily organ; nevertheless, its activity does depend on the internal senses—see 1a. 84, 7.

agent intellect (*intellectus agens*), a faculty of the soul, according to St Thomas; its function is to render potentially intelligible objects actually intelligible, by way of an 'illumination'—see *illumination* and *intellectual light*.

analogy (*comparatio*, in one of its senses), see *comparison*.

appetitive part of the soul (*pars appetitiva*), shorthand for the appetitional or motivational functions of the human soul; usually stands for so-called 'sense appetites' rather than the will or intellectual appetite.

class (*genus, species*), logical category; Aristotelean logic organizes particulars under *species* under *genera*, up to the ten supreme *genera*, the categories; modern terminology refers to classes, and when *genus* and *species* are referred to together, the latter can be translated as 'sub-class'.

cogitativa (*vis*), see *internal senses*.

comparison (*comparatio*): (1) most often used in ordinary sense of comparing two (known) things with one another; (2) sometimes used in place of analogy, i.e., the process of discovering something unknown (say about God) from what is more directly known.

complete knowledge (*perfectum judicium, scientia completa, cognitio perfecta*), includes everything proper to the object; contrasted with *scientia imperfecta*, incomplete knowledge, and *cognitio confusa*, confused knowledge—these latter being knowledge that is vague or in terms of general principles only.

compositio et divisio, St Thomas's term for the second act of the mind, that in which it combines the objects of simple understanding and asserts something to be the case in reality; only in this act are truth and falsity, in the strict sense, to be found; see Appendix 3.

conditions, material individuating (*materiales conditiones individuantes, principia individualia*), principles explaining the individuality or singularity of a material being; not to be construed as forms or additions to the specific nature, except in the order of explanation.

conserved species (*species conservatæ*), concepts or species stored in the intellect; the basis for intellectual memory.

contingent things (*contingentia*), contrasted with necessary beings, *necessaria*; contingent things can be or not be, whereas something necessary cannot not be.

convertendo se ad phantasmata, simpliciter intelligibilia, see *turn.*

corruptible-incorruptible things (*corruptibilia-incorruptibilia*), a distinction applied by St Thomas to material realities; the heavenly bodies were assumed to be incorruptible, made of a matter (*quinta essentia*) different from that of sublunary, corruptible material things.

deceptio, see *infallibility.*

demonstrative knowledge (*scientia*), certain and evident knowledge acquired by way of demonstration from self-evident principles or premises; see Appendix 4.

discernment, see *judicium.*

divisio, see *compositio et divisio.*

effluere, effluentes, see *influence.*

essence (*essentia, quidditas*), see *quidditas.*

experience (*experimentum, experimur*), argument for psychological or epistemological theories; only rarely used by St Thomas.

extremes (*extrema*), terms of a proposition.

faculty (*potentia, virtus, vis*), capacity to perform a given psychological operation or activity; not to be reified or taken in the static sense suggested by opponents of faculty psychology.

form of thing known (*forma cogniti, forma rei intellectæ*), some form must be in the knower for knowledge to be possible, because faculties go from potentiality to actuality and this requires an actualizing form; it must be the form of the object known if the theory of knowledge is realistic.

formæ separatæ, see *ideas.*

formation, formulation (*formatio*): (1) active power of imagination by which it can combine images in a creative way; (2) similar capacity in the intellect; St Thomas gives a brief explanation that is difficult to match: 'In the sense part of man there are two kinds of activity. One takes place by way of a change effected from outside. . . . The other activity is "formation" by which the faculty of imagination formulates for itself a model of something

189

absent or even of something never seen. Now both of these activities
are joined in the intellect. For (1) there is indeed an effect produced in the
possible intellect in so far as it is informed by a species; (2) further, when
it is thus informed, it formulates either a definition or else an affirmative
or negative statement, which is then signified by words. Thus the meaning
(*ratio*) which a name signifies is a definition, and an enunciation signifies
the intellect's combining or separating' (1a. 85, 2 ad 3).

genus, see *class.*

habitual disposition (*habitus*), quality difficult to change, deeply ingrained in
whatever it is that becomes habituated; often simply transliterated as
'habit', but the exclusively moral connotation in English makes this
rendering unacceptable.
habitudo, relationship; but see *immobilis habitudo* under *rationes universales.*
habitus scientiæ, demonstrative knowledge which has become a habitual disposition in the mind (and materially in the internal senses); sometimes less
restricted, meaning any intellectual knowledge possessed as a habitual
disposition.

ideas, Platonic (*ideæ separatæ, formæ separatæ, formæ intelligibiles separatæ,
formæ immateriales subsistentes, substantiæ abstractæ, universalia subsistentia*), St Thomas simply adopts Aristotle's interpretation of Platonic
Ideas or Forms, according to which they are assumed to exist somewhere
apart from the world of sense; the sensible world then gets its existence
and its meaning by *participation* in the Ideas.
illumination (*illuminatio*): (1) of sense images (*phantasmata*) by the agent
intellect, whether in the process of abstraction or in the use of species
previously abstracted; (2) of a created intellect by divine light, for which
see *species infused by God.*
image (*imago*), more precise term than *similitudo*, likeness (in any respect);
an image is supposed to imitate or reproduce the imaged thing as closely
as possible—see 1a. 93, 1; see also *sense images* (*phantasmata*).
imagination (*imaginatio, vis imaginaria, imaginativa*), see *internal senses.*
immaterial substances (*immaterialia separata, substantiæ separatæ;* in Avicenna
and Averroes, *intellectus separatus, intellectus agens* or *possibilis separatus*),
any substance or substantial entity that can exist entirely apart from matter
—thus Platonic Ideas or neo-Platonist 'intelligences' would be immaterial
substances; St Thomas generally, when he is speaking in his own name,
restricts the term to God and the angels, or even only to the angels.
immateriality required for knowledge (*immaterialitas, immaterialiter cognosci,
ratio cognitionis*), the very essence of knowledge, according to St Thomas;
since matter restricts a form to one individual, the form of a thing known
can actualize a knower only in so far as it is in some sense free from this
restriction; thus even the knowledge of the external senses must be immaterial in this minimal way.

immutatio organi, see *passio*.

impressio sensibilium in sensum, see *passio*.

individuating conditions (*materiales conditiones individuantes*), see *conditions, principle of individuation*.

infallible knowledge (*infallibilitas*, contrast *deceptio*), that knowledge of its proper object which a faculty must attain if it operates at all; applied specifically to the simple understanding of essences, but this doctrine should not be misunderstood—see Appendix 2.

influence (*per influentiam, influere, effluere*), an obviously metaphorical term, used by St Thomas in much the same way that it was used by neo-Platonist and Augustinian upholders of an illuminationist theory of knowledge—light 'flows' from a source to illuminate an object for a knower, and the light is received by the knower along with what is illumined; St Thomas, however, denies the illumination theory for natural knowledge and, at least in this treatise, restricts illuminative knowledge to the separated soul receiving infused species from God; nevertheless, the very *intellectual light* of the agent intellect is spoken of as a participation or sharing in the divine light.

innate species or ideas (*species* [*naturaliter*] *inditæ, species innatæ*), knowledge not acquired by experience or from the senses, but possessed naturally, from birth; in the Platonic view, as interpreted by St Thomas, innate knowledge needs to be recollected, especially by freeing the mind from distracting sensations and emotions.

intellect (*intellectus, mens, virtus intellectualis*), man's highest spiritual faculty; St Thomas simply assumes that the objects of intellect as such must be necessary and unchanging, as distinguished from the changing objects of the senses.

intellective or *intellectual part* of the soul (*pars intellectiva*), shorthand for those operations of the soul which take place apart from (though not completely independent of) the senses and emotions; willing pertains to the intellective part as much as understanding.

intellectual light (*lumen intellectuale, lumen intellectus agentis; impressio, similitudo participata luminis increati, primæ veritatis*), by analogy with the physical light that makes sensible objects visible, the mind is presumed to have its own light in itself, as a special faculty (though this agent intellect is a participation in the light of divine truth) which 'lights up' or illuminates potentially intelligible objects to make them actually intelligible; note that this light must function in all intellectual knowledge, in forming enunciations or propositions, in assenting to truth, and in reasoning—as well as in the obvious case of abstraction.

intellectus: agens, see *agent intellect; possibilis*, see *possible intellect*.

intelligibilia (*intellecta*) *speculata* of Averroes, see *ideas*.

intelligible objects (*intelligibilia* [*in actu*]; *intellecta in actu, res intellecta*), things either in themselves intelligible or rendered such by the agent intellect; once understood they can be referred to indiscriminately as *intelligibilia in actu* or *res intellecta(e)*.

intentio intelligibilis, see *rationes universales, formation.*

intention of universality (intentio universalitatis), the quality of being abstract attaching to a universal concept, idea or species; see *universality, abstraction.*

internal senses (vires sensitivæ: imaginativa, cogitativa, memorativa), imagination (re-presentation of sense images in perception, often in synthesized form), cogitative faculty ('instinct', *ratio particularis* or concrete reasoning process, etc.) and sense memory; all three produce *sense images (phantasmata).*

judgment, see *judicium.*

judicium, discernment, discrimination according to a standard; sometimes judgment (in the modern sense, as standing for the second act of the mind), though even here the sense is normally that of a judgment based on a prior discernment, say of one of the senses; see Appendix 3.

knowledge: (1) in general (*cognitio* or [frequently] *scientia*); (2) demonstrative knowledge, see *scientia.*

ligamentum, impedimentum sensus, a 'binding' of the senses (for whatever reason), impeding their use.

likeness (similitudo), necessary requirement for created knowledge; equivalent of *forma cogniti*, reducing faculty from potentiality to actuality, and guaranteeing knowledge of the object as it is (at least in some respect); see *form of thing known, image.*

lumen: intellectuale, see *intellectual light; divinum*, see *species infused by God.*

material individuating conditions (materiales conditiones individuantes), see *conditions, principle of individuation.*

material things (whose 'whatness' or essence is proper object of the human intellect), see *quidditas.*

matter in intellectual knowledge: *materia sensibilis*, corporeal reality in general, anything that can be perceived by the senses; *materia intelligibilis*, substance as prior (in the order of explanation) to quantity, which is prior to all the sensible qualities; *materia sensibilis communis*, sensible realities abstractly considered, say the required texture, colour, etc. for a human body; *materia sensibilis signata vel individualis*, the peculiar sensible qualities of a given individual body; *materia intelligibilis communis*, substance in the abstract as the necessary condition for the existence of quantity; *materia intelligibilis individualis*, a given substance as subject to given quantitative determinations—see Ia. 85, 1 ad 2, for the relation between these as objects of the various speculative sciences.

memory (sense) (*vis memorativa*), see *internal senses;* referred to once in the treatise as *reminiscentia.*

mind (mens), see *intellect.*

mode of understanding (modus intelligendi), a term used primarily to distinguish different modes (or *gradus*, degrees or levels); sometimes St Thomas distinguishes three, divine, angelic, and human; at other times he merely distinguishes the abstractive mode from understanding by infusion of species from God.

name (*nomen*), see *words*.

nature of thing understood (*natura rei abstractæ*), that to which is attached the quality of abstractness, *intentio universalitatis*; see also *rationes universales*.

object of knowledge, see *proper object*.

opinion (*opinio*), uncertain, dialectical knowledge, often based on common beliefs of men in general or experts; see Appendix 4.

order of understanding (*ordo intelligendi*), the natural process of development in human understanding, from vague to precise knowledge, from general principles to more and more exact (*propria*) knowledge; this order is determined, not by empirical investigation, but by an analysis of necessary presuppositions.

organs of sense faculties (*organa sensus et imaginationis*), the material component of a cognitive faculty, the eye for instance with respect to sight; the organ is functional and instrumental to the faculty, without which the organ cannot perform its function—the eye of a corpse, shortly after death, may be functionally perfect, but it can no longer be said to 'see' in any proper sense.

pars appetitiva, intellectiva, sensitiva, see *appetitive part* (of the soul), *intellective part, sense part*.

participation (*participatio*), a technical term in Plato's thought; though Aristotle claims Plato never clarified its meaning, St Thomas gives a brief explanation: 'Having [a Platonic] Idea by participation means that there is a likeness of the Idea in the thing that has it by participation, just as the original model is contained in a copy' (1a. 84, 4); for *participata similitudu divini luminis*, see *intellectual light*; for *species ex influentia divina participatæ*, see *species infused by God*.

particulars particularia, in this volume approximately equivalent to *singularia*, contrasted with *universals*.

passio: (1) *organi*, effect produced in a sense organ by the activity of a sensible object; synonymous with *immutatio organi, impressio sensibilium in sensum*; (2) *intellectus possibilis*, of the possible intellect, a similar passive aspect of intellectual knowledge, though there is an essential difference: the possible intellect, like a sense faculty, receives the form or likeness of the thing known (*species impressa*), but actual knowledge does not take place until the intellect, thus informed formulates a concept (definition, *compositio*, etc.)— see *formation*, and Appendix 1; note that introspection will not reveal this aspect of intellection, which must be arrived at through a reasoning process going from activity to necessarily presupposed condition.

per essentiam (*per seipsam*), *per speciem* (*similitudinem*), St Thomas notes that all intellectual knowledge must be either by the presence of an intelligible object to an intellect essentially, or else by a likeness or species; the distinction usually serves to indicate that human knowledge requires a species (even in the case of the intellect itself and its contents).

phantasmata, see *sense images*.

possible intellect (*intellectus possibilis*), the knowing intellect, distinct from the *agent intellect* which prepares the matter for knowledge.

potency, power (*potentia, virtus, vis*), see *faculty*.

primum cognitum, the first thing known by the human mind; St Thomas denies that this can be God, asserting that our understanding must begin with sensible realities (and indeed with their vaguest and most general aspects).

principle of individuation (*principium individuationis, singularitatis*), that which explains the individuality or singular character of material beings— not as efficient cause but as formal explanation or logical presupposition; matter, in some sense, is the principle of individuation.

principle of knowing, of being (*principium cognoscendi, essendi*), principle by reason of which we know, principle explaining the existence of a thing; St Thomas employs the distinction to emphasize that the two need not be the same.

proper object (*proprium objectum, primo et per se cognitum*), the object to which a faculty is essentially ordained; either it is attained or the faculty does not operate; see Appendix 2 for one instance.

quidditas: quæ est proprium objectum intellectus nostri; in materia corporali existens; rei materialis quæ sub sensu et imaginatione cadit; rei materialis abstracta a phantasmatibus, the proper object of the human intellect in this life, the essence or 'whatness' of a material thing, abstracted from but understood only in a sense image; this essence need not be the specific essence, and indeed usually is not—see Appendix 2.

quod, quo intelligitur, that *which* is understood as distinct from that *by which* understanding takes place; species are not *what* is understood directly, but the means *by which* the realities of which they are likenesses are understood.

rationes universales (*scibilium*); *ratio quam significat nomen* (*vel enuntiatio*); *conceptiones intellectus; intentio intelligibilis; immobilis habitudo*, the universal aspect or meaning attained in abstractive knowledge; this *ratio* exists in a singular way in material realities, but it can be understood by an abstractive intellect only in universal form, only in a state of abstractness; note, however, that in St Thomas's understanding of the process the universal, to be understood, must be seen *in* the particular, in relation to the sense image from which it was abstracted (see Ia. 84, 7).

reflection (*reflexio*): (1) on the concrete knowledge of the senses, internal and external—this is the way an abstractive intellect can know singulars or particular things: (2) by which the intellect knows itself and its contents (its species for instance) in the process of knowing external things.

res intellecta, see *intelligible objects.*

scientia: (1) frequently used for knowledge in general; (2) for special sense, see *demonstrative knowledge.*

sense images (phantasmata), material likenesses of material things (*similitudines materiales quæ sunt phantasmata*), the products of the three *internal senses,* often the result of a synthesizing process.

sense part of the soul (*pars sensitiva*), shorthand for the functions of the soul that are forms of bodily organs, i.e., the internal and external senses, and the emotions.

senses, sense knowledge (*sensus, sensibilia* [*in actu*]), the ultimate source of all man's knowledge according to the Aristotelian–Thomistic theory of knowledge; see 1a. 84, 6–8.

sensible objects (sensibilia), objects of the five external senses: sight, hearing, smell, taste, and touch (and, we would add today, their sub-divisions or variations); these constitute the 'sensible or material world' of everyday experience, but it is as objects of the senses that they are most properly called *sensibilia*; note that it is these same objects that are represented in the sense images (*phantasmata*) of the internal senses, now usually combined and reconstructed.

sensus communis, sometimes translated 'common sense', but best left in the Latin; a special but unique faculty, its function is to correlate and combine the data of the senses to serve as *species impressa* for the internal senses (especially imagination).

separated soul (anima separata a corpore), St Thomas's term for the soul as it remains in existence after death; he distinguishes the knowledge connatural to this state (treated here) from the knowledge of the beatific vision.

similitude (similitudo), see *likeness.*

similitudines materiales (phantasmata), see *sense images.*

simple understanding (simplex et absoluta consideratio, simplex intelligentia), the understanding of an essence or 'whatness' (*quidditas*); see Appendix 2.

singulars (singularia), individuals, approximately equivalent to particulars. A man is a particular, this man an individual.

species: (1) (*species*) logical class (or sub-class when arranged below a *genus*); (2) (*species*) natural class or collection of things of the same kind; (3) (*species intelligibilis*) St Thomas's customary term for the form or likeness of the thing known in intellectual knowledge; in the present treatise he does not often distinguish between *species impressa* and *species expressa* (the concept) —see Appendix 1.

species inditæ, innatæ, see *innate species or ideas.*

species infused by God (species divinitus influxæ, similitudines divinitus impressæ, species ex influentia divini luminis participatæ), the means of knowing proper to immaterial substances; the human soul, when separated from the body, shares in this mode of understanding according to the opinion of St Thomas.

speculative sciences (*scientiæ speculativæ*), according to Aristotle these include natural science, mathematics, and metaphysics or first philosophy; these are distinguished from 'rational science' (logic) and the practical sciences, ethics, politics, etc.

turn to (*se convertere ad phantasmata, simpliciter intelligibilia*), a metaphor used by St Thomas in a technical sense; the mind's taking heed of a meaningful object in what is presented by the imagination.

universalia subsistentia, see *ideas*.

universaliora, universals with greater logical extension; the term can also stand for *principia universaliora*, more universal principles (whether logical statements or causes), but St Thomas is always careful to distinguish and safeguard the prior sense.

universality (*intentio universalitatis*), the state or quality of abstractness belonging to objects of the human intellect by reason of its mode of understanding; see *abstraction*.

universals (*universalia, universale, universale abstractum*), the opposite (logically) of particulars or singulars; generally speaking the sense is universal concepts, natures understood abstractly, see *intention of universality* and *rationes universales*.

via remotionis, way of knowing something (especially God) by recognizing that it does not have a quality found in our experience.

virtus, vis (synonyms of *potentia*), see *faculty*.

voces, see *words*.

words (*voces*, including *nomina*, names, and *enuntiationes*, the verbal expressions of *propositions*), expressions of concepts directly, of things only indirectly; with respect to species (*species intelligibiles*), St Thomas says quite clearly that it is the *species expressa* that words signify, not the *species impressa* (1a. 85, 2 ad 3)—see *formation* and *rationes universales*.

Index

(Numbers refer to pages, italics to notes and appendices)

J

K

L

M

N

O

P

possible intellect *25, 29,* 127, *169*
pre-Socratic sensism xix
Pre-Socratics *6*
principium 12

priority in knowledge 65
properties manifest natures *170*
proportion of faculty and object 41,
  51, 129

Q

quidditas 81, 155, 170, 172

quod quid est 81, 170

R

ratio
  as *immobilis habitudo 168*
  and *quidditas 172*
  as *rationabile 168*
  signified by definition *167*
ratio particularis 5, 169
realism
  Aristotelean-Thomastic *38, 185*
  naive *185*

realist epistemology and naturally
  known axioms *21*
realistic theory of knowledge xx
reflection 61
Régis, L. *174*
Reid, T. *185*
representationalism 57
Russell, B. *183*

S

scepticism xix
Scholastics' use of abstract terms *124*
science as system *176*
scientia 6, 151, 176
second act of mind *173, 174*
second intentions *62*
sense images
  as composite *5, 169, 174*
  as translation of *phantasmata 5, 169*
senses awakening mind 27
sensible and intellectual knowledge 37
sensus communis 47, 115
separatum 7
singulars known indirectly 91, 151
soul separated from body

soul—*continued*
  objects of knowledge 141, 145,
    151, 161
  understands by infused species
    143, 147, 151, 159
species
  as likeness *167*
  as principle *167*
  as translation of *species intelligibilis*
    4, 54, 168
species impressa-expressa 4, 62, 168, 169, 174
species sensibilis 169
Steiner, G. *185*
subsistent immaterial forms 23
substantial forms as unknown *170*

T

theological sources *179*
Thomas Aquinas, St
  on abstraction *49*
  and Aristotelean *via media* xix
  defence of natural knowledge xix,
    121, 136, 180, 182
  on dialectical reasoning *177*
  and history of theories of knowledge
    181

Thomas Aquinas, St—*continued*
  on intelligence as dependent on
    body *26*
  against representationalism 57
  as theologian *179*
  treatise on man *3*
truth 78
turning to sense images *5, 39, 139, 141,* 145, 153, 157

U

V

W